"I was appalled that Smith did not have a cell mate for seven and a half years, for my time in isolation was pure hell—I hated every second of it. Each day seemed to never end, and each month was an eternity. . . . This is a story that needs to be told, and Phil Smith and Peggy Herz have done a bang-up job!"

—Colonel Ben Pollard, USAF (Ret),
former POW; President, NAM-POWs Inc.,
the largest Vietnam POW organization

"I found it inspirational. You will too."
—General Bill Creech, USAF (Ret),
former Commander, Tactical Air Command

"Smith went through a test that none of us ever want to take. I couldn't put the book down."
—General John T. Chain, USAF (Ret),
former Commander, Strategic Air Command

"A compelling story of a tough fighter pilot's perseverance and courage demonstrated by a great American during some extraordinary times in our history, most of which we would like to forget."
—Thomas G. McInerney

"Phil Smith's ejection from his F-104 . . . began a violent descent which ended . . . in seven and a half years in a hell on earth. . . . His ordeal is unique to the Southeast Asia War in that he was held as an enemy of the state by a power not directly involved in the conflict. This circumstance added to the constant uncertainty about his future which he was forced to overcome. . . . An extraordinary account of human will in the face of adversity.

—Major General Robert W. Clement, USAF (Ret), former Commander, 16th Air Force (Europe)

"Moving . . . powerful."

—General Charles L. Donnelly, Jr., USAF (Ret), former Commander, US Air Forces in Europe

"The intensity and the momentum increase the deeper you get into the book until you feel you are a participant in the deprivation, degradation and brutality. Courage, determination and faith in God are Col. Smith's mainstay."

—General Robinson Risner, USAF (Ret), former POW, author of *Passing of the Night*

"Powerful . . . a wonderfully tough, intelligent recall of solitary imprisonment. . . . Phil reawakened my bitter emotions. . . . Best yet of the Vietnam-era prison experiences. . . . Three cheers for Phil Smith."

—Colonel Hervey S. Stockman, USAF (Ret), former F-104 fighter pilot and POW, past President of NAM-POW

JOURNEY INTO DARKNESS

Col. Philip E. Smith
and Peggy Herz

POCKET BOOKS

New York   London   Toronto   Sydney   Tokyo   Singapore

An *Original* Publication of POCKET BOOKS

POCKET BOOKS, a division of Simon & Schuster Inc.
1230 Avenue of the Americas, New York, NY 10020

ISBN: 0-671-72823-7

First Pocket Books printing February 1992

10 9 8 7 6 5 4 3 2 1

Journey into Darkness is dedicated . . .

To my loving family and dear friends, whose courage and steadfastness never wavered during the long years of my captivity. Their faith and strength were beacons of light during my darkest days.

To the U.S. Air Force and the men and women I served with during my career. From them, I learned what it means to be a proud soldier and a proud American.

To John Downey, Richard Fecteau and Robert Flynn, who shared those dreadful years in China with me and taught me what courage is all about.

To my fellow POWs, who suffered so brutally at the hands of the enemy in Southeast Asia and still upheld the honor of their country and the Military Code of Conduct.

And most of all, it is dedicated to those comrades who did not make it back from Vietnam. I was one of the lucky ones. I survived. I came home, while thousands of others did not. My country did not forget me during the long years of my captivity in China; I pray that we will never forget any of those we send off to serve our country.

Col. Philip E. Smith,
USAF (Ret)

Acknowledgments

We are deeply grateful to our families and friends, who were so supportive during the writing of this book. They helped us beyond measure with their spirited words of encouragement and enthusiasm, and to each one of them, we send our love and our heartfelt thanks.

Special thanks to our agent, Philip Spitzer, who believed in this project from the very beginning; and to Paul McCarthy and Eric Tobias, editors at Pocket Books, whose help and guidance and enthusiasm were so invaluable.

And we pay loving tribute to Ed Herz, who read, listened, advised, and was totally committed to this book. He was a man of grace and humor and great intelligence who instilled a sense of balance and perspective in everything he did. He died in 1989, but the influence and inspiration of a beloved husband have not been forgotten.

Peggy Herz

Contents

CONTENTS

JOURNEY
INTO
DARKNESS

1

"We've Lost You"

September, 1965: Da Nang Air Base, South Vietnam. The stillness of the night was increasingly being shattered by the sound of enemy rockets flying over the base. The constant shelling had been going on for weeks, making us wonder when we'd be hit. The sound became so common, the pilots in The Hooch were able to distinguish between those shells approaching the compound and those going away from it. The joke was a nightly one: "Incoming!" "Outgoing!"

The hours of darkness were disturbed by small-arms fire as well. For more than a year U.S. forces had been intensifying their efforts to defend this key military installation, and still small bands of Vietcong were managing to sneak onto the base. They crept in to destroy whatever they could: equipment, supplies, aircraft, ammunition, fuel, personnel. During the previous few weeks the VC had destroyed a C-130 Hercules aircraft sitting on the ramp and had burned and shelled other equipment. They'd killed some of the base guards, and some of them, in turn, had been killed.

For all of us on the base these attacks brought home the terrible truth: We were in a war zone, and even our highly guarded air base was not secure. Initially we believed these losses could occur on the ground, but not in the air. Those of us who flew the F-104 considered our sleek little airplane a bastion of invincibility. Once it was airborne, it could not be brought down, or so we wanted to believe.

In early September the invincibility myth, like the night's stillness, was destroyed. Our entire squadron was jolted when R. E. Smith returned from a combat mission in the north with large holes in the wing of his 104 caused by antiaircraft fire. It was a shock, and it meant several things to us: Enemy gunners were getting more accurate, and we weren't as safe, even in the air, as we had once thought. On the ground and in the air, the war was intensifying.

September 19, 1965. As acting flight commander, I spent the warm September afternoon in the squadron building scheduling two missions for the following day: an air patrol mission out over the Tonkin Gulf and an afternoon bombing mission in North Vietnam. I scheduled myself to be ground spare (standby) for the morning mission and to lead the more dangerous afternoon bombing mission.

I wasn't being altruistic in my choice of assignment. I was a TAC (Tactical Air Command) fighter pilot, trained to fly the sleekest, most beautiful fighter plane of them all, the single-seat, single-engine F-104. All of us who flew that plane were eager to fly at every opportunity and to go on the most challenging and most dangerous missions. It had been drilled into us that fighter pilots must be lean and mean, trained killers who, if we were any good, would fly right to the edge of our nerves, our abilities, our equipment, and the dangers around us.

We had to have confidence in ourselves and in one another, and we'd learned that by training for years to fly combat missions anywhere in the world. In 1965, at the age of thirty, I believed I knew myself, my airplane, and the talents and temperaments of the other men in my flight. We had come to Vietnam together, seven of us, from George Air

Force Base in California, as part of the 436th Squadron. We were fighter pilots ready for action; so far there had been no air battles in the many missions we had flown in North and South Vietnam.

I was short of pilots in scheduling the next day's sorties because two of our seven flight members were away. Flight Commander Harvey Quackenbush would be back in time to fly, but not in time to plan or lead either mission. I assigned Ken Kerwin, Harvey Quackenbush, R. E. Smith, and Don Madonna to the morning flight, with Kerwin as flight leader, hoping that all four men and their machines would be able to fly so I could continue working on planning the more dangerous but gratifying mission into the north. Bombing missions in North Vietnam were always dangerous, but we preferred them to the air patrol missions. Our chances of being shot down were greater, but so was our sense of accomplishment. Dropping bombs on railroad yards or military installations gave us the feeling we were actually fighting the enemy.

Late in the afternoon I decided to call it a day. I'd flown a morning mission and spent the afternoon doing paperwork. I was tired and knew the next day would be a long, tough one. I had an early dinner in the Officers' Club and turned in at about ten o'clock.

There were few separate sleeping quarters on the air base. The seven of us who had come from George together shared a dormitory arrangement that we called The Hooch, an open bay area that slept thirty men in double bunks. There were a dozen such dormitories in the officers' compound, an area within the base that was separately fenced in and guarded, and considered reasonably safe during the day, though we all wondered about the cooks and maids who worked in the compound. Were they Vietcong? Perhaps, but at least they were all searched before entering or leaving, so there was some assurance that they didn't have bombs, guns, or knives.

* * *

September 20, 1965, Da Nang Air Base, South Vietnam. I was ready for a busy day. I got up at five o'clock, showered, shaved, dressed in a lightweight gray nylon flying suit and flying boots, and headed for the Officers' Club for breakfast. I selected scrambled eggs, bacon, toast, orange juice, and coffee and joined the four pilots scheduled to go on the morning air patrol mission. The five of us were friends of long standing, easy and comfortable with one another. We had trained and flown together for many years in preparation for the war we now confronted. Since arriving in Vietnam we'd discovered frustrations we'd never expected. That morning at breakfast we wondered once again how much longer it would be before the authorities allowed U.S. forces to strike hard at the heart of the enemy and bring the conflict to an end.

We ate quickly and then went outside and got in the pickup truck that took us the short distance to the flight line where the squadron operations building was located. It was a hot morning with scattered clouds, not a bad morning for a foray out over the Tonkin Gulf in a fighter plane, only 54.77 feet long, that could outrun anything else in the air on that particular morning—or any other morning.

As ground spare, I prepared for the mission along with the four pilots assigned to it. Air defense missions are long and tedious. The four pilots would fly for four hours, refueling from a tanker in the air. Often such a mission seemed like a long exercise in doing nothing but flying around and around over the water. We might get into an air-to-air battle and shoot down an enemy aircraft, and we all wanted to do that, but the chances of it happening were very slim. The main point of air patrol missions was to identify enemy aircraft and keep them away from U.S. ships in the Tonkin Gulf.

That morning we checked maps and the "frag" sent down by headquarters, which spelled out the details of the mission. Then we sat down and had a formal briefing during which the flight leader, Ken Kerwin, made sure we all understood every detail of the mission and how it was going to be conducted.

From there the five of us went out to the ops (operations) counter to check for last-minute weather and mission changes and the tail numbers of the airplanes we would fly that day. We copied all pertinent information and then got back in the pickup truck, which took us to the flight line where the airplanes were parked.

So far I had four able-bodied pilots suited up and ready to go. Now if their four airplanes had no problems, I could head back to the squadron and finish planning the afternoon bombing mission.

We started our engines. The call sign of the flight and its leader was Venus Five One. The call signs of the other flight members: Venus Five Two, Five Three, and Five Four. Flight members checked their radios and received ground clearance from ground control to taxi to the runway. I stayed where I was. My airplane and I were ready to go if we were needed, but so far we weren't.

The flight leader punched his mike. "Venus Five One, let's go channel two." Each of us acknowledged the channel change by giving our call sign, "Two, three, four, spare." We were now on the active runway frequency. The flight leader reported to the tower, "Da Nang tower, this is Venus Five One, number one with four."

"Venus Five One, taxi into position and hold." The flight taxied into position and waited momentarily. "Venus Five One, the wind is three one zero at ten, cleared for takeoff." Flight leader Ken Kerwin signaled for engine run-up. Four F-104s were ready to go. They streaked down the runway; three thousand feet later, at a takeoff speed of almost two hundred knots, they were airborne.

I was still parked on the ramp. So far all aircraft had checked out, but I knew any number of things could still go wrong. Gear doors were often out of adjustment; if a gear door wouldn't come up and lock, it could be damaged when the plane got to a higher speed. Another common problem was fuel tanks that wouldn't feed.

On that morning, however, the Venus Five One flight was in the air and appeared to have four good airplanes. Kerwin called back to Da Nang. "Okay, spare, you can shut down. We've got four good birds." I shut down my engine, unstrapped, and got out of the airplane, pleased that I'd have the time I wanted to work on the afternoon bombing mission. I walked back to the squadron building, got out the maps, and continued planning the mission. Ten minutes later the ops officer rushed in. "Grab up your chute, Smitty, Q-Bush has aborted."

On long air patrol missions aircraft must be able to refuel from the airborne tanker, called a KC-135 by the Air Force, which was a modified Boeing 707 used to provide aerial refueling for various types of aircraft. That morning the tanker, flying at a speed of about three hundred knots, was in orbit some 140 miles north of Da Nang. For the F-104s, each carrying about two and a half hours of fuel, the presence of the tanker out over the water meant they could refuel in five minutes or less and get back on station. Without the tanker they would have to return to Da Nang, get clearance to land, taxi in, wait for ground crews to refuel them from a truck, fill out a new flight plan—and it could be an hour or more before they were back on station. For all the planes the tanker support extended the time they could be on station and the distance they could be from home base.

The tankers were flown by Strategic Air Command (SAC) crews out of Thailand and Guam. It was well known that enemy radar, Chinese and Vietnamese, observed the tanker support for the fighter missions, and enemy aircraft knew better than to tangle with fighters with plenty of fuel. Throughout each mission the unarmed tanker was protected by two fighter planes.

F-104s used the probe and drogue system of refueling. The fighter pilot approached the tanker from the rear and slightly below. Once he received clearance from the tanker pilot to approach and hook up the fighter pilot slowed his speed from 450 knots to the tanker's speed of about 300 knots. The boom operator on the tanker lowered the boom, a huge metal pipe that came down from the back of the tanker at an angle of about forty degrees. Extended from the end of the boom was a flexible rubber hose and a funnel-shaped basket, which was called the drogue.

It was up to the fighter pilot to maneuver his aircraft into position so that the probe, a round metal tube attached to the left front side of the fuselage, would make contact with the drogue on the tanker. Making the connection wasn't always easy. In a thunderstorm or other heavy turbulence the tanker bounced around, making it difficult to hook up. In such cases the fighter pilot had no choice but to back off for ten feet or so, wait until the air was smoother, and then try again. Once connected he had to make sure to maintain his precise position, or he would disconnect from the basket, and both the probe and the drogue could be damaged.

When the boom operator told him he had a full load of fuel the fighter pilot retarded the throttle, similar to letting up on the gas pedal of an automobile, backed off, and disconnected. He was, in effect, letting the tanker fly away from him by slowing down his own speed.

Harvey Quackenbush was aborting the flight because his plane could not take on fuel. The tip of the probe was bent very slightly, and no one had noticed it before takeoff. The probe would not lock into the drogue; fuel therefore could not flow from the tanker to the 104. If he couldn't refuel, Quackenbush was no good for the mission. He was returning to base.

I knew I had to move quickly to replace Quackenbush and rendezvous with the flight. I grabbed my parachute, helmet, and survival gear. As I dashed for the door I met the squadron commander, who offered me a lift to the ramp where my airplane was parked. The ramp was only an eighth of a mile away, but I accepted the offer. It was faster to ride than walk.

There was no time for idle chatter, but I would never forget my commander's final words to me: "Have a nice flight, and be sure you stay away from Hainan Island," he said. I had no intention of going anywhere near there, I assured him. "Yes, sir," I replied, "I'll stay away from Hainan Island."

I understood his concern. In recent days there had been considerable air activity around that island belonging to Red China. The U.S. had no desire to provoke China into entering the war. Neither did it want Red Chinese planes flying over U.S. ships in the Tonkin Gulf. That was one of the reasons the F-104s had been maintaining a presence in the Gulf. We knew the Chinese on Hainan Island would see us on their radar, but no one thought the Chinese would tangle with us. We were there to make the Chinese stay away, not to shoot them down. It was understood, however, that if any enemy aircraft committed a hostile act, the U.S. fighter pilots would go after them with a vengeance.

Hainan Island wasn't my problem right then, however. Rendezvousing with my flight was. Radar controllers knew that Quackenbush had aborted the flight; they had him on their radar scopes and were working him back. I got in the plane I had preflighted earlier, and moments later I was cleared for takeoff. Once I was airborne I left the radio frequency of the Da Nang tower and switched to Panama, the radar station on top of Monkey Mountain near Da Nang. From then on I would be controlled by Panama, the ground station, and by a radar plane flying around over the Gulf relaying radar signals back to Panama. I established radio contact with Panama, requesting a steer to the tanker.

"Five Five, say your heading," Panama instructed. I did so. "Venus Five Five, turn left zero one zero degrees." I turned my aircraft to that heading, generally north, and Panama continued to control me until I had tallyho on the tanker. Once the tanker was in sight I thanked Panama and left their frequency.

My airplane was performing beautifully. It even had a good radar, which surprised me. Those of us who flew the 104 had learned that it was fast and deadly and that it occasionally had equipment problems, as did any aircraft. The 104 radar was designed to pick up a target twenty miles away, but it seldom did. But on this morning my radar was working well. It picked up the tanker at seventeen miles and locked on at ten miles. I was then getting accurate range information and had no trouble tracking the tanker as I came in. Once I was close I turned off the radar, hooked up to the tanker, and began to take on fuel.

R. E. Smith, deputy flight leader of Venus Five One, was beside me on the tanker. I knew the other two members of the flight were out patrolling their assigned area. On long air patrol missions two airplanes patrolled, two refueled, then they swapped. It was important to stagger this way so we didn't have four airplanes back at the tanker at the same time or leave the tanker alone and unprotected.

After an abort it was also important to get the flight back in sequence, Five One with Five Two, Five Three with Five Four. When I arrived at the tanker Venus Five One flight was not in sequence. To get the flight back in order the flight leader made a call. "Send Five Two up." That was my call sign. To my flight, and to radar controllers on the ground and in the air, I had assumed Quackenbush's call sign and was now Venus Five Two. R. E. Smith, Venus Five Three, would stay with the tanker to protect it and be joined by Venus Five Four as soon as I reached the two aircraft out on patrol.

I was being sent up to rendezvous with my flight—and no one had any qualms about the decision to send me up alone. I would be flying a short distance as a single ship, and this was a simple in-flight rendezvous. No one, not I nor anyone else, expected any problems with enemy aircraft. In those days, the North Vietnamese pilots were new and inexperienced and the war was just starting to crank up. Except in a few cases North Vietnamese aircraft had not begun to challenge U.S. pilots. Rarely had anyone in my squadron seen an enemy airplane in the air. They ran from us.

I reported to Panama that I was off the tanker and requested a steer to my flight. I knew generally where the flight was supposed to be, but I needed Panama to give me heading and altitude information.

From the tanker I tuned in channel twenty-six on my TACAN set. The TACAN system was a navigational aid—short for tactical air navigation. The station I was heading for was on a U.S. naval vessel out in the Tonkin Gulf off the coast of North Vietnam. Since North Vietnam wouldn't let enemy forces put a TACAN installation on their land, this one had been put in the water, and it would be the closest navigational aid that I'd have on the whole flight. When I tuned in that station cockpit instruments gave me heading and distance to the station.

I reached the station with no problems. Mission planning had already shown me what track to take outbound from there. I knew I must get on that track precisely and get the wind figured out before I lost contact with the TACAN station. From then on I would have to go by my heading indicator, an instrument showing the direction I was going. A radar controller back at Panama on Monkey Mountain would feed me the bearing and distance information I needed to rendezvous with my flight.

I reported my position to Panama. "We've got you," they responded. "Continue your heading. Your flight is approximately one hundred miles away." As I continued out over the Gulf Panama gave me minor heading corrections. Generally, however, they let me stay on the track I'd established outbound from the TACAN station. Periodically radar controllers gave me an update: "Maintain your heading. . . . The flight is now eighty miles away. . . . Your flight is dead ahead for fifty miles. . . . Turn right to a heading of zero five zero degrees. . . . Your target is now twenty miles away."

I was being directed to my flight with no difficulty—or so it seemed. But on that fateful morning nothing was quite the way it seemed. Everything appeared to be normal. When the radar controllers started giving me detailed information I was confident they really had me on their scopes. If they didn't, they would be telling me to change my squawk and make identification turns. None of that happened. As I got closer to the rendezvous point Panama asked, "Do you have Venus Five One in sight yet?" I scanned the air. "No joy." Nothing in sight.

I looked for contrails in the clear air. At higher altitudes, under certain atmospheric conditions, you could see what looked like white smoke coming out of the back of an airplane. That was moisture coming out of the engine that froze into ice crystals and made a white plume. If an airplane was contrailing, it was easy to pick up. I saw no contrails, nor did I see anything on my radar. Panama repeated, "Continue your heading. They're right in front of you."

For the first time I began to feel uneasy. I knew my F-104 had good radar. I'd picked up the tanker at seventeen miles. If the two planes I was trying to rendezvous with were right in front of me, I ought to be picking them up on my radar, but I wasn't. The only other navigational aid I had was the TACAN that had operated properly within a range of about 150 miles from its ground station. Now I was beyond that range. It had broken lock and was of no value to me anymore. I looked down. Far beneath me was a deck of clouds. I couldn't see the water, but up at 35,000 feet, where I was, it was as clear as a bell, with no clouds at all. It was a beautiful day, but where were those two F-104s I was looking for?

At that moment I was given even more unsettling news. Panama reported that I had merged with the target. The blips on their radar had come together, indicating that I and the two planes I was trying to locate were in the same immediate area. The news was both puzzling and alarming. If two other planes were nearby and I couldn't see them visually or on my radar, there was a good potential for a midair collision.

The other two pilots, I knew, were flying on headings assigned by Panama, waiting for me to join up with them. I also knew they'd be listening with interest as Panama gave me the final steers to complete the rendezvous. They, too, would be concerned about the potential for a midair. Obviously they couldn't see me, and they wouldn't like what they were hearing. Panama contacted the flight leader. "Venus Five One, do you have Five Two in sight?" Flight leader Ken Kerwin responded, "No, we don't have him yet."

All of that told me one thing: I could not continue the heading I was on. I had to turn. I knew the time I had posted out from the TACAN station; I knew I was flying 520 knots per hour. In a matter of minutes I would be right over the island belonging to Red China—and I could be flying right into the flight path of the other two F-104s. I knew the flight had to be going from my left to my right, and the island was straight ahead.

I turned to the right, rolling my right wing down. I was going generally south then, hoping to parallel the path of the other two airplanes. Dropping my right wing gave me better visibility below me, and the flash of the wing in the sun might help the other pilots pick me up.

At that point I was well aware that three seasoned fighter pilots were in the air, two of them flying in formation, one alone. Panama's equipment showed us together, and we were not. All three of us had flown high-performance F-104s at supersonic speeds; we had been trained to know our aircraft and what to do in every conceivable situation. And I was very sure that all three of us had begun to suspect that something was very much amiss. One thing was clear: I was not in an enviable position. I was a single fighter pilot; no wingman was flying beside me to provide visual lookout. And increasingly it appeared that I was being directed by radar equipment on the ground that might not be working properly.

The Venus Five One pilots reported their altitude. I noted that I was flying at a higher altitude. I asked for their heading. The flight leader responded, "Five One steady, one seven zero degrees." I turned to the same heading and rolled out, going almost due south now.

The radar controllers back at Panama, perhaps for the first time, also seemed to become aware that something was wrong. "We don't have you," they told me. "We've lost you. Change your squawk." I did so. It was not an unusual request. Squawk was a term for the IFF, Identification Friend or Foe, a piece of equipment carried by all military aircraft that provided positive aircraft identification to friendly radar. Enemy airplanes didn't carry the system.

Panama was trying to identify me on their radar scopes. When a pilot turned his IFF on it emitted a signal that the radar screen picked up. If I squawked two, they'd see two little marks on the radar screen. If I squawked emergency, radar would show four marks. These IFF markings were much clearer on the radar scope than a skin paint, which was a raw return that the radar got from any airplane, including enemy airplanes. If the radar scopes saw a blip and it wasn't squawking, they were suspicious that it might be an enemy aircraft. Under normal conditions U.S. pilots squawked all the time, squawking different codes depending on our location and stage of flight. We were asked to change squawks only when radar controllers wanted to clarify who we were.

On this clear, sunny September morning, I was told, "Squawk one. . . . Now squawk three. . . . We have you. . . . Now we don't have you. We've lost you. . . . Maintain your heading. We've got you again. Turn right for an identification turn."

The increasingly alarming dialogue went on for many minutes, and I began to suspect not only that Panama's radar might not be working properly, but that my own IFF wasn't working at all. The nickname for the IFF was parrot. Was my parrot broken? Why didn't Panama know where I was?

It wasn't the first time I'd been lost from radar contact. I'd been lost many times, in fact, and in most cases radar had picked me up again. Even if they didn't, fighter pilots were supposed to be able to make it back to home base on their own. The IFF was just an aid, an assistance. If we didn't have that assistance, we could usually figure out a way to determine where we were. We might have a hard time finding another airplane without radar assistance, but if we couldn't, we just went home.

This time, however, ten or fifteen minutes had gone by while Panama gave me confusing and conflicting information, and I knew that was highly unusual. Normally they had us or they didn't have us. And then, to complicate matters even further, during the time that I was flailing around, turning and squawking, I sighted another airplane. Briefly I thought it was my flight, but it was back behind me and high. That was not a very good place to have another airplane.

I reported to Panama that I had an unidentified aircraft back at my five o'clock, then I made a big whopping turn and rolled out so I had the airplane in sight in front of me. I increased my speed to 580 knots and gave chase. The plane was going away from me, heading toward China. I told Panama that further pursuit wasn't possible; I'd lost sight of the airplane and wasn't about to chase something I couldn't see.

I turned back around, realizing that the turn I'd made might have sent me even further away from my flight. For another few minutes Panama continued to request that I change my squawk. I sensed we were getting nowhere.

The only way I could tell what direction I was going was by my heading indicator. Underneath me was a solid undercast. I saw nothing but white down there—no land or water, only that big sheet of clouds. At that moment I knew what direction I was going, but not where I was. I might, in fact, be right over Hainan Island and not even know it.

I continued to follow Panama's directions to turn and change squawks. Then Panama said, "Turn right ninety degrees for identification." I did so and made an appalling discovery. During the past few minutes, in all the flopping around that I'd been doing, my heading indicator had stopped turning. It had frozen in position. I immediately tried to use the standby compass, which on the 104 is mounted on a hinge that folds down so it doesn't obstruct the pilot's view. I tried to raise the compass—only to find that the hinge was stuck. The compass could not be raised to the proper operating position, making it unusable.

I tried to keep my voice calm and matter-of-fact as I reported to Panama that I had just lost my heading indicator. I was now somewhere way out over the Tonkin Gulf. I didn't know exactly where I was, and without a heading indicator or a standby compass I didn't know what direction I was flying.

A wave of sensations washed over me. I had flown many missions. I was a veteran fighter pilot, as well trained, I believed, as anybody in the Air Force. I was old enough to have logged more than two thousand hours of flying time, young enough to feel invincible and unafraid, and experienced enough to know that my role in the mission was rapidly approaching disaster. I had not been able to rendezvous with my flight. I didn't know where they were or how to find them. Fighter pilots expect to succeed, and on the morning of September 20, 1965, I wasn't at all sure I was going to succeed. I had to face a terrible truth: It looked very much like I was not going to accomplish the mission. The very idea of that was bitter and demoralizing to me.

An even more critical problem was facing me at that moment, however, and I was well aware of it: I had better find my way home before I ran out of fuel.

2

A Sitting Duck

On a farm in Roodhouse, Illinois, a slight, dark-haired boy of eight stood listening to the sounds of airplanes flying overhead. It was 1942, and U.S. bombers flying out of Omaha, Nebraska, were preparing to go to war. I was that young boy, and I was playing one of my favorite games. I would stand there for hours holding a small aircraft recognition book in my hand that showed pictures of airplanes from different angles. On a clear day, when I could see the airplanes, I would look at the wings, the tails, count the engines, and try to identify the aircraft from my book. They were all propeller planes and not flying very high, so it was fine sport.

Seeing and hearing those airplanes gave me chills. I was a farm boy with chores that never ended. My life was rooted in the rich Illinois farmland and controlled by a harsh, austere, autocratic father. As often as possible, however, my eyes and ears were on the sky. Even on a cloudy day, when I couldn't see any airplanes, I listened for them and tried to determine whether I was hearing a B-17 or a B-24.

One day I heard a sound I had never heard before and

would never forget, and then I saw the airplane. It was a B-29, the biggest bomber flown in World War II. To my young ears, the sound of its four engines was awesome, much like a deep, dramatic, gut-wrenching growl.

Being able to fly an airplane like that was beyond my comprehension. A childhood dream, perhaps, but certainly no more than that.

As I grew older I recognized several things about myself and my family. I was the youngest of six children, born of strict, religious parents.

Ours was not a laughing, boisterous family. Our father frowned on his six children having fun; he believed in work, not play, but there were times when the six of us—Joseph, Paul, Irene, Robert, James, and I—managed to do both.

My only sister, Irene, was eleven years older than I, and she was very special. She hugged me all the time, and I liked that, and she washed my hair and checked my fingernails and made a fuss over me.

It was hard—impossible—for me to live up to my four brothers and one sister. They had all been the best in their classes. They were studious, they got A's, and the teachers liked them.

I preferred to play games and sports and chase girls and tinker with farm machinery with my dad.

As a child I wasn't allowed to dance, stay out late, go to movies, spend money foolishly—even for an ice cream cone on Saturday night—and most certainly, I was never permitted to drink or smoke, at least not at home or where my parents might catch me.

James and I were very close. The others graduated from high school and left home, and the two of us drew even closer together. James was three years older, and we were opposites in many ways. I liked the outdoors, riding the tractor, watching my dad repair machinery, looking for animals out by the stream. I learned from my dad. At an early age I knew about engines and carburetors and how all the farm machinery worked. James had to do his share of the work on the farm, but he preferred to stay inside, reading and playing the piano. He was stocky like our mother; I was small and slight. We were different, but as the years went by I found myself following in his footsteps. James liked theater, speech, music, and I discovered that I did, too.

My father was very hard on us. His fortunes increased as I got older, but he was never one to relax and enjoy himself. He couldn't stop working or demanding that his family work. I was permitted to play on the school basketball team, but none of my other brothers had been allowed to play on any school athletic teams. They'd had no choice: They were to go to school and then come directly home and get to work. There were chores to be done.

Our dad believed that if you did a job, you should do it right, if not perfectly. His rows of corn had to be the straightest, his fields the neatest, his fences free of every single weed. He had built the family home himself, doing wiring, plumbing, roofing, carpentry. Even if he was building a hog house, the boards had to be cut off squarely, the structure put together so that it was straight and sturdy. He wouldn't build a lopsided anything, and he was as hard on himself as he was on his children.

There were times when his children may have loved him, but we didn't always like him very much. Even then we knew, however, that at the core of our family was a strength, a bond, a belief in one another that was as strong and abiding as the land we farmed. This was the environment in which I grew up; I have never doubted that it had a profound effect on the development of my character and my personality.

September 20, 1965. As I flailed around high in the air over the Tonkin Gulf I knew for sure that rendezvousing with my flight was becoming less likely with each passing moment. The realization was a traumatic one. I was greatly concerned that I had lost my heading indicator and standby compass, that Panama couldn't identify me on their radar scopes, that my fuel was going down, and that neither I nor anyone else knew where I was.

More than all that, however, was the sinking sensation that I was failing in my mission. Fighter pilots are trained to be mission-oriented. We are taught to be proud, self-confident individuals who believe, not only in ourselves, but in one another and in our abilities to accomplish whatever missions we're assigned.

Only those who graduate at the top of their classes in pilot training can become fighter pilots. Out of my class at Bryan Air Force Base in Texas only two of us out of sixty-six had become fighter pilots. Failure wasn't a word we wanted to hear. In our profession failure could, and often did, mean death.

My mission had been to rendezvous with Venus Five One flight. Without me the flight was one plane short and could not efficiently conduct the mission.

I had not succeeded in my objective, and knowing that gave me a terrible feeling, as profound as any I had known in my career. I'd go back to home base with the stigma of failure on me, and I knew exactly what would happen. The others would raise hell. "Have you had your eyes checked recently?" they'd inquire, only partially in jest. I'd let my team down and had failed personally. That was a tough pill to swallow.

I was caught now in a situation beyond my control. That was not to my liking at all, and I knew I could not let it continue for many more minutes. Radar controllers at Panama asked me to make a right ninety-degree identification turn, which they hoped would help them identify me on their radar scopes. They knew that if I was going east, such a turn would head me due south, and they should be able to see that turn.

I tried my best to comply. Without a heading indicator I had to do it visually. There was no land in sight beneath me, but there were puffy clouds on the horizon. I looked off to my right at a ninety-degree angle and spotted a cloud with a dip in it. I would head for that. I reported to Panama that I was rolling out ninety degrees and squawking emergency.

Panama requested that I do it again, and again. Without a heading indicator I couldn't be sure of my accuracy; I hoped I was turning ninety degrees. I wanted to show Panama that I could make ninety-degree turns without instruments, and I wanted to do everything possible to help them pick me up.

The radio transmissions continued to be calm and businesslike, even though I was well aware that everyone on that frequency would know by now that there was a problem, and perhaps a serious one. Once again Panama admitted that they couldn't locate me. "We've lost you completely," they reported. "We do not have you on our scopes."

Boy, I thought, that's neat. I was on top of a heavy cloud cover, with inoperative heading instruments, radar had lost me, and I was near, or over, enemy territory. My options were limited, but my goal was clear. I must try to save my airplane and get my fanny back on the ground. I still had plenty of fuel, but I needed to find myself quickly and get to the tanker or back to home plate at Da Nang.

I continued to receive directions from Panama asking for numerous changes in my IFF squawk. It began to sound like a broken record leading nowhere. Panama reported that they had me, then they didn't have me.

Even though I flew every day and knew the voices of the radar controllers working out of Panama, I had never met any of them personally. In the few months I'd been in Vietnam, however, I'd been impressed with their competence. Normally they picked us up immediately, knew our mission, and knew how to direct us to it.

For them to be having this kind of trouble locating an airplane was unusual. They, and I, knew my position was becoming more precarious by the moment. I needed help, and Panama wasn't able to give it. Finally I called the tanker and requested an emergency direction-finding steer to them.

The tanker, I knew, carried direction-finding equipment

consisting of a radio and an automatic direction-finding antenna that turned in the direction of the transmission being received. A needle on the dial in the cockpit of the tanker indicated the direction from which the transmission was coming.

The tanker asked me to transmit on my UHF radio for ten seconds. I punched my mike button and held it down. During those ten seconds my radio sent out the electronic transmission signals that activated the direction-finding equipment on the tanker. Once I let up on the mike button the needle on the dial in the tanker went dead.

The tanker continued on its course. Minutes later they asked me to transmit again. Their equipment showed only direction; by triangulation they hoped to be able to compute my distance from them.

The tanker crew was well qualified for this kind of action. Flight members on the tanker included a pilot, copilot, navigator, boom operator, and flight engineer. The navigator, I knew, would be checking maps spread out before him and monitoring his instrument panel as he coordinated the tanker's search for my missing aircraft.

It was not a day when things went right, however. The domino theory was clearly in effect: When one thing went wrong, everything went wrong. The results of the tanker's direction-finding fixes were not conclusive. They could guess where I was, but they couldn't be sure.

My mind was racing as I took further action on my own and jettisoned the fuel tanks that were attached to my wings. The fuel in those tanks had been used first. At this point they were simply causing additional drag, which increased my fuel consumption. Then I warned Panama of my next step: "I'm going to declare an emergency here pretty quick if I can't get contact with anybody."

"Understand," Panama responded.

Once I declared an emergency, everyone listening would know I was in serious trouble and would make every effort to assist me. This would include air traffic controllers on the ground and in the air, all other planes in the area, and any ships down in the Tonkin Gulf.

Over and over we had been instructed to declare emergencies when we were in trouble and to do so quickly, while there was still time for us to be helped. I had arrived at a dangerous moment; my fuel quantity was decreasing, and I needed help that I wasn't getting. Finally I took action. "Panama, this is Venus Five Two declaring an emergency NOW!"

My message was relayed to Panama by another plane somewhere in the area. Panama responded to the other pilot: "Roger. Understand. We can't maintain contact with him. Even his emergency squawk is out at this time."

The emergency call had been made. Supervisors and controllers at every level would maximize their efforts to find me. The tanker, continuing to try to take fixes on my whereabouts, had already realized the urgency of the situation. "We're coming around toward you," they reported, and they turned toward where they believed me to be.

My voice, I hoped, continued to be calm and steady throughout all my radio transmissions, but in my belly I had an empty, queasy, very uncomfortable feeling. A thought flashed through my mind: I'm not going to make it. I'm going to run out of gas before they find me out here, and I don't know where in the hell I am. There was no time, however, to dwell on such thoughts.

I contacted Panama again, asking them to scramble any available aircraft with automatic direction-finding equipment that could come up and try to home in on me.

"Roger," replied the radar controller, indicating that he had heard the request, but not whether it could be accomplished.

I knew there were F-102s sitting alert back at Da Nang that could be scrambled on a moment's notice. They were air defense airplanes carrying airborne radar equipment with a range of one hundred fifty to two hundred miles, compared to the F-104's range of twenty miles. Their usual mission was to go out and find or intercept enemy airplanes. Why the hell couldn't they be sent up to help find me? A desperate, last-ditch effort, maybe, but why not? And what about the Navy? They had the capability to launch aircraft that might be of help. Should Panama ask for their assistance? Should I? Events were moving so quickly I had little time to consider all the possible steps that might be taken.

I knew the other pilots in Venus Five One flight were listening, and I knew that if they could detect anything I was doing wrong, or offer any constructive suggestions, they would do so. We always evaluated and commented on one another's performances throughout our flights and once we got back on the ground. After all our missions we debriefed, sometimes for an hour or more, telling one another what we had done wrong and how the mission might have been more successful. At this moment I heard no suggestions. I knew there was little they could do. Their radar sets didn't extend out very far on a good day, and so far this hadn't been a good day at all. Increasingly my communications with Panama were breaking up, indicating to me that I was probably more than two hundred miles from Da Nang, which meant I could be anywhere in a vast area of more than a thousand square miles. The other pilots could relay radio transmissions between Panama and me when necessary, and they could wait with mounting concern as my troubles deepened.

Throughout my career I had been known to be meticulous and to plan each course of action carefully and methodically. I knew now, sitting high in the air in my F-104, that the moment of truth, and action, had arrived. I could wait no longer for help from anyone else. It was up to me to use every resource I had to find out where I was. I feared I was near Hainan Island. If I was, I needed to get away from there and fly west, back across the Tonkin Gulf. Once I got back on the western side of the Gulf I would hit the coastline of either North or South Vietnam, and I had flown up and down that coastline many times. I knew it well, from Saigon in the south to Haiphong in the north.

Haiphong, a northern port city near Hanoi, had distinguishing markings that I had never seen anyplace else in the world. Off the coast of Haiphong Harbor, out in the water, was an outcropping of black lava rocks that was visible from 30,000 feet. I had often used those rocks as checkpoints for my location. If I hit the coast north of there, I wouldn't recognize any landmarks and would know that I must turn south toward Da Nang.

At this point I needed to find out which direction I was flying and head west. That shouldn't be too difficult, I thought. I had been one of the few to be selected to attend the most prestigious school in the Air Force, the Fighter Weapons Instructor School, and we'd been trained extensively in figuring out complicated bombing and navigational computations. Actually, though, what I really needed at the moment wasn't sophisticated equipment and training. What I needed was a plain old sundial.

Sundials had intrigued me as a child. On walks with my dad I'd been fascinated with sundials and how they worked. "Sundials measure the angle of the sun at any given time," my dad had explained. Now, at this crucial moment in my life, the use of such a simple instrument might well mean the difference between life and death.

The sun was glaring in the cockpit as I looked around for something that would cast a shadow. Around the canopy bow and windscreen area were various metal bolts and protrusions, but none of them was long enough to cast a satisfactory shadow to determine direction. I needed something longer. A pencil? I pulled one out of my pocket and tried it. It didn't work, and then I realized why. It was almost noon. The sun was nearly overhead, and the shadows were too short to be usable. I couldn't find anything in the cockpit that would work, and I knew what that meant. There I was in an airplane with all kinds of fancy equipment, capable of going twice the speed of sound, and even my pencil sundial wouldn't help me find my way home.

I needed something magical to happen, and it did. The

clouds parted, and I was startled to see a coastline. It was as if someone had pulled a curtain to help me find my way home. I got a brief look at the coastline, and then the clouds closed in again and I couldn't see anything.

Then, miraculously, there was another break in the clouds. I reported seeing it to Panama. Perhaps the information would help them in their search for me. By now, I knew, dozens of people in the air and on the ground were aware that an emergency existed. During my career I had probably declared emergencies thirty times, usually because of mechanical malfunctions. In those cases air controllers directed the stricken aircraft to the nearest airfield, telling all other aircraft to stay away and stay off their radios. Ambulances and fire trucks were called; all the resources of an air base or airfield were called upon, giving top priority to getting the plane and its pilot back on the ground.

On this day nobody could do any of that for me because they still didn't know where I was. The tanker had me at one location, Panama at another. Venus Five One flight leader Ken Kerwin tried to be of help. "Venus Five Two, say your fuel state," he requested, and I responded. I had three thousand pounds and a coastline in sight.

"Okay, Five Two," he directed, "suggest you jettison your external stores and retain the tips and follow the coastline south." He was assuming that I was seeing the coast of North Vietnam.

The transmissions began to reflect growing concern and anxiety, although the voices I could hear remained calm. "Say present heading," Panama instructed, and I tried not to show anger or frustration with the radar controller, although obviously the question wasn't answerable. "I don't know what my heading is," I answered. "My heading indicator and standby compass are both out."

The tanker, now heading in what they believed was my direction, requested another direction-finding steer. "Transmit for ten," they instructed.

"Roger, transmitting for ten," I replied, holding my mike button down for ten seconds.

The tanker called again. "You're off to our right at the present time, so head for the coast and you'll probably intercept us. We'll keep checking your position."

"Okay. I'm parallel with the coast."

Twice I reported that I had a coastline in sight. My first instinct was to put the coastline directly behind me and get out of there. But I did not know what coastline I was seeing and I realized that flying away from it might in fact take me further away from Da Nang. The tanker thought I was talking about the coast of North Vietnam, but was it that coast? No one knew for sure. The confusion was apparent when the tanker reported, "Venus Five Two, this is Rickshaw One Two, we're taking up a collision course. Our altitude is two four zero. We should intercept you." That interception never took place. I wasn't where everyone thought I was.

"Venus Five Two, (this is) Panama, are you squawking flash now? Are you squawking Mayday?"

"That's affirmative."

The transmissions continued as the minutes wore on. Once again Panama thought they had me. "Five Two, an aircraft that should be you is about 140 miles out of Da Nang. Do you have a wingman holding hands with you?" A wingman is a second airplane flying almost abreast and slightly behind the leader. Panama saw two blips; perhaps another aircraft had joined up with me, or perhaps they weren't seeing my aircraft at all. And there was a third possibility: Maybe they were seeing me and an enemy airplane that no one else had spotted.

I answered their question. I had no wingman. I was still a solo aircraft.

"Roger, we still have you," Panama reported. "Strangle your parrot [don't squawk anything] for positive ID" I did as instructed, and then I heard Venus Five Four transmit that he had left the tanker and request a steer to Venus Five Two. I was instructed to squawk flash, then emergency. Once again Panama couldn't pick me up. They'd lost me again—if they'd ever had me in the first place.

I continued to follow Panama's directions, but it was becoming increasingly clear that if I was going to get out of this mess, I'd have to do it myself. It had been almost an hour since I had departed the airborne refueling tanker. When Panama told me for the last time that they had lost me again, I had only one thought: I had to go down and take a look at the coastline. I had no choice. I could stay up high and run out of fuel, or I could go down and try to determine where I was.

Suddenly a big hole opened in the clouds beneath me. I could see ten miles of coastline. I pulled the power back, lowered the nose, and made a steep descent to get down below the clouds quickly. The clouds closed around me as I headed down. Once I could see land again I would use dead reckoning to try to determine where I was. My maps were out and unfolded; I'd try to find a landmark on the ground—a railroad track, a cliff, a river—that I could identify on a map.

At ten thousand feet I broke through the clouds and was in the clear. I leveled off at nine thousand feet, wanting to stay as high as possible. As I did so the queasiness I'd been feeling for some minutes disappeared. I was taking positive action, and that changed everything. I felt renewed hope when I saw the coastline, even though I knew immediately that I had never seen that coastline before. It must be the northern part of North Vietnam, I thought, or perhaps mainland China or Hainan Island.

One thing was sure: I was in enemy territory, and I'd better find something on the ground that was identifiable on my maps and get the hell out of there. As I leveled off I increased my power to maintain a speed of 350 knots. Then I made two big, hard turns so I could see behind me. Had enemy aircraft happened to be passing along as I popped out of the clouds? If so, I wanted to see them before they saw me. I turned hard to the left, looked around, and then pulled hard to the right. Then I rolled out parallel to the coast. I'd cleared my six o'clock position and was relieved to have seen nothing. I rolled out straight and level and looked down at the coastline, my maps spread out on my lap.

Down below, on the coastline, I saw just what I needed. A gigantic cliff rose some three thousand feet up from the sea. It was an incredible sight; surely that cliff would be shown on my maps. I was busy watching the coast, looking at my maps, trying to confirm my position. I was alone, flying straight and level, no wingman, no eyes in the back of my head.

I had no way of seeing an airplane that was in the clouds above me. My lone F-104 was a sitting duck. Not more than twenty seconds after I had made my clearing turns my aircraft took direct hits and shrapnel grazed my right arm. At that moment I didn't know the extent of the damage done to me or my aircraft, and I didn't know who was shooting at me.

3

Carnival Ride in a Panic Situation

I felt heavy thumps on my airplane as I was hit, as if someone was banging on it with a sledgehammer. How stupid could I be? I had never once looked down at the water. I'd been so busy checking my six o'clock position, looking directly behind me for enemy aircraft, that I had neglected to look down. Then *whammo*—I was getting hit. I cursed myself for being so negligent as I monitored my instruments and watched the warning-light panel come ablaze with red and amber lights. I had no time to worry about those lights right then, however. First I had to find out who was shooting at me. I'd seen no enemy aircraft during my clearing turns. It had to be a ship.

I reported to Panama that I'd been hit, then I rolled the wings to the left to look down at the water. My airplane was vibrating, but I needed to find the ship so I could turn away from it, or I'd get hosed down for sure as I got closer to the enemy guns. Rolling left, I looked down. There was no ship in sight. Nothing. I rolled the wings to the right to look on that side. No ship. Where the hell was it?

Then, out of the corner of my eye, I spotted the aircraft that had been shooting at me breaking off from his firing pass. I didn't know where that airplane had come from or how it had gotten behind me, but there it was, a MIG-19 with the red star of China on its tail. Ships were forgotten. There was the enemy. How many other MIGs were closing in behind me? Clearly the Red Chinese pilot had come down from the clouds at a high rate of speed to put my F-104 in firing range. If he didn't turn or break off, he'd be out in front of me. The enemy pilot was moving fast as he broke off.

My shock at being hit was gone. My right wing had holes in it, and the missile and missile rail had been blown off that side. The MIG-19, I knew, had two guns. One of them was a .37-millimeter cannon, which fired large projectiles. No wonder I'd felt such heavy thuds on my aircraft when I was hit. Enemy shells had penetrated the fuselage. I knew there was a hole somewhere in the side of the airplane because I was losing pressurization in the cockpit. I could hear the depressurization and feel it as my ears popped.

Right now the warning lights in the cockpit indicated extensive damage to many of the aircraft systems. All that was unimportant, however, for there, turning away from me in a fast, steep climb with both afterburners going, was the enemy aircraft. Instantly I rolled into a right turn and pulled back on the stick as hard as I could to increase my turn rate. I wanted that Chinese fighter directly in front of me, not behind.

It was a supreme moment for a fighter pilot. Shooting that MIG down would be the ultimate achievement for any fighter pilot, and I was going to do it. I was going to get a kill. I'd be the first one in my squadron to shoot down an enemy aircraft in Vietnam. That's what aviation history was all about. How lucky could I be? I'd been fired on and hit, but I hadn't been blown out of the sky. Now, with deadly intent, I concentrated on just one thing: getting behind that MIG and bringing him down.

I pushed the throttle full forward to increase my speed. As I did so, new warning lights came on. Instruments in the cockpit indicated exhaust temperature was increasing and the engine rpm was going down, and I felt no thrust increase. I knew what that meant. I had an engine stall. The F-104 was equipped with a J-79 engine, which had a history of compressor stalls. Instantly I shut the engine off so there was no fuel going to it, hit the air-start switches, positioned the throttle to full military thrust, and felt great relief when the engine restarted and accelerated. Although the stall had been cleared, the engine wasn't running properly. It was rough and sounded terrible, but at least it was running, and I could get enough thrust out of it to go after the enemy.

I was well aware of the warning lights illuminated on the instrument panel, but I couldn't do anything about them at that moment. I had more important things to do. I was going in for the kill. My own safety didn't enter into my thoughts at all. If I got into an air-to-air battle with the enemy and had to light my afterburner, I might run out of gas and not make it back. None of that mattered. I wondered about other enemy aircraft, however. Where were they? Had this one MIG been sent up alone? It didn't make sense to me, but I had seen no other aircraft, and no one else was shooting at me. It was strange, I thought, and it made that MIG very vulnerable. My 104 was coming in around behind him and closing. I could barely breathe in anticipation. I just hoped my airplane would hang on long enough for me to shoot that bastard down.

I was a lame, wounded duck. But all of my malfunctioning equipment was nothing compared to a sound I heard at that moment. My fighter plane was equipped with AIM-9B missiles, called Sidewinders. And my remaining missile was growling. It was the most wonderful sound I had ever heard. When the missile detected a heat source it emitted a growling noise that I could hear in my headset. The closer and more nearly aligned the missile was to the heat source, the louder it growled. Once launched, these air-to-air missiles locked on the heat source and automatically guided themselves to the target.

My right missile had been shot off, but the left one was still there and it was . . . oh, yes . . . it was growling. What a glorious moment. Sidewinder missiles can home in on the heat of an engine, but when afterburners are lighted, flames come out the tail of an airplane. In trying to get away from me the enemy pilot had lighted his afterburners, making him a perfect target. My feelings of anxiety and panic turned to ecstasy. By damn, I was going to shoot that MIG out of existence, and that was any fighter pilot's number one objective. Dropping bombs on targets was one thing; the absolute ultimate achievement would be to shoot this MIG down and get credit for a kill.

I was concentrating intently as I continued turning toward the enemy aircraft, my missile growling. The enemy was off to my right at about a thirty-degree angle, not a good enough angle to be sure of a successful hit. Ideally I wanted to be directly behind that target so my missile was aligned with the center of the heat source; then a hit would be virtually assured. I wanted to turn my aircraft just a little bit further for a perfect shot. My one remaining missile had to do the job. Once it was fired, the missile would take off like a giant corkscrew, its eye seeking the source of the heat. If its eye lost that source, it wouldn't track or guide itself in. It would simply fly unguided until it burned out, and then it would self-destruct. That must not happen.

I had practiced this maneuver many times. I had already flipped the missile select switch to the armed position as I continued to turn toward the MIG. Suddenly I felt something horrendous. My flight control stick had gone dead. I could no longer turn my aircraft at all. In that second the enemy MIG climbed into the clouds and disappeared. The 104's Sidewinder missile quit growling. I couldn't believe it. Never in my life had I felt a more empty, sickened, dejected sense of failure and defeat. The enemy had escaped! All that I had trained for, dreamed of, had just slipped out of my grasp. In that moment I knew total, terrible defeat.

My F-104 had two independent flight control systems that

were activated by hydraulic fluid pumped under pressure through a series of lines and valves. I had lost that Chinese MIG because both those systems had failed, and I had no control over the flight of my aircraft. The nose of the 104 was going down, and I couldn't pull it up.

I knew I was going to have to eject, but I hoped to delay that moment as long as possible so that I could get away from the enemy coastline. If I could head the airplane further out to sea, I figured I'd be increasing my chances for survival and rescue. Get away from land, and friendly forces could pick me up.

My airplane was descending at a twenty-degree dive angle. The water was coming up fast. Staying with the airplane any longer would only decrease my chances for a successful ejection and might even send me crashing into the Tonkin Gulf. I had no time to lose. I had never jumped out of an airplane before, but I'd practiced it many times in a simulator on the ground. I estimated my airplane was going to crash into the sea in about ten seconds. It was time to bail out. I made a last transmission to Panama from my descending aircraft: "I'm ejecting, and I'm ejecting NOW!"

I assumed the ejection position, sitting back erect in the seat to avoid spinal injury when the seat was forced out of the aircraft. I put my head back against the headrest so the ejection force wouldn't snap my neck, and I pulled my feet back from underneath the instrument panel. Then I reached down with both hands and pulled the ejection ring on the seat between my feet. There was no turning back now; from then on, everything was automatic. In an instant the canopy was blown off by two small explosive cartridges that released the locks; once the canopy was loose the wind stream blew it away.

I had ejected at an altitude of six to eight thousand feet, hoping the high altitude would increase my chances of survival, and I had pulled the throttle of the airplane back to idle to reduce the speed as much as possible before I ejected.

The ejection procedure had begun. The canopy was gone. If I hadn't already pulled my feet back from under the instrument panel, they would have been pulled back by cables on a reel. All of us wore metal spurs on the heels of our flying boots; each time we flew, we attached those spurs to the cables. If our feet were extended when the seat was blown out of the airplane, our legs would be crushed by the instrument panel. My feet were back and in the footrests, which would help stabilize them once I got out in the wind stream.

I knew the entire ejection procedure was controlled by powder cartridges that had different burning rates. One might take a tenth of a second to activate, another two tenths of a second. Everything was timed to happen in the proper sequence. The canopy had to blow off before the seat went up.

I knew all about these timed sequences, but for one brief moment I was alarmingly aware of the pause before the next step, and I came close to panicking. It was one thing to learn all about the ejection procedure in the classroom, another to be going through it out here in enemy territory.

The canopy blew off, and the wind hit me in the face. Then nothing happened. The ejection seat's not going to work, I thought with horror, and this plane is about to crash. At that moment a rocket motor attached to the seat went *whoosh* and forced the seat up and out of the airplane. It was one of the most hair-raising sensations I had ever had. For one brief second it was almost fun in a death-defying way—like a carnival ride in a panic situation.

As soon as my head cleared the windscreen there was a strong tug on my throat from the helmet's chin strap as a tremendous blast of air hit my face. The seat had been blown some four hundred feet away from the airplane; there I was, tumbling through the air, still attached to my seat.

Rationally, I knew what would happen next, but each time there was a delay I panicked. Why hasn't my parachute opened, I wondered, and then I realized it had better *not* open when I was still in the seat or anywhere near the seat. Sufficient time had not elapsed for that to occur, but within a tenth of a second the lap belt released and the seat separator activated. Pilots call the seat separator the butt snapper because it actually snaps your butt out of the seat by tightening the tension of the webbing you're sitting on. I was hurled from the seat like a slingshot.

So far, I realized, everything had worked perfectly in my ejection, but the time delays still scared me. I had never fully realized how long three tenths of a second could seem during such a critical time. I was still tumbling through space, now a free-falling body. "Oh, my God," I thought, "after everything else that's happened today, now my parachute's not going to open!" Just as I reached for the D-ring to open the parachute manually I felt a hard jolt, and the parachute deployed automatically. As it did it blossomed out, giving me a strong tug as it slowed my fall through the air. This, I knew, was called the parachute opening shock, and what a tremendous relief it was to feel it.

And then everything stopped. Up to that moment the world had been spinning, tumbling, and reeling. Now, with the parachute open, I was floating down like a feather. For the first time I opened my eyes, which had been forced closed by the wind blast at ejection, and noted that the day was warm and beautiful. Off in the distance I could see rolling green mountains and the steep cliff I'd spotted from the air. The water below was blue and crystal clear. For one brief moment I was physically comfortable as I floated down, though still feeling the trauma of the whole ejection experience. I assumed the land I was seeing was Hainan Island or part of mainland China. Since I'd been shot down by a Chinese plane, it made sense that this was Chinese territory, not North Vietnamese.

I was amazed at how I felt. I was coming down calmly and quietly, and even the ejection itself had not been as terrifying as I had expected. Pilots often have to eject so low to the ground after takeoff, in a panic situation, that they are injured or killed. But I was more fortunate.

I was descending slowly, secured in the parachute harness, a series of straps that attached me to the parachute. I knew I could have been blown to bits; I also knew the ejection system might not have worked. It had worked, and I was alive. Momentarily I felt a sense of euphoria. Then reality set in.

On this fateful day in September of 1965 my airplane had been shot out of the sky, and I had seen the smoke after it crashed into the sea. Now I was parachuting into enemy territory and I hoped with all my being that I was prepared for what lay ahead. With cold clarity I knew, even without conscious thought, that everything I had learned and become over the years would be called upon before this day was over. Coming down in the parachute was a sensation I could never have imagined. There was a deadly calmness to it. I could hear the flutter of the parachute and the wind whistling through the risers. Otherwise it was an eerie, quiet descent into . . . I didn't know what. Death, perhaps. Capture, more likely. I dared not think too far ahead. Consider your options, I told myself, knowing they were terrifyingly limited.

I had almost no hope of being rescued. If I were off the coast of either North or South Vietnam, there might be U.S. helicopters in the area that could pick me up. Here I was probably only a distance of three to five miles from the enemy coastline, and I figured my chances of being found quickly by friendly forces were just about zero.

I had better do what I could for myself, I knew, as I began to recall survival techniques that I'd learned over the years. Many of them were steps that I had not consciously thought of for a long time. Coming down in the parachute, I had a vivid recollection of an instructor I'd had in survival school years before. I could hear the instructor say, "When your parachute opens the first thing you do is look up to see if you've got a good chute; if you don't, you've got to do something about it." I looked up to make sure none of the risers was twisted and the parachute was fully inflated. It was open and operating properly.

I remembered something else I'd learned in survival school: "If you're parachuting into enemy territory, take advantage of the height you have while you're in your parachute to observe your surroundings and develop an escape and evasion plan. Try to decide, while you're up high, what direction to take when you hit the ground." It had all sounded logical in school.

I looked toward the coast in the distance and noted a wooded area off to the left. If I could reach that thicket, perhaps I could hide there for a few days and use my radio to make contact with search-and-rescue teams.

The plan might have worked had it not been for two rather sobering obstacles. I had intentionally headed my airplane out to sea, hoping to get thirty miles or more away from land to facilitate possible rescue. I hadn't succeeded in doing that, and now I was coming down over water near the coast and was highly visible. Unless I was picked up immediately, I couldn't remain undetected out in the sea for long; I'd be seen and captured. I needed to get to shore.

The other obstacle was even more formidable. I'd been surveying the land beyond the coastline to try to develop an escape and evasion route. Suddenly I looked down at the water beneath me, and I couldn't believe my eyes. I was coming down right in the middle of a big Chinese fishing fleet.

4

An Unexpected Catch

During our early days in pilot training the other cadets and I began learning basic survival techniques. We were young men who were eager to fly and fight; we knew survival training was necessary and important, but we hoped we never had to use any of it. We were taught to wear the proper flying equipment and to know the environment into which we were flying and how to cope with it if we had to bail out of our comfortable cockpits.

I graduated second in my class in pilot training and thus received one of the two assignments to become a fighter pilot. It was a great moment for a young man who had loved airplanes for so long. I went into advanced pilot training and gunnery school and then was assigned to Europe and discovered that all pilots going overseas were sent to combat survival school. This was no longer just survival in the wilds of the Arctic or the jungle or the desert, this was survival in a combat environment.

The Air Force Combat Survival School was at Stead Air Force Base near Reno, Nevada. I spent three weeks there in the most extensive survival school I ever attended. We had two weeks of classroom instruction, and then fifty of us were sent out on a mountain trek that none of us would ever forget. For a week we lived in the mountains, sleeping in sleeping bags in a tent, catching rabbits to eat, drinking melted snow for water. It chills me to think about it, for it was horrendously cold, and the snow was eight feet deep in most places.

Toward the end of our stay in the mountains we were dropped off in pairs at various points along the side of the mountain, given a map and a compass, and told to find our way over ten miles of rugged mountain terrain at night to a termination point where we would be picked up. We were dropped off at three o'clock on a dark winter afternoon, knowing we must reach the rendezvous spot by nine o'clock the following morning or we would flunk that part of the course.

We had to move fast and quietly. We were learning to survive in enemy territory, and we must not be caught. Instructors in snowmobiles were searching through the darkness for us. If we were caught, we'd be downgraded. We wore snowshoes and backpacks; it was indeed a grueling test of endurance in the wind and darkness and deep snow.

After that sojourn in the mountains we were sent to a mock prisoner-of-war camp. To all of us this seemed impressively realistic. We were captured, interrogated, and put in cells in a camp surrounded by barbed-wire fences and guard towers. The guards wore Russian uniforms, and there were sweat boxes for solitary confinement. It was very apparent that the Air Force was going to great efforts to prepare us psychologically and emotionally for what we might expect if we were ever captured by enemy forces. We went through the training, but the prospect of actually being captured by enemy forces seemed very remote to us during those training sessions.

Now, years later, that prospect didn't seem at all remote to me. As I was descending in my parachute I had hoped I could land in the water and stay in my dinghy until darkness set in, then head for shore and hide in the wooded area off to the left. But, oh, damn! My heart sank as I looked down at those fishing boats. I'd never make it to shore. Those boats were scattered over an area several miles in diameter. Under any other circumstances I might have laughed. What an unbelievable sight. I was descending slowly, so I had ample opportunity to observe the motley armada. Most of the boats appeared to be so small they held only one or two fishermen, and unless those men were asleep there was no way they'd miss seeing this big orange-and-white object come drifting down out of the sky.

As I looked down at those boats they were still fairly far below me, and for one moment I felt a stabbing sensation of something I had never felt before, something that survival schools could never teach anyone. Drifting down in my parachute, I was totally, completely alone, cut off from any world I had ever known. What I did in the next few minutes might well determine whether I lived or died.

I dared not dwell on the dangers. That ragtag collection of fishermen might look ludicrous to my American eyes, but I had no illusions. They were the enemy, and they could see me coming down.

I took the battery-operated radio out of my vest pocket and began transmitting, reporting that Venus Five Two had ejected, I was coming down in my parachute some distance off an unidentified coastline, I could see a steep cliff, and I was uninjured. I was giving a blow-by-blow narration of what I was seeing, hoping it might help friendly forces find me.

There was one thing wrong with the whole scenario, however, and I knew it when I released the transmitter button. I could hear the beep, beep, beep of the personnel locator beacon through my radio receiver. That locator activated automatically when the parachute was deployed. What it meant was that my voice and that beeper were transmitting on the same frequency, the international guard channel, designed for emergencies, and they were blocking each other out. This is nonsense, I thought. I had to get that beeper turned off. I put the radio back in my vest pocket and strapped it in so it wouldn't fall out. Then I looked up at the beeper, attached to the riser of the parachute, and reached out to try to turn it off. Even though I could see it in its pouch, I couldn't quite get to it, so I pulled the riser down to bring it closer. As I did so I realized I'd made a mistake. Air spilled out of the parachute canopy, which caused the parachute to swing alarmingly and descend faster, and I still couldn't reach the beeper. The hell with this, I decided. I'm too far away and too low for anybody to hear me anyway. I'd better concentrate on getting this thing in the water.

I'd had lessons in water landings in survival school. We'd been taken out to sea in a big boat with all our gear—rubber dinghy, parachute harness, helmet—and told to jump off the back of the boat and hit the water as if we were coming down in a parachute. Once we jumped we were left out in the water in our dinghy for the rest of the day. Every now and then a boat came by to see if we were okay.

Oh, God, I thought, remembering all that. I hadn't really expected to use any of it. Another part of the lesson had been taught from the hanging harness. I'd jumped off a platform in a simulated parachute jump, and the harness caught me; then I'd learned which buckles to unsnap if I was going to hit in high winds or in water or on land. At other times the other pilots and I had been required to go to the officers' swimming pool at a base and jump off the diving board wearing all the equipment we'd have on if we had ejected from an airplane.

I thought about those years of training. Since I was coming down into water, the crucial considerations were staying afloat; making sure the parachute didn't collapse on top of me, suffocating me; and avoiding entanglement in the risers.

My parachute harness had a mechanism on each shoulder

that would release the parachute risers and canopy. The minute my feet hit the water I pulled those release mechanisms, and my parachute blew gently away. I had already inflated my underarm life preservers, which would act as flotation gear. I dropped into the water; the underarm life preservers stopped my fall, holding my head above water.

My dinghy, a small rubber boat attached to me by a twenty-foot lanyard, had inflated automatically and been the first object to hit the water. I'd hoped I wouldn't land right on top of it and puncture it, and I hadn't. The dinghy was off to the side; I found the lanyard and pulled it toward me. I moved quickly. There were sharks in this water; I needed to get into that dinghy as fast as possible.

I grabbed the dinghy and turned my body around to pull myself into it on my stomach. I'd belly in, then roll over on my back and sit down. As I followed the procedures I'd practiced so many times in training I felt a sharp dig on my left leg. I looked down, puzzled, and saw that one of the cables on the spurs of my flying boots was still there. It was this raw cable that had rubbed me on the leg as I twisted around, and I knew it would puncture the rubber dinghy if I pulled my feet in. I was surprised. Nowhere in any of the extensive training we'd received had there been any warning of this possible hazard. Raw cable was dangerous, to me and to the dinghy. I couldn't leave it there.

I slid back into the water, using my underarm life preservers as floats, and pulled my foot up to remove the cable, wondering as I did so how many times this had happened to others. Lives could be lost because of dinghies punctured by this raw cable. I got the wire off and dropped it into the water, then climbed back into the dinghy. I sat for a moment, feeling relieved just to be in the dinghy.

I was still alarmed by the possibility of sharks circling my little rubber raft. Part of the dinghy's equipment included a shark-repellent kit. I opened the kit, pulled out the repellent bag, which looked like a tea bag, unsealed it, and swished it back and forth in the water. The repellent was a chemical compound that turned the water green; the smell and color were supposed to chase sharks away. I saw movement in the water around me and assumed it was sharks. I hoped the repellent would work, and it did.

The dinghy's survival kit was in the water, secured by a short strap. I pulled it in. The survival kit was a waterproof canvas bag packed with a variety of survival equipment, including sunburn lotion, fishing hooks and lines, medicines, water purification tablets, and a rescue mirror. In all, the bag held some thirty or forty items designed for sea or land survival. I looked through it quickly, saw nothing I needed right then, zipped it back up, and put it to the side.

I was trying to remain calm. I knew I must not let my emotions get away from me, or I'd be overwhelmed by a sense of dejection and despair. It wasn't easy. I couldn't help remembering all the stories I'd heard of people who had been out on the water for weeks and weeks and finally died. I didn't expect that to happen to me—I was too near the coastline—but that didn't prevent me from feeling horribly frightened and apprehensive. And most of all I felt great uncertainty. The outcome of this disastrous misadventure had not been decided by any means. I could still starve, drown, be eaten by sharks, be captured by the enemy, or be beaten down by the sun. Not pleasant alternatives, any of them.

And yet I'd come this far, and I mustn't waste precious moments, even if I was scared to death. If the Chinese captured me, what would they do to me? How would I be treated? One thing was certain: I'd be interrogated, and I'd better be prepared. I looked down and saw my Fighter Weapons School patch on my sleeve. With my survival knife I cut the patch off and threw it in the water. It was one of my most prized possessions, a symbol of achievement that my captors must not see. It didn't sink, so I grabbed it back, cut it into little shreds, and watched the pieces disappear.

If my captors knew anything at all about U.S. Air Force operations, and I assumed they did, they would know what the Fighter Weapons School was all about. Those of us who had been selected to go to that school had been taught intricate details of all weapons, including nuclear weapons. We knew much more than the average pilot about nuclear weapons, in fact, and China didn't have nuclear weapons yet. It could make for some uncomfortable interrogation if they discovered my background. I must not let them know that I had been exposed to sensitive classified material. I made very sure the pieces of that patch disappeared down into the water.

Then I pulled the radio out of my vest pocket. As I attached the power cord to the battery I cursed my stupidity. Everything was wet, the battery was fully charged, and I got a hell of a jolt. Be more careful, I warned myself.

The beeper, still attached to the parachute, was off in the water somewhere and no longer a problem, so I decided to try a radio transmission. Once again I gave pertinent information on my surroundings and my condition. I knew that it was probably futile, but I wanted to be sure I did everything possible to increase my chances of being picked up. I didn't want to omit any step that might help. Finally I stopped transmitting. I didn't believe anyone had heard me when I was up high in my parachute because of the beeper interference; how could they possibly hear me now, when I was riding in a little rubber dinghy right at sea level? I knew I must not run the radio battery down with useless transmissions. I might need it very badly at a later time.

Off in the distance I could see the fishing boats drawing closer. Even though I was floating low in the water, I knew they could see me and were coming after me. And at that moment I felt fear . . . and sadness. I had been so proud to be a member of the F-104 unit and Harvey Quackenbush's flight. Now I was letting all of them down. I was about to be captured by a bunch of ragtag fishermen, and nothing in any of my training could really have prepared me for this moment, nor could I ever have imagined it in my most dreadful nightmares. I sat watching them close in on me.

The first person to reach me in the water was an old man who came paddling toward me in a little boat that was more raft than boat. I held my breath. At least the old man wasn't shaking his fist at me or brandishing a knife or gun. I watched him warily. Then the old man grinned, and in this moment of extreme danger I couldn't help noticing that he had no top teeth. He stuck out his hand and pulled me into his boat, along with all my equipment, including the dinghy.

Other boats were closing in as the old man paddled toward shore. We eyed each other suspiciously. It appeared the fisherman was trying to look friendly, but he was being very cautious. It was a one-on-one situation; none of the other boats was close enough yet to be of help if he needed them. The old man had no way of knowing I wasn't going to pull a gun and shoot him, and he had no way of knowing who I was. Clearly I wasn't Chinese, but might I be a friendly force? A Russian? Or somebody who was friendly to the Chinese military? The fisherman was being very, very careful. I knew I could overpower him, but what would that accomplish? If I resorted to violence with those other boats approaching, I'd definitely never reach shore alive.

Thirty minutes later a larger boat drew near. I was motioned into it, and the old man paddled away. His boss seemed to have taken over. The fishing fleet, it appeared, was fairly well organized. The atmosphere, however, began to change. There were no longer any attempts to be friendly. The mood had become official and hostile.

Five fishermen stood on the larger boat, motioning me to sit down. Then they rigged the sails, and the boat headed toward shore. The five of them eyed me and my equipment but made no move to search me. And suddenly, as I sat there in that old, crude, rickety boat, I felt an icy chill. I was more frightened than I had ever been before. I might have known how to respond to military captors; this group of wild-eyed civilians scared the hell out of me.

I was out in the open sea off a coastline that appeared to be uninhabited. Laws of the civilized world, as I knew them, just might not apply out here. The fishermen had no shirts on; they looked dirty and sweaty and mean and reminded me very much of the terrifying pirates I'd read about as a kid. I watched them carefully, trying not to do anything that would cause them to attack or harm me.

Moments later an even larger boat came on the scene. It appeared I was being worked up the chain of command of this scary bunch of Oriental fishermen. Okay, I thought, play all the musical boats you want to with me. And then, just as I was about to be transferred to the bigger boat, something seemed to go wrong in the chain of command. The fishermen in the two boats began to scream at each other. The mood turned ugly very quickly, and I didn't have any idea what was happening. Everyone seemed hysterical and confused, and nobody appeared to be in charge.

Finally the men who had possession of me motioned me out of the boat. One of them jumped into the water and helped me slide down; others on that boat followed, evidently intending to lead me to shore.

The men in the larger boat were infuriated; the intensity of their voices increased dramatically and frighteningly. As I stood in water up to my waist I got a good look at them for the first time. Oh, my God, I realized, they have guns. There were eight or nine of them up there with rifles and pistols, and they were all pointed at me.

At that moment I knew with absolute certainty that I was going to die. This was it, and what a horribly unfair way to go. I'd thought about death, sure—a plane in flames as I chased enemy aircraft, one last daring dogfight as I showed my skill and flew to the very edge of my nerves and beyond. But this? There was nothing glorious about this. These Chinese barbarians were going to execute me right here in this godforsaken spot with no trial, no judge, no chance to defend myself.

I stood, paralyzed, but as the intensity of the fishermen's quarrel grew I became confused. Was I reading this scene wrong? Why were the men in the two boats yelling at each other? Why didn't they just shoot me? Was it possible that maybe, just maybe, the men with guns simply wanted me to be transferred to their boat, and the people who had me refused to turn me over?

As they argued among themselves I took a slow step to the side. Several of my captors were standing in the water right in front of me; another was off to the side motioning for me to come in his direction. I took another step, moving very slowly, and watched the barrels of the guns that had been pointed directly at me. As I moved I couldn't believe what I saw. The guns didn't follow me. They hadn't been pointed at me at all, but at the fishermen who had been standing directly in front of me. I felt dizzy from fright and relief. They weren't going to kill me right there; they simply wanted possession of me. It was unbelievable.

Finally the power of the gun prevailed. I was ordered onto the larger boat and, for the first time, was searched very carefully. I knew one thing they were looking for that they weren't going to find. My gun. In my rush to rendezvous with my flight I had left my .38 revolver back at Da Nang. During their search they also didn't find the big survival knife that was strapped to my leg.

The boat sailed the final few hundred yards to shore, and I was ordered to disembark. I jumped off the boat, bewildered and shaky. Was this nightmare never going to end? Feelings of fright, apprehension, fatigue closed down around me.

The Chinese had stripped me of my belongings. As we left the boat everyone around seemed to be carrying something of mine, as if to proclaim his role in my capture. At gunpoint I was marched a short distance to a crude-looking little fishing village with three small bamboo huts and told to go in one of the huts. Frightened or not, I was rational enough to realize they wanted to get me out of sight. I could be seen out on the open beach by friendly or enemy forces, and the fishermen didn't want that.

I was surprised to see an old woman sitting in the hut I entered. She jumped up off the dirt floor where she'd been sitting and smiled at me, then motioned for me to sit down on the little rug on the floor. She brought me a cup of water, the first thing I'd had to eat or drink for many hours, and I nodded my thanks. I could hear talking outside, and then a man came in and motioned for me to go through a door into a back room. I did as I was told and was even more surprised to see a girl of eighteen or nineteen sitting in the room. I was dumbfounded. What in the world were they doing? Any number of possibilities flashed through my mind. She was an attractive, neat, pretty young woman. Were they setting me up, hoping I would make advances toward her so they would have an excuse to kill me? Or were they friendly to the U.S. and planning to hide me until I could be returned to American forces? I had no way of knowing.

The young woman and I sat in silence in the back room of the small hut for ten or fifteen minutes. I could hear the Chinese jabbering among themselves just outside. This couldn't be happening! What the hell was I doing sitting on a dirt floor in a hut in China? I'd started the day at five A.M. back in The Hooch at Da Nang. I'd been shot down shortly after noon. It was now two P.M., according to my wet but still-operating watch. At this very moment, I should have been dropping bombs in North Vietnam. We'd been briefed on Vietnam, but China? Nobody had told us a thing about China, except to stay away from it.

I took a deep breath. From the beginning of my Air Force career I had accepted all the risks that being a fighter pilot entailed. Capture was one of them. I had wanted a life beyond Roodhouse and the farm, and I had found it. Flying

49

fighter planes had touched something very deep within me. Now I was tired, wet, in shock, and very frightened. That would pass. I was alive, and my mind was functioning. I heard a new voice, and an older-looking man appeared at the door and ordered me outside. The talk had ended. Evidently they had decided what to do with me.

5

A Dark Day

From the first moment he ran into trouble on that fateful morning in 1965 U.S. Air Force Captain Philip E. Smith had used his radio to try to help himself and others find him and get him back to home base. Many of those radio transmissions were never heard by Panama, his fellow pilots, or any ships down in the Tonkin Gulf. By the time he was shot down he was flying low and was several hundred miles away from Da Nang. The crew of the KC-135 airborne refueling tanker, which had tried so hard to find him, thought they heard his last transmission, and they responded: "Understand you're bailing out." They heard no reply.

Ken Kerwin, leader of Venus Five One flight, also gave it one last desperate try. "Venus Five Two, Five One here," he transmitted. Six seconds later he repeated, "Venus Five Two, Five One here."

Thirty seconds later, with a sinking heart, he admitted it was hopeless. "Panama, [this is] Venus Five One. Have you got the Air Sea Rescue alerted for a possible pickup?"

Panama: "Roger. We're talking to them right now, Five One."

51

Five One: "Okay, and try to give them his last known position."

Panama: "Roger. We only have a rough approximation. We'll pass that. He should be within twenty miles of that. We never heard Five Two on Guard [the emergency radio channel]."

Five One: "Roger, understand. You can alert the Navy, too. They may be in that area."

Panama: "We've already alerted the Navy, Five One, thank you."

Five One: "Roger."

The drama in the sky had ended. The missing pilot had ejected. Where he was, no one knew.

At three o'clock that afternoon Air Sea Rescue efforts were launched out of Da Nang Air Base to find the downed Air Force pilot. Two of the first to volunteer to take part in that rescue mission were Smith's fellow F-104 pilots, his flight commander, Harvey Quackenbush, and his longtime friend and flight member, Dale Carlson. If Phil Smith was alive somewhere out there in the waters of the Tonkin Gulf, they wanted to be there to find him.

Hours of anguish led up to that moment when the rescue effort was actually launched, and they were especially poignant for Harvey Quackenbush, whose place Smith had taken in the flight. Normally Quackenbush would have led the flight, but he had been out of town, and the rules specified that he had to be the wingman when he first came back. After he aborted the flight he headed back to Da Nang and talked to Phil Smith briefly on the radio as he was letting down. He didn't see Smith as he was climbing out to go to the tanker. They made passing comments, and that was it.

Quackenbush was having a snack in the Officers' Club when the news came in. Phil Smith had not rendezvoused with his flight, and radar controllers could not find him on their scopes. Smith's flight commander felt a tightening in his chest as he headed for the command post. Word of the emergency had spread quickly. The room was filled with full colonels, lieutenant colonels, the wing commander, squadron commander, operations officers. Telephone lines were open to Panama, and a great confusion of information was coming in. Quackenbush could hear some of the transmissions, though he never heard Smith's voice.

There was nothing at all that he could do except stand and pace and listen, and that was agonizing for him. Harvey Quackenbush was a man of action, a natural-born leader who was eager to take on any assignment or tell off any pompous bigwig. Others in his flight were more polished than this bear of a man who had grown up milking cows on a big farm in Ohio, but none of them was more highly regarded or respected.

He was there in the command post when he heard the worst. His friend was down. It was a confusing, emotional moment. No one knew for sure what had happened. Had Smith been shot down? Had he run out of fuel? Most of all, *where was he?* Information was pouring in from all directions. The Navy reported spotting a raft in one area; others thought they saw one a hundred miles away. Tension in the room mounted as those in charge tried to piece together the facts.

Quackenbush knew the Search and Rescue (SAR) effort, being organized as quickly as possible, would be much more difficult than those they had conducted in North Vietnam. In most of those efforts search teams knew where the downed pilots were. Their flight members had seen them bail out. Rescuers didn't have to go search for them.

This would be altogether different. No one knew for sure where Smith was, and they couldn't rescue him until they found him. Quackenbush had a grim thought: Radar hadn't been able to find Smith when he was up in the air; how in the hell were they going to find him now, when he was probably bobbing around like a cork on the high seas? Clearly there were only two ways—they'd have to spot him visually or hear him on the radio if they got close enough for him to call for help.

It was decided to launch two SA-16s, amphibious aircraft that could land in the water if they spotted the downed pilot. Quackenbush and Carlson, in their F-104s, would provide cover in case a MIG showed its face and tried to take a shot at the old two-engine, slow-moving amphibians.

The two fighter pilots were eager to get going. One other problem faced the mission, however. The Air Force KC-135 tanker didn't have enough fuel to stay up in the air much longer, and the F-104s had to be able to refuel in the air or they'd lose precious hours of daylight. No other 135s were available, except in Thailand and the Philippines, and they couldn't get on the scene fast enough to help.

This, however, was not just an Air Force emergency. An American military man was in deep trouble; all the friendly forces in a huge area were on alert to provide assistance. At this moment the Air Force turned to the Marines for help. The Marines, they knew, had aircraft on the field at Da Nang that they could launch within minutes. One of them was a Marine C-130, with a capability of aerial refueling. The Marines were eager to help and ready to move fast. The C-130 would be airborne immediately, they responded; it would be in orbit when it was needed.

It was time for action. Quackenbush and Carlson took off from Da Nang in their 104s and refueled once from the Air Force KC-135 tanker that had been in the air all morning. From then on they refueled from the Marine C-130.

Where was the search effort going to take them? All the information correlated at the command post pointed in one direction. The commander believed the place to search for Phil Smith was off the west and southwest coasts of Hainan Island.

Quackenbush and Carlson flew cover for one of the

SA-16s; the other was sent off in another direction. It was heart-wrenching flying for the two fighter pilots. The SA-16 flew low, lumbering along at 150 knots in a prescribed search-and-rescue pattern. To the fighter pilots it looked as if the enemy could throw rocks at that plane and knock it down.

The 104 pilots stayed high, making S turns to keep the amphibian in sight and make sure no strangers got in there with them. The weather had started to clear. There were still layered clouds above them, but Quackenbush and Carlson were in the clear at about ten thousand feet. When they ran low on fuel they alerted the tanker and then told the SA-16 to head out into the middle of the Gulf until they got back; then they'd move in closer again.

It was slow, painstaking, frustrating work. The amphibious plane was in contact with Panama; Quackenbush and Carlson stayed off their radios, hoping they might pick up a transmission from below. The afternoon progressed, and they saw and heard nothing. Finally the dreaded moment arrived. It was beginning to get dark, and the SA-16 had to go home. Oh, God, Harvey Quackenbush thought, we can't leave Phil Smith out here alone. Both 104s had full loads of fuel. The two fighter pilots decided they'd make one more pass by themselves before heading back to Da Nang.

September 20, 1965, Enemy Territory. As I was led out of the crude fisherman's hut I knew the long day was far from over. Since my early breakfast in the Officers' Club in Da Nang I had been lost in the air, shot down by a Chinese MIG, and captured by ragtag fishermen, and it was still only early afternoon. The old woman in the hut had given me a little water to drink, but nothing to eat. Now, as we left the hut, it appeared we were going on a march; where, I couldn't imagine. My gray nylon flying suit and flying boots were wet and uncomfortable, my right sleeve ripped where flying metal had hit me during the shoot-down.

The march got off to a ragged start. My captors were simple fishermen, not soldiers or policemen, and this was an extraordinary moment for them. They had captured an enemy bandit! Having captured me, however, they didn't know what to do with me. They'd obviously been told to take me someplace, but none of them wanted to get out in front of me to lead the way. From behind they prodded and poked me in one direction and then another. I tried to follow their directions without helping them out too much. What the hell, I thought, how was I supposed to know where to go? This whole thing sure hadn't been my idea. Finally one of the braver fishermen stepped out and took the lead, and the march got started.

I looked for landmarks as we moved along, heading away from the beach at about a forty-five-degree angle. It was a clean beach, a working beach, with crude huts and fishing paraphernalia sitting in the midst of great unspoiled natural beauty. I noted we were heading in the direction of the steep cliff I'd seen from the air, and I also noticed that all my gear was still with me. Some distance behind, six natives were carrying my dinghy like it was a casket. In all there must have been forty people following me, many of them with rifles slung over their shoulders. I wondered about those people. Were they merely curious onlookers, or bloodthirsty natives coming along for the kill?

The group continued to grow as we moved inland. I knew these natives couldn't possibly have radio or television sets in this primitive spot, but word was sure spreading quickly that something unusual was happening, and whatever their reasons, everyone was tagging along to see what would happen next.

I couldn't help but recognize the lunacy of it all. I'd seen many survival films on how to escape if you were ever captured. Now here I was—in China, I assumed— surrounded by dozens of people, including women and children, and not one survival film I'd ever seen had come close to being of help in this macabre situation. This band of keyed-up Orientals was not about to let me escape.

On and on we walked, the land becoming steeper and steeper. Almost three hours passed, and deep fatigue was setting in when I realized where we were. We were indeed at the base of the high cliff that I had seen from the air. There, for the first time, I was confronted by three uniformed soldiers, and I was aghast when I discovered what they were going to do with me. They were going to make me climb that cliff. I looked up. My God, I thought, how could I possibly do that? I was already exhausted. How much more could I take in one day?

They were not asking me, however; they were telling me, just as they were telling the civilians in my entourage to go back and tend to the rice paddies or cut off the fish heads or whatever. The civilians turned back. Whatever was on top of that cliff was off limits to them, and they knew it. I watched them go with some regret. They, at least, had not harmed me.

Briefly I wondered why these people were going to all this trouble. Why didn't they just shoot me and get it over with? Later I'd have plenty of time to realize why they weren't about to do away with a captured American pilot. At that moment, however, I'd had no food, and I was about to collapse. The three uniformed soldiers looked to be about twenty-five, and a hell of a lot more agile than I felt right then. One of them took the lead, moving quickly and easily. It was immediately apparent that he wasn't the least bit sympathetic to me or my physical condition. Watching him convinced me that he'd probably been jumping up and down these cliffs all his life.

I tried to keep up with him, but it wasn't possible. The terrain was so rough that I had to stagger up two or three feet, then walk parallel to the cliff for another few feet, then climb over enormous rocks, moving sometimes on my hands and knees. My flying suit had dried during the march; it quickly became soaked again with heavy perspiration.

My feet and legs began to hurt badly, and I simply couldn't keep up. Finally I just slowed down and moved at my own pace. It was midafternoon and hot, and my wet, heavy flying boots made it increasingly difficult to scrabble over the rocks. The other three in the impromptu hiking party were wearing canvas shoes and scurrying up the cliff with no difficulty at all. Too bad, I thought, that when I'd dressed at Da Nang that morning I hadn't dressed for cliff climbing in China that afternoon. I slogged along, tired, sore, and out of breath.

At last we made it to the top, and I wasn't at all surprised by what I saw. It was a military outpost, neat, clean, orderly, with several buildings flying flags, military insignia in various locations. I knew without looking that this observation post on top of the cliff would have a fine view of the sea and the coastline and any enemy activity out there. And I knew that China, with its millions of people, could keep such watch posts along all the borders of the country.

I was led into one of the buildings, where I met a young officer who spoke some broken English. For one rash moment I felt a twinge of optimism. Perhaps I could convince this young soldier of the truth, that I had had navigational problems and had gotten lost. Then he'd let me go. It was a fleeting dream, however, for the young man began to ask questions in his broken English. Was I injured? Did I hurt anyplace? Was anyone else with me? I could see what he was doing and had to admire him for it. He'd asked first about my physical state, in an effort to soften me up. Then he'd hoodwink me, if possible, into telling him if there were any other enemy pilots out there that they should go out and capture. It was smart interrogation.

I answered carefully. I was uninjured, I said, not admitting that my feet were killing me from that long march in my heavy flying boots. The Chinese soldier seemed to sense something wrong, however. He gestured for me to take my boots off and bent down as if to help me. I pulled them off just as another soldier entered the room carrying a bucket of warm water. Putting my aching feet in that water was a soothing sensation, and I was grateful.

Another man, apparently a cook, came in carrying a bowl of noodles, a spoon, and a cup of water and handed them to me. I thanked him and meant it. The noodles had been boiled in water and were tasteless, but I was so hungry, I ate them quickly.

As I ate I tried to think rationally and analyze the bizarre situation in which I now found myself. I'd been captured by the enemy; now I was being fed and soaking my feet in warm water. It really wasn't the reception I might have expected or feared. The officer with me seemed too young to be in charge of this small military outpost, but he was certainly in command at the moment, and so far he had shown no belligerence or aggressiveness. Nor had he shown any indication of letting me go.

I knew there was one thing I could try. I reached into my pocket and took out a piece of silk cloth that was part of the standard blood chit package issued to pilots flying in enemy territory. On one side of the cloth was a map of China and Southeast Asia, on the other a number of questions and phrases written in fifteen different languages. This was to be used to communicate with foreigners in just such an emergency as this and was, in effect, a voucher with my blood at stake.

I pointed to the first line in English, which read: "I'm an American fighting man. Please help me. I mean no harm to you. If you will help me, you will be rewarded by my government." Then I moved my finger across the page to the same line in Chinese. The young soldier ignored that line and pointed to another. This "conversation" went on for some minutes, using the Chinese officer's smattering of English and the blood chit. He continued to ask me questions: Was I alone? How many were with me? Was there another airplane? I was relieved, and somewhat surprised, that he didn't ask me what my mission had been or where I had flown out of that morning. He seemed concerned only about my condition and any other Americans who might have been with me. Throughout it all we were cautious and polite with each other.

But there was one piece of information, more than anything else, that I desperately wanted. With great care I asked one simple question and held my breath that I would get an answer, and I did. It was a moment of triumph that would help hold me together for a long time to come. One of the questions on the silk cloth was, "Where am I?" I pointed to it and turned the cloth over to the map. Instantly the young Chinese pointed to Hainan Island and the spot where the military outpost was located. I took a deep breath, trying not to show my elation. Learning my precise whereabouts was of extreme value to me, and I didn't want the young Chinese to suspect how exhilarated I felt at gaining that information.

I knew I would be interrogated . . . today, tomorrow, perhaps for many days. Knowing where I had ejected would be crucial to my responses. Had I been shot down over mainland China? Hainan Island? International waters? The information I had just received would make it possible for me to develop a plausible explanation for being anywhere near China. I had been out over international waters, I would claim, and was shot down by a trigger-happy fighter pilot who had knocked me out of the sky when I was minding my own business.

After about an hour the young Chinese soldier left the room. He had done his duty. My immediate needs had been taken care of, and I had been questioned at length. Two armed soldiers came in and stood by the door, and I could

also see armed guards outside the building. They weren't
taking any chances that I might escape. I sat, feeling tired
and dazed, and waited for whatever might come next. If
they were trying to wear me down, they were succeeding. I
watched the daylight fade away, knowing the darkest day of
my life wasn't over yet.

6

Hainan Island

As it began to get dark two F-104 fighter pilots, Harvey Quackenbush and Dale Carlson, were making one last effort to find their missing flight member, Phil Smith. They took their airplanes down to five hundred feet above the water just off the coastline of Hainan Island. They knew they were flying over Chinese territory and could be shot down at any moment, but they figured the odds were in their favor. There were two of them, they were flying low, and the Chinese communists would have to catch them before they shot them down. They didn't intend to be caught or hit by antiaircraft missiles.

They searched two thirds of the coastline of the island at that low altitude, flying at an airspeed of about 480 knots. Flying faster at that low level, they knew, would use up too much fuel. They'd been in the air more than five hours, and both of them were becoming increasingly depressed. It appeared that Phil Smith was just . . . gone. They didn't know if he was alive or dead or if they were even looking in the right area. They believed they were, but they didn't see anything, and it was one of the worst feelings either had ever experienced. One of their flight members was missing, and there was nothing down there, no indication of life whatsoever.

They'd hoped to hear a radio transmission or see a flare or make some kind of contact, but darkness was falling, and they were running low on fuel. They had no choice; they had to go home. The tanker had already left. Tired and sick at heart, they climbed back up to twenty thousand feet for the flight back to Da Nang. And then, at just about the same moment, they turned on their cockpit and navigation lights, and both gasped at what they discovered.

Harvey Quackenbush would describe it in detail in years to come: "We had not flown at night at all. All of our flying in Vietnam had been in the daylight. We were flying the butts off our airplanes. We put more hours on those 104s in a month there than we would have in six months back home. We were flying the bloody wings off them. So little things like lights that we didn't need—nobody worried about lights! Everybody was too concerned about keeping guns and engines and bombing systems and other equipment working. To hell with the lights. We didn't need lights; we were day fighters."

On September 20, 1965, Quackenbush and Carlson were flying at night, and they made a grim discovery: Neither of their lighting systems was functioning properly. Carlson had some navigation lights on the outside of his plane, but no illumination in the cockpit except the thunderstorm lights, which were used during thunderstorms so a flash of lightning wouldn't blind the pilot. The problem was, Carlson wasn't going through a thunderstorm, and those lights weren't suitable for penetration and landing at night.

Quackenbush, in the other 104, had instrument lights, but only two navigation lights, which he knew was not ideal for formation flying. Nonetheless, the two decided that Quackenbush would lead them back. Quackenbush could see no other alternative: "I at least had interior lights and could see the instruments. We were going to come back in formation and land at Da Nang. We knew that to fly formation at night you should have navigation lights in three locations so the wingman could judge where you were. But we didn't have three lights. We figured we'd get back all right anyway. So we had a couple of lighting problems—no big deal."

The two veteran pilots headed for Da Nang. Quackenbush reported to Panama that they were coming down and would land in formation. "Little did I know," he would later report, "that during the previous week, while I was on assignment in Taiwan, a new policy had been established at Da Nang directing that there would be no more formation penetrations and approaches and landings. Even if I had known, though, what was I going to do? Leave Carlson up there with no instrument lights? He wouldn't be able to see his airspeed indicator, his attitude indicator, or anything else."

Carlson was flying on Quackenbush's wing and could see him just fine. Then, as they were letting down to land at Da Nang, they went through a thick layer of clouds. Carlson was on Quackenbush's right wing as they went into the clouds in a left-descending turn. As they came out the bottom Quackenbush heard Carlson say, "Harve, I've lost you, light the burner."

"So I lit the afterburner real quick," said Quackenbush, "and of course, Christ, the afterburner puts out a sheet of fire that you'd see for forty miles. Carlson said, 'I've got you.' So no sweat. I told him, 'Okay, I'm holding 350 knots in a left turn,' and he responded, 'Okay.'"

That was the last thing Quackenbush heard before his whole world came unglued. "My airplane went four hundred different directions in about three microseconds. It was the wildest ride I've ever had. I was going to bail out as soon as I could get hold of the goddamn ejection ring, but I was flailing around in there so badly, I couldn't get hold of it. The airplane went bloody wild."

One thought flashed through his mind. He had no way of knowing for sure, but Carlson must have hit the tail of his airplane. It was totally out of control. Quackenbush had always felt he fit into the 104 rather neatly; when he came out of this one he looked like he'd been through a meat grinder, beaten black and blue. It seemed as if he'd been spinning around like a whirling dervish for three days; in reality, it had only been a matter of seconds before he was able to grab the ejection ring and give it a hard pull.

The next few moments were a blur. He was conscious but badly shaken up, and he couldn't quite focus on everything that was happening. One minute he'd been cruising along just fine, then *wham!* Everything came apart. Now he was coming down in a parachute, and he realized how dark and quiet it was. And suddenly his mind clicked back on. He could hear the flutter of the parachute and nothing else. But he knew there could be grave danger beneath him, for even though he wasn't too far out of Da Nang he remembered a series of pictures that the pilots had been shown, taken off radar scopes at night. He had been astounded at those photographs.

"There wasn't a Ho Chi Minh Trail at that time," he'd said after seeing those photographs, "and the bad guys were moving all their supplies down to South Vietnam in junks and any little thing that would float. Down they'd come, just off the coast at night, then they'd put into some inlet just before sunup and hide all day. Maybe they'd only cover a mile or two each night, but that's how they were moving everything south. And we had radar pictures showing thousands of little blips of light. They were using anything that would float, including fifty-five-gallon barrels tied together to move fuel."

Ingenious and dangerous. They moved in darkness and might well be in the water beneath him. "Harve," Quackenbush told himself, "you're in big trouble. The minute you hit the water the Vietcong will be there with guns and blow you away." There was nothing he could do about it, however, as he continued his quiet descent. Everything was pitch black as he hit the water. "God damn," he thought, "they had to have heard me hit." He stayed very quiet for a moment. There were no sounds. Perhaps he hadn't been detected.

He knew he must get into his life raft. He grabbed the lanyard and pulled it toward him. As he reached for it he felt a glob of . . . what? It was an unformed mass of some kind. "It figures," he sighed. "The damn raft is supposed to inflate automatically, and mine didn't. Great."

He'd had classroom instruction in what to do in such a situation, but he hadn't paid much attention. Now he wished he'd listened to old Jack Glover a little more closely instead of sleeping through the class. He fumbled and fiddled, and it was all very eerie because there were large swells in the sea, and he was bobbing up and down helplessly. As he came to the top of one swell he saw a couple of lights off in the distance and a helicopter down south toward Da Nang. And then he was swept back down to the bottom of the swell, and oh, God, it was black down there. The only good thing was that the water was warm.

He knew he was going to have to blow up his raft himself. "Here I am in my flying suit and boots and all this other crap, and I'm huffing and puffing trying to blow up my dinghy," he thought in disgust, and then he noticed that his feet were tangled up in something and realized it was the shroud lines from the parachute. He loosened his feet as he continued to blow up the raft. "When you're scared, you'd be surprised at what you can do," he noted. Finally the dinghy was inflated, and Quackenbush climbed in, a feat he didn't find easy at all. He was being as quiet as possible, but as he sat in his dinghy he noticed helicopters had come closer, and he could see ships off in the distance. The next time he rose to the top of a swell he saw searchlights. Hallelujah! Then he went crashing back down into the dark hole at the bottom of a swell.

Enemy patrol boats might be nearby, but he had to alert those rescue teams. He had pen flares in the pocket of his uniform, which he pulled out and fired. There came a helicopter! And he could hear the putt, putt, putt of a small boat. He hoped those were the good guys who were fast approaching. He saw the boat coming toward him, and incredibly, he still hadn't gotten his .38 revolver out of its holster, an oversight he realized later. People in the boat turned a hand-held searchlight in his direction as he paddled around to face them. And then, as he rode up to the top of one of the swells, he saw Dale Carlson lying flat in his dinghy some forty feet away.

He couldn't believe it. He had automatically assumed that Carlson was dead. He knew the statistics; almost never did two people survive a midair collision. The chances of both of them coming out alive, he figured, were probably about one in one hundred. And there was Carlson! He paddled toward him as quickly as possible. "I've hurt my back," Carlson whispered. "Is somebody shooting at us?"

"No, no," Quackenbush reassured him. "That was the popping of the flares I fired. Help is coming." Just then the small patrol boat pulled up; Quackenbush was relieved to see American and South Vietnamese personnel on board. "Be careful," he warned them as they reached for Carlson, "he's injured." He helped lift Carlson into the boat. His flight member was groaning in misery, but they had to get him out of the dinghy.

The patrol boat took them to a Navy communications ship anchored out further off the coast of Da Nang, where they spent the night in the sick bay. It was a dreadful night. Navy doctors checked them over and x-rayed Carlson's back, finding nothing seriously wrong. Then they were put together in a room in the sick bay, but there was very little they could say to each other. They were thankful to be alive; in many ways it was a miracle that they were.

But as Quackenbush lay in his uncomfortable hammock-type bed, tired and sore and miserable, he couldn't recall many worse days in his life. Harvey Quackenbush was a proud leader—proud of his men, their machines, their accomplishments. When the toll of this day was added up it would be one of the most dismal days in the history of the squadron: Three F-104s had been lost, two pilots had had to eject and be rescued from the water, and one pilot was missing. No, he couldn't think of many worse days.

And he couldn't help recalling other nights back in The Hooch. The seven men in his flight had bunks off in the corner, away from the others in The Hooch. And often, before they went to sleep, these fighter pilots asked Phil Smith to tell them bedtime stories. He complied with great enthusiasm. He loved telling stories, and everyone knew it would take him ten minutes to tell something that would take someone else ten seconds.

They loved listening to him, and almost always they wanted him to tell the same stories—about his sexual escapades in his younger days. His parents had frowned on dating and dancing, but at a fairly young age Phil Smith had discovered sex—and young girls who were as eager and compliant as anyone could ever want. The stories he told about those years of his youth were about wonderful, realistic, juicy, down-home sex in the car, in the park, under the bushes, anywhere at all . . . all about young, exuberant, uncomplicated pleasure. Phil Smith could lie in his bunk in The Hooch in South Vietnam and hold the others spell-bound with tales of his adventures. Were his stories true? Who cared? He was an intriguing storyteller whose tales helped them escape the realities of their lives. These were men, separated from their loved ones, who were living in a combat zone in the stinking heat of the tropics. However briefly, Phil Smith and his vivid imagination could take them away from all that.

Tonight, on this Navy ship off the coast of Da Nang, there wouldn't be any bedtime stories. Quackenbush and Carlson and all the others had always accepted one basic principle of combat: You've got to expect losses in a big operation. But this was not a loss that Harvey Quackenbush had ever expected. He drifted off to sleep thinking about his friend and what a terrible day it had been. He could only hope that tomorrow would be better, and that somewhere out there they would find Phil Smith.

September 20, 1965, Hainan Island. Just before dark I heard the clatter of trucks arriving. Moments later I was taken outdoors to where three military vehicles had pulled up. They were similar to American jeeps, only larger, each capable of carrying six people in the back, three on each side. Soldiers motioned for me to get in the back of the front truck; armed guards climbed in with me.

And though my senses were dulled with fatigue, I couldn't believe what happened next. I assumed I had been through the worst the day had to offer, but I was wrong. The driver of my vehicle took off like a madman. Never have I had such a ride. We flew over rough, bumpy, unpaved roads, careening around corners with the rear wheels sliding sideways, zooming across little bridges, bouncing around with the wheels coming completely off the ground at times. For almost two hours I gritted my teeth, closed my eyes, and wished I had my ejection seat and parachute. After all I had been through on this terrible day I was convinced I was going to be killed right here in this stupid jeep. I hung on for dear life, wondering what in the world they were doing.

Finally, thankfully, we pulled into a fairly good-sized town. The driver was still going like crazy, but the roads were better, and I figured—prayed!—the journey must be coming to an end.

It was dark when we finally pulled into an area of lush vegetation. Off in the distance I could see a building and what looked like thousands of people gathered around it. Were they waiting for me? I had a sinking feeling that they were.

The jeep pulled to a stop, and I was ordered out. As the guards and I descended from the truck we discovered we couldn't get through the crush of people and had to wait momentarily as the police cleared a pathway for us. Instinctively I knew this was a dangerous moment. I was trapped in the middle of enemy civilians whose mood I couldn't immediately determine, and it was a terrifying sensation. I stayed close to the guards as we made our way slowly into the building, our every move watched by that huge mob of Chinese civilians.

The building we entered consisted of one big room, maybe thirty by sixty feet, with open, screened-in walls. The crowds outside could stand on all four sides of the building and watch what was happening inside. I saw a raised platform at one end of the room, and out in the middle, all by themselves, sat one chair and a small table. My immediate reaction was chilling: This looked very much like the setting for an inquisition.

Guards led me to the chair and motioned for me to sit down. Three dignitaries were seated on the platform at the end of the room, some twenty feet away from me. I looked up at them, feeling queasy and uncomfortable sitting there all alone in the middle of that room, surrounded by restless spectators on all sides. Hours before, my airplane had been a sitting duck as it came down out of the clouds; now I was an even better target here in the middle of this mob of people. I could hear low mumbling coming from all directions.

My mind was whirling. Would this dreadful day never end? Was I to be put on trial right here and now? Amazingly, as I sat pondering my plight, a man entered carrying a plate of food that he put down on the table by me. Obviously I was expected to eat that food under the scrutiny of this huge, hostile crowd. On the plate were vegetables, rice, and a little piece of meat. I was handed a knife, fork, and spoon and told to eat. I took a deep breath and did so as cameras flashed. This was all propaganda, I knew. I was at center stage and was expected to play my role properly.

When I stopped eating I was brought a pack of cigarettes, which I declined. Then it was time to get down to business. The three men on the platform were dressed in dark Mao jackets. They didn't appear to be military. There was no military insignia on their collars. I guessed them to be civilian authorities, judges or magistrates.

None of them spoke English, I discovered as they began to ask questions, but the interpreter spoke flawless English. The senior-looking official began the questioning; the others added to it as they went along. What was my name? Where had I come from? Was I in the military? Why was I here? Why had I intruded into their territory? I answered their questions briefly and politely.

Then they changed their tactics and began accusing me of deliberately trying to provoke the Chinese government. "You've committed a crime against the Chinese people," they said. "You're a spy."

I knew my responses were being recorded and would be heard by communist officials. What was I going to say? For the first time I was being seriously interrogated, far beyond the earlier questioning. Keep your wits about you, I reminded myself, we're getting into some sensitive areas.

My training from day one as a pilot had taught me that if you land in the hands of the enemy, according to the Geneva Convention you're only required to give name, rank, serial number, and date of birth, and you should resist further interrogation to the best of your ability.

I had also been taught that if you were captured by the enemy and felt it necessary to go beyond those basic facts, you should carefully plan your responses in advance if you had time. Construct a plausible story and stick to it. During the terrifying jeep ride, even though I had been fearing for my life, I had had time to do some thinking and had decided that I should explain why I was there, figuring it would be in the best interests of the U.S. government, the Air Force, and myself to tell them the truth—at least part of it. I wouldn't give them the details of my mission, but I would tell them that I'd had instrument failures, and I would admit that *if* I had intruded over their land or their territorial airspace, it was a mistake. I hadn't been sent to do that. My squadron commander, in fact, had told me to stay away from Hainan Island.

Isolated as I was, and had been since my shoot-down, I knew my capture by the Chinese would cause an international incident, and I wanted to minimize the significance of my shoot-down by explaining what had actually happened. I answered each question very carefully. Nonetheless, the tone of the interrogation gradually became more hostile. The officials didn't like my attitude, they said. I was being cocky. I had been captured by the great Chinese people, and they wouldn't tolerate any arrogance. I softened my tone even further; a confrontation would help nothing. Over and over I repeated that I was sorry, I hadn't meant to cause an international incident, I didn't mean to be there, they should turn me loose. Tell me how to get out of there.

It didn't work. The magistrates looked stonier than ever. You'll not get out of here, they declared. Justice will prevail. You must be punished for your evil ways. We don't believe any of what you say. This went on for more than thirty minutes. I stuck to my story. My being near Hainan Island was a mistake. Then, finally, it was over. The magistrates rose and walked out. I was led back outside and told to get in the truck, the massive crowd watching my every move.

It was late at night by then. Mentally and physically I had never felt so exhausted. I was not to rest yet, however, for a man I hadn't seen before got in the truck beside me and started asking questions in English. He appeared to be a reporter of some kind.

As we bounced along the darkened roads the man handed me a photograph, and there was just enough light to see it. I tried not to show my surprise. It was a photograph of my F-104 taken from the gun camera film on the MIG-19 that had shot me down. There was no doubt in my mind. It was my plane. When I had jettisoned the pylons the left one had not been released, and the enemy had shot the missile and the launcher rail off the right wing tip. That was exactly what

72

I was seeing in this photograph. It was the precise configuration of my aircraft at the time I ejected.

I tried not to react. They had shot me down and had a picture to prove it, and I knew how proud and elated they must be to have this photographic proof. I didn't want to do anything to add to their delight. I looked at the photograph impassively and then looked away.

The reported continued to ask questions, which I ignored. I rode in silence as the jeep bounced along through the town for thirty minutes and then approached an airport through a back gate. It looked very much as though they were trying to get me into the airport and off the island without anyone knowing it. A small road ran through high weeds; our driver slowed down only slightly as we bounced along. Moments later we came out on a ramp where a DC-3 was sitting. I could see buildings in the distance, but no other aircraft. It looked to me like a military airport of some kind.

I recognized the DC-3, an old American-built gooney bird. As we got out of the jeep and stood near the airplane I saw that my gear was spread out on the ground. All of it had been opened and searched by the plane's crew, including the survival kit that held the medicine, bandages, sunburn lotion and other supplies that I hadn't needed when I'd opened it in the dinghy. The kit also contained six big flares that resembled shotgun shells.

The Chinese were looking at those flares, not knowing what they were. One of them turned to me and asked a question, which a man standing nearby translated: "We're going to get on this airplane for a trip of several hours. We want you to tell us if there is anything dangerous in any of this that we ought to know about before we put it on the airplane."

I took a quick look at everything on the ground, knowing full well that only the flares might be dangerous. Then I explained what they were and told them not to activate the trigger mechanisms or the flares would ignite and burn. The crew seemed satisfied and loaded all the equipment on the airplane. Then they told me to board.

The interior wasn't what I had expected. It was a DC-3, all right, but a plush one that must have been used by high-ranking military officers. The floors, sides, and ceiling were covered with carpet; big, wide, comfortable seats had replaced the typical military webbed benches.

I was motioned into a seat and told to sit down. As I did so I realized that fatigue had settled in every part of my being. I had had no sleep for almost twenty-four hours and was almost beyond caring what happened next. In my weariness I knew I had lost control of my life, and this was incredibly frustrating and antithetical to all my training and experience as a fighter pilot. Now I was on a DC-3, airborne out of Hainan Island, a prisoner of the Chinese communists. An official, apparently an intelligence officer, sat down beside me and gave me some chocolate. Then he began to ask the same questions I'd been asked so many times. What was my mission? Who was with me? On and on he went. I answered at first, then stopped. I was too tired to continue.

Events of that disastrous day had transpired so quickly, I'd had almost no time to think. I worried that I hadn't responded properly to my interrogators on Hainan Island. Had I done the right thing in going beyond name, rank, and serial number? I'd had no lawyer, no counsel, no help at all except my instincts and my years of training as an air force officer.

Sitting there in that old American-built plane, I thought about home and family and friends. My wife, Judy, would be furious if I didn't make it home for the birth of our third child in December. I'd been away on assignment when the second child was born, and she'd never completely forgiven me. Our marriage wasn't nearly as strong as it had seemed in earlier years, and I wondered what effect my capture would have on it. I hoped I'd be released quickly and no harm would be done.

And I thought about my parents. Had they been notified

that I'd been captured? It would cause them so much pain. More than anything else, right then I wished I could put my arms around my mother and assure both my parents that I was okay and would be home soon. I had wanted to live my own life, but I had never wanted to cause them any pain or grief. During the past twenty-four hours, though, control of my life had slipped away from me, and I couldn't spare them or myself the agony of what had happened or the fear of what lay ahead. I couldn't alter the events that had transpired during this one dreadful day, but I could try to find out what might happen in the days ahead.

"Where are we going?" I asked the intelligence officer sitting beside me.

"Mainland China," he replied. "Canton."

7

Mainland China

September 21, 1965, China. It was approaching three A.M. when the DC-3 came in for a landing at Canton Airport. The weather was clear and calm, so I was totally unprepared for the landing. The plane came close to crashing; I bounced up in the air and then came thudding back down as we hit the tarmac. Welcome to Canton, I thought, wondering what had gone wrong. I looked out as we taxied in and saw an American-built cargo plane, a C-130 with Pakistan markings on it.

Then I saw several dark hardtop sedans pulling up right beside us as we came to a stop. I was led off the airplane by the officer in charge and directed into one of those cars, where a man was sitting in the backseat. "Are you Smith?" he asked as I got into the car beside him. "Yes," I replied. "How do you feel? Are you tired or hungry?" He spoke excellent English as he inquired about my general well-being, and he seemed sympathetic to my plight. "Are you cold?" he added, noticing the early-morning chill. "Yes, as a matter of fact, I am," I said, and he took off his coat and put it around my shoulders in an unexpectedly kind gesture. For hours I had been questioned and badgered, and this man, whose name, I learned, was Shu, did none of that. He was considerate and professional, not trying to extract any military information from me or berate or antagonize or scare me in any way.

The cars sped quickly away from the airport. In the darkness of the early morning we encountered very little traffic as we headed into the city. After his initial pleasantries Shu said very little, seeming to understand that I was fatigued almost beyond speech.

Our motorcade pulled up before a modernistic hotel with large glass doors and windows, marble columns and marble steps, and stopped. I was puzzled as Shu led the way to the front door, which was opened for us as we neared. Was I to be put here for the night?

I was led into a large room, one apparently used for banquets, and told to sit down at a long table covered with a white tablecloth. I hoped they weren't going to feed me again. Food didn't seem very appealing at the moment.

No food arrived, however. Shu and I sat at the table for twenty minutes, and nothing happened. I couldn't begin to guess what we were waiting for or what all this meant, and that frightened me.

Then a man entered wearing a black Mao jacket, black trousers, and a black hat. I sighed inwardly, knowing this must be another magistrate of some kind. He asked me my name, nationality, and whether I was in the military, and I answered his questions. Then he said, "I am here to inform you that you are under arrest by the authorities of the People's Republic of China for intrusion and violation of our airspace." He was very official, reading the charges from a piece of paper, a man with him interpreting. The magistrate then said, "You've committed crimes. You must not try to escape. Do you understand that?"

I said I did. "Do you have any questions?" he inquired. "Yes," I replied. "When will I be released? I'm here by accident." He was in no humor to respond or negotiate. "I will not answer your questions," he replied sternly, almost arrogantly. "You're under arrest, and you will be here until we decide what to do with you." That was it. He got up and stomped out, and I was led back out to the car in which I'd arrived.

In the dark hours just before dawn the car headed toward the outskirts of town. I sat in the backseat with Shu, watching out the window, and I was surprised by what I saw. I knew Canton was an old city, and I had expected to see buildings that were deteriorating and crumbling, but on this night the city looked better than I had anticipated. There were green trees and streets that were wide and clean; perhaps, I thought, because Canton was in the south of China, near Hong Kong, and had always been an active trading center.

After about forty minutes our car drove into a residential area of old Canton. The streets were lined with big homes that had apparently been taken over by the military when the Communists came to power in 1949. They were no longer in good condition, but clearly, in their day, the homes had belonged to the very wealthy of the city.

The car drove through a big old wooden gate leading into the compound of large homes and stopped before a three-story building that looked like a large dormitory, which it turned out to be. Shu led me into one of the dormitory rooms and told me to rest. They left me alone for a short time, and then, just as it was getting light outside, Shu and two guards came and got me. We walked outside and down the street for several blocks, staying within the compound walls. Shu, walking beside me, moved briskly, apparently wanting to get me inside without anyone seeing me. Daylight was coming, people were beginning to get up, activity was increasing. Shu led me into a bedroom in one of the big houses. "This is your room," he said. "You can sleep now."

I had expected a dungeon or a prison cell, not a room with a double bed, a chair, and a desk. The bed even had sheets, a cover, and mosquito netting. I took off my clothes and climbed in, exhausted and confused.

So many things had happened in the past twenty-four hours. Again and again I relived that scene in the open-air building on Hainan Island where I was first questioned. Had I done the right thing there? It was the first time I had explained why I was near the Chinese borders, and everything I said and did had been recorded and photographed. I had made the decision to tell more than name, rank, serial number, and date of birth, but that decision haunted me, and I tried to remember exactly what I had said so the Chinese couldn't trick me later on. I must not be caught in any inconsistencies.

I understood that I was in a battle with my captors—a mental battle. My arms were laid down, my airplane was gone. The battle would be fought now, not with speed and firepower, but with wits and intelligence.

8

A Family in Illinois

Roodhouse, Illinois, 1965. Carrie and Oscar Smith, simple, hardworking farmers, lived in Greene County in west central Illinois. Everything was typically midwestern about their farm on Route 1. They raised almost all their own food and did all the work themselves. They were frugal, conservative, God-fearing. They knew their son Philip was in a dangerous profession, and they accepted that. But nothing really prepared them for the news they received on an autumn day in 1965. A neighbor heard a bulletin on the radio and rushed to telephone the Smiths. A USAF fighter pilot had been shot down somewhere off Vietnam and was reported missing in action. He was identified as Captain Philip E. Smith.

It was a stunning blow to this quiet midwestern family. For something to happen to their youngest son was beyond their worst nightmares. They did the only thing they knew to do: They turned to God and to their family.

New York City, New York. Jim Smith was living on East 81st Street in Manhattan in the fall of 1965, although he had spent most of the past ten years working out of the country.

At heart, Jim was a wanderer who enjoyed exotic locales and jobs, learning new languages, meeting different people. He'd worked for a government intelligence agency in Europe and in Washington, D.C., and for an import-export company in the Far East. By 1965 he was thirty-three years old and had already seen more of the world than many people would ever see. He wasn't crazy about living in New York City, but he didn't expect to be there for long, so he didn't mind it too much. Then one morning he answered the telephone and everything changed. It was his mother, in tears. Phil had been shot down and was reported missing in action. Jim hung up quickly, unable to talk. There was no one he loved more than his younger brother Phil. They had grown up together. They both enjoyed danger and excitement; after all, they were young and indestructible, or so they had wanted to believe.

He walked out into the streets of New York City, and nothing looked the same to him. A film covered his eyes. God, he prayed, please don't let anything happen to Phil. He tried to think positively. Maybe rescue teams had picked him up. Somehow, though, Jim didn't believe it.

By nighttime he knew the truth. The story was headline news around the world. The Chinese communists announced that one of their planes had shot down a U.S. F-104 Starfighter jet over Hainan Island and captured its pilot. Captain Philip E. Smith's official status was changed from missing to "detained by hostile forces."

Jim made a trip to Washington, D.C., to see if everything possible was being done to get his brother back. Then he headed home to Roodhouse for an emotional, tearful reunion with his family. He knew what a difficult time it was for his parents. Carrie and Oscar wanted to bear the pain of their son's capture privately and silently, but that wasn't possible. Phil Smith was the first American to be captured by the Chinese since the Korean War. It was news everywhere. Reporters from all over the world kept calling, and Jim's heart ached for what his parents were going through, especially his mother. Carrie Smith had always been the mother figure of old, cooking enormous meals, baking breads and cakes, taking care of her home and six children, working in the fields when necessary. She had tried hard to soften Oscar's harshness to his family. Oscar's rigid rules had dictated the lives of all of them, but Carrie had always been there to give her children extra money, food, and sizable quantities of care and love and understanding. All the family went to church Sunday morning and evening; Carrie also went to prayer meetings on Thursday night. Her church and her family were her life. She had always believed she could take whatever life had in store for her, and she wouldn't waver now. On a September day in 1965 she got out a map and looked at it carefully. Where exactly was her beloved son being held captive? She saw what Jim already knew. China was a very long way from Roodhouse, Illinois.

9

A Firing Squad and a Scraggly Christmas Tree

For a brief time I dozed restlessly, then was awakened by someone rattling my bed. I longed for the oblivion of sleep, but it wasn't to be. I opened my eyes and saw a young Chinese kitchen worker putting a tray on the table in the room. So it hadn't been a nightmare after all. I was a prisoner of the Chinese.

I got out of bed, put on my flying suit, and walked over to the table. I was surprised when I lifted the cover of the tray. My Chinese captors had given me a Western-style breakfast: fried eggs, bacon, toast, and coffee. I sat down and ate the food, feeling dull and dazed, and thought briefly of my mother. She had often laughed that I would eat anything, anytime; maybe that would help me now. The door of my room was open, as it had been since I arrived. A guard stood in the door or paced in the hall nearby, and I could see armed guards in the yard outside.

I looked more closely around the room where I was being held. It wasn't the bamboo cage I might have expected. At one time it must have been quite pleasant, in fact. Nonetheless, I was a prisoner, and—surroundings aside— everything I had lived, worked, and hoped for might well end here in this miserable, godforsaken country. Bleakness, despair, fear, apprehension, fatigue . . . I sat, nearly overwhelmed by the enormity of the emotions flooding through me.

I looked up as the Cantonese lawyer named Shu walked into the room. Shu, who had met me at the airport in the early hours of the morning, had been born and raised in Canton and spoke the Cantonese dialect as well as excellent English. He came in carrying an armload of clothes. "Put these on," he said, not unkindly. "We want to wash your flying suit."

For a moment I was surprised, then I realized what they were doing. They wanted to get their hands on my flying suit so they could check it over very carefully. What the hell, I thought, let them have it. It would tell them nothing. I had stripped it of all military insignia while I was in the life raft, and there was nothing hidden in it. I put on the Chinese clothes that were clean but not new: dark blue lightweight cotton pants and a hip-length military jacket with a Mao collar. Obviously someone had sized me up and scurried around to find the right clothing, and I had to admit that the new wardrobe was more comfortable than my hot flying suit.

"We're going outside now," Shu said, leading the way out of the house. As we walked around the yard we were closely watched by several guards, and I was surprised by their attitude. They were armed and in uniform, but they were very polite and had stood aside as we walked out the door. Throughout our walk they showed no hostility or belligerence. Clearly they were there to make sure I didn't escape, not to manhandle or antagonize me.

As we walked, even though I was feeling unsteady and almost overcome by so many raw emotions, I realized something about Shu. The small, thin lawyer was genuinely doing his best to be kind to me. In a calm, compassionate, soft-spoken way he was trying to answer my questions and bolster my morale. He himself was asking no questions; he was simply listening patiently as I poured out some of the questions that were tormenting me. There were so many things I desperately wanted to know. I was accused of being a criminal. What did that mean in Chinese law? What was going to happen to me? Would I have a lawyer? Be put on trial? See the charges in writing?

"I don't know," Shu replied to all of my questions. "It will depend on you and your cooperation. You must not resist." And on that first morning Shu used the phrase that I was to hear over and over again: "Your case will be determined by your cooperation and friendly attitude."

Cooperation and friendly attitude. Meaning what? I assumed it meant that if I did everything they wanted me to do and told them everything they wanted to know, I would be helping my case . . . maybe. And maybe not. It didn't really matter. Whatever the Chinese meant, I wasn't about to confess to any of their charges or give them any more information than necessary. I was an American military officer, and I wasn't about to make deals with the enemy, no matter what they promised. Knowing I was trapped made my spirits sink even lower. There was nothing honorable I could do to get out of there except wait and hope.

"Don't worry," Shu kept insisting. "Just cooperate, and everything will turn out fine." I had grave doubts about that platitude. I knew so little about this country, but to the best of my knowledge I was the only member of the American military forces being held by the Chinese.

China's relations with the U.S. and most countries of the world had been in a steep decline ever since the Chinese communists took over in 1949. As a consequence, in 1965 the outside world knew little about what was going on behind the Bamboo Curtain. The communists were secretive and hostile to the Western world, and even to some communist countries. I would have bet, however, that they would very quickly recognize the enormous propaganda to be gained from the capture of an American pilot and waste no time in taking advantage of it. Their achievement was something they could, and did, flaunt to the entire world.

I was sure of that on the second day of my captivity, when I was taken outside and saw that still and movie cameras had been set up on the lawn. I was going to be filmed, I was told, and I was surprised at the preparations that had been made. A lot of work had gone into the staging for what I knew would be a phony piece of propaganda. I was to be the leading man, whether I wanted to be or not.

"You're to come out this door and walk down the steps," the man in charge informed me. "Then pause, look at the cameras, and keep walking." I did as I was told. We rehearsed once, then the cameras rolled. Two other segments were also included, one showing me being examined by a doctor and two nurses who asked me various questions about my health, the other showing me eating a meal. As the filming continued I began to feel more and more used and manipulated. I wanted to look into the cameras and tell the rest of the world, "Don't believe these communists! I'm not a spy!" Instead I sat docilely as I was served a plate of food and a glass of tea and told to eat while the cameras were operating.

It infuriated me to have to participate in such specious nonsense, but I had no choice, and I hoped there were some advantages to be gained by me, as well as by my captors. The Chinese wanted to show the world that they were treating their prisoner well. I resented having to help them do that, but perhaps my family would see the film and have visual proof that I was all right. I held myself together and cooperated with what they wanted me to do. Ten days later, in Roodhouse, Illinois, my family did see the film clip on national television and gained some comfort from it. My purpose had been accomplished, and so had the enemy's. Doctors, good food, a stroll about the grounds . . . let the world see how compassionate the Chinese were, or wanted to appear.

From the first day of my imprisonment I tried not to let the Chinese know how despondent I felt, or how fearful and uncertain. Anything they learned about me could be used against me, so even with Shu I did my best to appear calm and in control. That facade almost slipped on September 23, two days after I arrived in Canton, when Shu came into my room and gave me stationery, saying I could write two letters. The results of that kindness affected me greatly. It was still early in the Vietnam conflict, but I knew that American military men had already disappeared into the horrendous prison system of North Vietnam and were never heard from. For years, and sometimes forever, their families didn't know if they were dead or alive. To be able to write to my family was a godsend. I thanked Shu and then sat down and wrote to my wife Judy in Victorville, California, and to my parents in Roodhouse, Illinois. I knew the letters would be read and censored; I wrote very carefully and found the first letter to my parents especially difficult to compose. A son in captivity can do little to ease his parents' pain, but I tried my best.

Thurs., 23 Sept. 65

Dear Folks,

I know what a shock it must have been for you to be notified of such terrible news. No matter how bad things turn out, it can always be worse.

I worry constantly about what a shock this must be to you, and I don't see how I can ever make it up to you for causing you so much grief and pain. As you know, there is nothing to do but wait and let things work out as best they can.

To try to tell you not to worry about me I know will not help you or change your feelings—because I know how much you will worry.

Please try to believe me and realize that I am not being harmed and I am being well taken care of. All I can ask of you is to take care of yourselves and try to pull yourselves together. I know everything will work out all right in the end.

I have no idea how long I will be here. All I do know is, for sure, the Lord is here with me every step of the way. I know he will protect me and keep me from all harm.

Try to take care of yourselves.

I Love You,
Phil

Two days later the Chinese began their official interrogation of me, and I grew to dread these sessions. They exhausted me physically, because they went on for so long, and mentally, because I had to be so careful of what I said. The interrogators came in pairs; one team would come for several days, then they'd be replaced by two new people. Shu and three other interpreters were assigned to me; they did the translating during these interrogation sessions. All of my answers were written down.

It was a long, grueling, laborious process. The interrogators had their questions prepared in advance and written down in notebooks. They began with military questions: Why was I where I was? I was lost, I responded. I'd had instrument failures, navigational problems, the weather was bad. I had not intended to violate their air space, and as far as I knew, I had not done so. I was over international waters. I shouldn't be criticized; their trigger-happy fighter pilot ought to be blamed for shooting me down over international waters.

What kind of aircraft was I flying? How fast would it go? How high would it climb? Those questions I did not fully answer. They had nothing to do with my case, and I was not about to give them detailed information about the performance of my airplane. Maybe they knew and maybe they didn't that the airplane I was flying had held three world records at the same time, a feat matched by few aircraft before or since that time. The F-104 had held world records for top speed, greatest rate of climb, and highest altitude. The highest altitude had been set in the 1950s: 103,395½ feet.

Over and over I said I realized the U.S. and China were not at war and the U.S. had no intention of provoking the Chinese. If I had strayed into their territory, which I didn't believe I had, it was a mistake. I was sorry. I apologized for creating an international incident. I was willing, I said, to tell them how it happened, but I would not reveal any military information that could be used against my fellow pilots.

I was asked repeatedly about the mission I was flying that day. I told them the mission was to maintain a presence in the Tonkin Gulf to prevent Chinese and North Vietnamese aircraft from harassing U.S. ships in the area.

What time had I taken off? How long had I been in the air? Was this a typical mission? Yes, I said, it was a typical mission. Was I on a bombing mission? None of your business, I replied.

Day after day it went on. The interrogators were not happy with me. I was lying, they claimed. I had been on a bombing mission. I was not helping my case, they said. I was being stubborn. I should cooperate and answer. They continued to ask sensitive questions; I continued to refuse to answer them, and they did not force me to do so.

One time one of the Chinese made a mistake that gave me a big psychological boost. I had been asked repeatedly if my airplane carried cameras or spy equipment of any kind, and I had said no. Then one of the interrogators told me they had recovered my airplane from the sea and had found all kinds of exotic spy cameras and equipment on it. I knew they were bluffing. My airplane was in bits and pieces at the bottom of the sea. I had seen the smoke when it crashed, and I knew that aircraft, especially F-104s, disintegrate on impact. I also knew my airplane carried absolutely no spy equipment.

I couldn't believe the interrogator would be so stupid. He

had lost all of his credibility, and I couldn't resist telling him so. "Get serious," I said in disgust. "I know very well what equipment my airplane carried. You say you found spy equipment? You're the one who is lying." I wasn't surprised that I never saw that interrogator again.

Initially I asked the interrogators questions of my own, as I had asked Shu. What was going to happen to me? Would I be released? Would I be put in prison? Nobody ever gave me any answers. It was always the same: "That is to be determined. The outcome of your case depends on your cooperation and friendly attitude. You're not doing anything to help your case. You're being stubborn, you're resisting, you're not answering our questions."

Throughout all the interrogation I tried to be formal and serious in my responses and attitude in an effort to let the Chinese know that I was sincere in telling them what had happened. I tried not to let my frustration show, though at times I slipped. "You've already asked me that," I said angrily. "Obviously you're trying to trick me. You're on a witch-hunt." Inwardly I wondered how well I was doing. There were times when I deliberately gave them erroneous information about our patrol missions over the Tonkin Gulf and the air assets and defenses at Da Nang Air Base, but they were so persistent, and they kept asking the same questions in so many different ways, that I wondered how consistent I was being in my responses.

There was never any clear pattern to the interrogation sessions. Sometimes I'd be questioned for six hours a day. Then days or weeks went by with no interrogation at all. During those times I assumed the interrogators and others were analyzing and reviewing everything I'd said, trying to find flaws and inconsistencies. Then another team would appear in my room, and the questioning would begin again.

As the weeks passed I became convinced that the interrogators didn't know what was going to happen to me, and perhaps their communist leaders didn't know, either. I'd come falling out of the sky into their laps, and they couldn't figure out what to do with me. Meanwhile, they never stopped trying to find things to use against me.

I was told I might be put on trial, and that frightened me. Who was to stop the Chinese from trying me and sentencing me to life in prison? I knew I had little chance of getting out until the war was over. And in my heart I knew the Chinese really weren't going to release me no matter what I said or did. They knew I would go back on active duty in Vietnam, and they weren't about to return an enemy flier to the battlefield.

Then one day after I had been in Canton about six weeks the interrogation changed. I was taken into another room of the old house where I was being held. Gathered there was a group of ten or twelve people, a tape recorder, and movie and still cameras. "Sit down," I was told. "We have important things to tell you." Then, for the first time, a man in black read the official detailed charges against me. With cameras rolling I was told I was being charged with espionage, sabotage, endangering the people of China, endangering the security of the country, aiding and abetting those forces trying to overthrow the government, and for crimes against the people of the world for taking part in the Vietnam War.

I responded to those charges in a polite, respectful way, denying them all. They were trumped-up charges, I insisted. There wasn't a thread of truth to any of them. I was a military man, not a criminal, and they were violating international law by holding me. The Chinese official was adamant: "Your case will be dealt with according to Chinese law, nobody else's law. International law means nothing. Only Chinese law counts." I sat watching him impassively.

Then the other men in the room began to ask questions as cameras continued to record the session. All the questions pertained to my actions and flight path just before I was shot down, and it took me only a moment to realize that these people were experienced in flying airplanes. Maybe they weren't pilots, but they knew airplanes, and they had obviously reviewed if not actually observed on radar my maneuvers prior to ejection. Why did I turn back and forth? Why did I circle? I was following radar instructions from the ground, I told them. Why did I descend from the high altitude? Why hadn't I tried to outrun the Chinese fighter, since my F-104 was so much faster than the MIG-19? Because I didn't see him, you nitwits, I wanted to say, but I didn't, continuing to be polite in my responses.

As an adult, and even as a child, I had always tried to be cool and in control and to keep my emotions in check. Never had I expected to lose control of my life the way I did in Canton. My months there were unbelievably difficult and emotional. I was so apprehensive, uneasy, uncertain of the future—and afraid of what was going to happen to me. I didn't know whether I was going to be thrown in prison, executed, released when the war was over. If I was released, what effect would my shoot-down and capture have on my military career? I continued to feel humility and loss of face for being shot down. My military future worried me, and so did my personal life. I worried about Judy and whether I would be home for the birth of our third child in December.

I knew I was tormenting myself by going over and over all my fears and uncertainties, but I couldn't seem to stop. I worried, not only about the future, but about everything I'd said in all the interrogation sessions. Was I saying the right things? How would the Air Force and the U.S. government feel about my responses to the questions of the Chinese?

After several weeks I no longer saw Shu, but three other interpreters were assigned to me. One of them was a short, fat Chinese whose name I never learned. The man was always in uniform; he wore very thick glasses, chain-smoked, and loved to talk. When he learned that my cigarettes had gotten wet during the ejection from my airplane he brought me some Chinese cigarettes, which I smoked for three days. At the end of those three days I noticed with horror that my fingers had turned black. If those cigarettes had done that to my fingers in such a short time, what would they do to my lungs if I smoked them for twenty years? On the spot I decided to stop smoking. I knew there were two major reasons why I should do so. One was health. I didn't want to spend years in a Chinese prison, be released, and then die of lung cancer the following year. I was buying myself an insurance policy of sorts. I knew that some time—years, perhaps—was going to be taken out of my life, and I wanted to be as healthy as possible for the years remaining after I was released.

The second reason was equally important to me. If my captors got me hooked on their cigarettes, those cigarettes could be used as a tool against me, to be taken away as a means of punishment or to force me to do something I didn't want to do. I didn't want to give them that kind of leverage.

The fat interpreter offered to get me other brands, which I declined. He finally gave up, but every time he came into my room he took out his own cigarettes and made a big production of lighting them.

On days when there were no interrogation sessions the interpreters often came in and talked to me. They seemed genuinely interested in me and my life in America. Sometimes one came in the morning, another in the afternoon, and these were rather pleasant interludes for me. The interpreters weren't trying to extract military information from me, they were just asking me about myself. One Sunday one of them noticed that I seemed dejected. "If you were home, what would you do on a Sunday?" he asked, and I described a typical Sunday to him—church, brunch, a ride, a visit with friends. The man listened with interest, then asked where I had traveled. Germany, France, Tripoli, Paris, London, Rome, I told him. These were places that none of the interpreters had ever been, and they were intrigued by tales of life beyond their borders.

These same interpreters read and censored all my incoming and outgoing mail, and by doing so they got to know my family and the people in the photographs they allowed me to receive. Their curiosity was insatiable, and it helped pass the time for me without my fearing I was giving important information. They called these sessions "friendly conversations."

My months in Canton were a time of great contrast. I was charged as a criminal and kept under the surveillance of armed guards twenty-four hours a day. The door to my room was always open, a light left on at night so the guards could look in and see me. "Friendly conversations" or not, I never forgot that I was dealing with the enemy. My life was in their hands, and I knew this was psychological warfare of sorts. Treat me nicely and then threaten me with life imprisonment or worse.

The Chinese took care of my basic needs. Three hot meals a day were delivered to my room: eggs in the morning; vegetables, maybe a little meat, and fruit at lunch; soup, possibly meat, and a vegetable in the evening. Meals were served on china plates with knives, forks, and spoons. It was obvious that the Cantonese were trying to provide me with Western-type food and utensils rather than their own Chinese-style food and chopsticks.

Next to my bedroom in the old house was a bathroom where I was permitted to go under the watchful eyes of the guards. The toilet and cold-water faucet worked; several times a week hot water was brought in and poured into the bathtub, and I was permitted to bathe.

The Chinese also tried to take care of my spiritual and reading needs by giving me a Bible, after repeated requests, and copies of a magazine, similar to *Life,* called *China Pictorial,* which was written in English. And they took care of my basic health needs. Before my capture I'd had a sore ingrown toenail, which became much worse after my long march in flying boots. The toe became infected, and Shu sent for the doctor, who managed to cure it after several painful attempts, and then they gave me sandal-type shoes to wear.

If my feet were comfortable, my mind was in a whirl as the roller-coaster treatment continued. You're a criminal, a liar, you're not cooperating, the interrogators insisted.

On October 15 something totally unexpected happened: I couldn't believe my eyes when the interpreters appeared in my room carrying a little birthday cake and singing "Happy Birthday" in English. It was the last thing in the world that I would ever have expected. It was thoughtful of them, and I appreciated it, but I wished they hadn't done it. They were still the enemy and I their captive. I couldn't be rude; I thanked them and took the cake and cut it into small pieces for myself and each one of them. I don't believe I could have a stranger birthday celebration than that one.

Christmas was even more astonishing. I knew the Chinese communists didn't recognize the birth of Christ. Yet somebody went out and found a scraggly-looking little Christmas tree, which they brought into my room. "What do you put on a Christmas tree?" they asked. In amazement I told them, and the Chinese responded, "We don't have lights and those other things. What can we substitute?" I thought for a moment and then suggested they get colored craft paper. The next day the interpreters returned with scissors and paper, and we sat and cut out bells and other ornaments, which we hung on the little tree. Then they took a picture of me sitting by that tree, which I later sent home to my family. Again, a strange and rather unnerving experience.

When I was alone I continued to ponder my case and worry about what I'd said through all the long interrogation sessions. I'd sit, stand, walk about the room . . . trying to remember what questions the Chinese had asked and what I had answered. I did this after each interrogation session, telling myself that if I was released in the near future, I wanted to be able to recount in detail everything they had asked me, hoping that this would help U.S. intelligence analyze Chinese interrogation techniques.

I continued to hope that I'd be released. After all, I kept reminding myself, the U.S. was not at war with China. And I had been kept in Canton; if they were to release me, it would no doubt be through nearby Hong Kong. They hadn't put me in prison; they fed and cared for me better than they would most prisoners. Perhaps the Chinese communists were weighing the consequences of releasing me and would decide in my favor very soon.

And then one day, out in the yard where I could see it from my window, Chinese soldiers set up for target practice and began shooting at the cardboard silhouette of a man's head and shoulders, with concentric circles going around. It was the kind of thing you'd see on a rifle range. They had put the silhouette up on the fence in clear view of my room, and each day an increasing number of soldiers took turns practicing, firing without bullets. I could hear the click of the triggers and the sergeant giving orders in Chinese: Ready, aim, fire!

I knew why they were doing it. To scare me. I asked the interpreter, just to see what he would say. "They're training," he explained. "Soldiers have to train." Sure, I thought, they have to train right outside my window.

As the days wore on, though, the target practice began to unnerve me, and the interrogators added to my unease. "We've asked you questions over and over, and you refuse to answer them," they repeated. "You're lying to us. You're withholding information. We want you to come straight and answer these questions. Are you willing?" My answer didn't change. No.

The target practice went on for more than a week. Then one day the chain-smoking interpreter with the thick glasses walked into my room. Usually when he came in he would smile and say, "How are you today, Captain Smith?" But on this particular day he was not smiling, and he looked very serious. "What's wrong?" I asked. "Are you not feeling well?"

"Don't joke today," he replied. "I've got something very important to tell you. It's been decided that you need to be punished for your crimes and your hostile, bitter attitude. Tomorrow you're going to be shot."

Shot? He's bluffing, I thought, but I couldn't be sure. My heart dropped as he began to reiterate the case against me, going through all the charges I had heard before: I had aroused the indignation and wrath of the Chinese people for my crimes, and the people were demanding that I be put to death. My stubborn attitude and refusal to confess to my crimes gave the Chinese authorities no choice but to yield to the demands of the great Chinese masses. Therefore, tomorrow I would be executed by the firing squad.

And maybe, I thought, that was how this whole debacle was going to end. Maybe he wasn't bluffing. I went to bed that night, but not to sleep. Several things didn't make any sense to me, most of all the statement that the Chinese people were demanding my death. Why would they do that? The people on Hainan Island knew I hadn't harmed anyone. They'd seen me come down in the parachute, they'd captured me and handed me over. The Chinese people wouldn't be demanding my death unless I had killed a Chinese. Would they?

As I contemplated the death threat through the long night it didn't seem to me that the timing was right. The Chinese had extracted no military information from me. To the best of my knowledge, I was the only U.S. military man to be captured in recent years. If they killed me, they'd be losing a valuable prisoner and a possible source of information. And if they shot me in public, their claims that they were humanitarian would be blown to bits, leaving them open to condemnation by most of the world.

The long night finally passed, and my breakfast was delivered as usual the next morning. I ate it, figuring it might be my last meal. Then I sat and waited. And waited. At about four o'clock in the afternoon a different interpreter came in. "Hey," I asked him, "what happened to the firing squad thing we were going to have this morning?" The words were out of my mouth before I realized how foolish I was being. I was making myself look stupid and arrogant, and things were shaky enough without deliberately antagonizing my captors. "Don't be insolent," the interpreter said, and then he changed the subject. I shut up, realizing to my great relief that the Chinese had been bluffing all along and didn't have the guts to admit it. The next day the target practice came to an end, and I realized that if they had been trying to scare me, they had succeeded.

Gradually, as the months passed, the interrogation began to wind down, and then it stopped. The Chinese were no longer trying to extract information from me. I also sensed a change in the mood of the people around me. They seemed to be waiting for something, making me feel increasingly uneasy and uncertain. Something was about to happen.

I had known that I would not be kept in this house in Canton indefinitely. Keeping a single prisoner in this environment was taking the time and effort of too many people. I knew they would eventually release me or move me to a place where they could imprison me with fewer people and less effort on their part. I also knew I had not cooperated the way they wanted, and they were probably going to put me in prison.

Thinking that brought on a whole new set of worries, and I was increasingly depressed. My third child had been born on December 21, and I had been notified by a telegram from the International Red Cross. I had not made it home for the birth or for Christmas, no one was interrogating me anymore, and time was passing more slowly than ever.

I didn't realize it at the time, but I was beginning to prepare myself subconsciously for what I suspected lay ahead. Reality was beginning to rear its ugly head, and I wasn't sure I was ready or able to accept it.

The interpreters had gotten to know me and my family, and I didn't believe they thought I was a spy. I was convinced they knew I was a victim of circumstances, there by accident. They also knew, I suspected, that their government was not going to turn me loose without making an example of me. I saw pity in their eyes, and nothing frightened me more than that. The interpreters' routine didn't change, but they seemed to have accepted the fact that I was a lost cause and would soon be slipping into the bowels of the Chinese prison system, and there was nothing they could do about it. They looked at me with empty expressions, and I could guess what that meant. They knew I was going to be severely punished or killed, and even if they didn't think I deserved it, it was going to happen. Their communist government had come to a decision.

10

Going the Wrong Direction

I came awake feeling tired and dazed. As I opened my eyes fear and exhaustion settled over me. I'd slept little; at some point during the long night a terrible, desolate cry had startled me awake. Was I dreaming? Or had I cried out in my sleep? I couldn't be sure. From the moment of my capture I'd tried to hide my agonizing sense of fear and desolation from my captors. I hoped I hadn't revealed anything in my sleep.

I looked around the room where I had been held captive for four months. The light on the table was still on, as it had been throughout every dreary night. The mosquito netting was no longer pulled around the bed. It was January, and even in southern China, in Canton, it had turned cold. One day I made the mistake of asking if there was heat in the building. "No," the interpreter replied. "It doesn't stay cold long enough to need heat." And then he added an apparent afterthought: "If you want to request that you be sent to a colder place, you would have heat inside."

It was a dirty trick, I soon learned. The interpreter had probably known all along that I was going to be sent north.

He'd simply wanted it to look as if I had requested the transfer. No, thanks, I had responded. I would make no such request. If I asked to be moved and my conditions worsened, I would forever blame myself.

Now none of it mattered. I was being moved anyway. Two days before, on January 25, one of the interpreters had come into my room looking grim. "Your case has been transferred to Peking," he announced in solemn, official tones. What does that mean? I asked. "The authorities concerned have decided that you will be moved up there." But why? I persisted. Was I going into prison? Would I be put on trial? Would my treatment be about the same as it had been in Canton? The interpreter would say no more.

For months I'd been waiting for some kind of decision. His pronouncement that I was going to be moved indicated some action was being taken by the authorities. My heart beat faster; I knew most of the possibilities were not good. Once a decision had been made there would be no turning back. I had already pleaded my case at length. There was nothing I could do at this point to change their decision. I looked at the interpreter, trying to get an indication of what was happening. His face was stony. The Chinese had insisted many times that I would be put on trial. Peking seemed a logical location for a trial, military or civilian.

I had been in Canton for four long, uncertain, unsettling months, and I knew one thing for sure: If I was being sent south toward Hong Kong, it might have meant release. Peking was far north in China. Oh, God, I thought, a decision had been made all right, and it had gone against me. This time they weren't bluffing. It was a devastating blow to be sent to Peking.

Now, on this last morning in Canton, I lay in bed, waiting for the first light of dawn. Then I would pack my few belongings in the cardboard boxes they'd supplied. I didn't have much—only the few clothes the Chinese had given me during my time in Canton and the letters I had received from my family. My toothbrush, toothpaste, washcloth, and towel would go into a small green plastic bag with a drawstring that I'd been given. That was all I had.

Only the letters and photographs from my family meant anything to me. Learning how to write the letters that were exchanged hadn't been easy for me or my family. At first many of my letters were returned by the Chinese, and I was told to rewrite them because I was giving information about my case that they would not allow. In one letter that came back I had told my parents that my case was being treated as that of a criminal, rather than a prisoner of war. "You're not permitted to say that," I was informed.

I couldn't fight them on the issue. Do it their way or don't do it. Gradually I learned what would be accepted. When letters were returned to me to be rewritten they were delayed that much longer in getting to my family. I quickly decided that it was more important to keep the lines of communication open than to try to include information that would be censored. I felt especially sorry for my mother, knowing the pain she was going through because of me and my predicament. And yet every month she sat down and wrote me a letter, trying to keep my spirits up.

At times I knew my family was taking me a bit too literally when I said I was being treated well. I wanted them to know I wasn't being beaten, but sometimes I went overboard. I winced a bit when I received this letter from my dad.

Roodhouse, Ill.
Nov. 6, 1965

Dear Phil,

We got your letter of the 22nd October, and it sure was good to hear from you, and especially that you were trusting the Lord. His promises never fail to those who fully trust and obey Him.

We are thankful that you are being treated fairly. I know it is unnecessary to tell you to show your appreciation for kind treatment.

We have had nice weather for about two weeks and have our beans and corn harvested. Crops were very good this year.

Many people are praying for you, and we just hope the will of the Lord be done in all of our lives and that we will meet for a better day before too long.

We'll be waiting to hear from you.

Love,
Mother and Dad

If I was misleading them a little bit, I never regretted it. The truth wasn't very pretty. This wasn't really some temporary assignment in an exotic foreign country. I was a prisoner, stripped of all freedom of choice. Only my mind was free to roam at will, and even that had to be kept in check at times. So I gave my family a rosy picture of my conditions; better to do that, I decided, than to frighten them by being overly negative.

On this day in late January 1966, I arose at daybreak after a restless night. I knew this day represented the beginning of a new era; the wheels were in motion, and I had no way of knowing how or where I would end up. Feeling nervous and apprehensive, I packed my few belongings, ate my breakfast, and waited. Dreams of the night, and the cry I'd heard, had left me upset and disquieted. Forget all that, I warned myself; things were bad enough when I was awake.

Later, the events of that day in January when I left Canton would become blurred in my mind. The pain and fear of the day were ultimately blotted out. I was going into hell, and I knew it.

At midmorning I was led out of the house and into one of two waiting cars. I was to be accompanied on the two-day train ride to Peking by one of the interpreters who had been with me for most of my time in captivity and by five Cantonese guards. As we walked to the cars I noted that none of the guards were in uniform, although all five carried guns in their waistbands, which they made sure I saw. They wanted to hide the fact that a prisoner was being moved, but they didn't want that prisoner to try anything funny.

We pulled up to a side entrance of the station in Canton, and I was quickly whisked onto the train. Casual observers would not have known a prisoner was being transported. There were no uniforms, handcuffs, or guns in sight. I was dressed in my Chinese-style clothing, but even if I hadn't been, I probably wouldn't have been noticed. Foreign diplomats, businessmen, journalists, and other non-Orientals were frequent visitors to Canton.

I was led rapidly into a compartment meant to hold four people. I'd been warned not to talk to any foreigners as I boarded or while on the train and was told I could leave the compartment only to go to the rest room, which was a short distance down the corridor, and I could go there only under the watchful eyes of the guards.

I spent the next two sad, depressing days in that compartment, alone much of the time. My emotional state was precarious, confused, unfocused. What was going to happen to me? What did this trip mean? I thought back on all that had happened the past four months, looking for clues as to what might lie ahead. I couldn't foresee the future, except I knew this move wasn't a good one. I was going north to Peking, and there was a constant red flashing light in my mind: *I am going the wrong direction.*

With every mile my heart sank lower and lower. I tried to pull myself together. You've made it this far, I reminded myself; you'll have to take whatever lies ahead. And so I sat, staring out the window at the countryside. At times the interpreter sat with me, pointing out the sights and cities as we moved along. Sometimes, in the cities, the interpreter pulled down the shades in the compartment so no one could see me from outside, but most of the time I was permitted to look out the window. Food was brought to me on a tray from the dining car, and I was pleasantly surprised to find that it was very good. The train carried tourists and business people from many countries; the food was obviously prepared to appeal to the international palate and was served on china plates with Western-style utensils.

At night my seat unfolded into a bed. I undressed and lay in the bed but didn't sleep. The bouncing train and my own precarious mental state made it impossible to do anything but doze restlessly. I knew the guards were in the compartment next door, and one was stationed in the hallway outside at all times.

The authorities in Canton had given me a small notebook, and on this dismal train ride I began writing in it. I was horrified by the poverty and backward conditions, and I tried to capture in words what I was seeing out the window.

At last, after two days, the train pulled into the large train station in Peking. The day matched my mood. It was cold, gray, forlorn-looking. Give me strength, I thought as I was kept waiting on the train until all the other passengers had departed. Then, once the area around my compartment had been cleared, I was led off the train and turned in the direction away from the train terminal. No one was in sight in the terminal as we left the station through a side exit. Cars were pulled up directly beside the exit. I was motioned into the first car, and it was then that I noticed that the Cantonese guards had not come out of the train station with me. Five Peking guards had been waiting for the train to pull in; I was now their responsibility. A new interpreter had also joined the group, a strange-looking woman who got in the car with me and the Cantonese interpreter. During the ride the two interpreters talked at length in Chinese. I could guess what they were saying even though I didn't speak Chinese. The Peking interpreter asked a number of questions: Does Smith speak any Chinese? No. Has he ever tried to escape? No. Is he a troublemaker? No. Has he ever gotten into a fight? No. What's his overall attitude? Uncooperative. Hostile toward our system. Is he suicidal? No. I could only surmise what was being discussed as I listened intently to the jabbering of the two Chinese.

As we drove through the streets of Peking I was shocked at

what I saw. The capital city looked unbelievably old and rundown. Most of the buildings were crumbling and in total disrepair. I hadn't expected such a depressing sight, and I felt even worse when I looked at the people. It was mid-morning, and there were hordes of people in the streets, on foot and on bicycles. If possible, they looked even more poor and hopeless than the buildings of their city. Seeing them was a jolt. If the natives of this city looked like that and lived in this dreadful environment, the life of a captive would surely be much worse. My life-style, I suspected, was going to be the pits.

The cars drove for a long time through back streets of Peking, finally reaching the outskirts of the city, where there were fewer and fewer buildings. In several places I saw sad-looking little vegetable gardens. Then, suddenly, a big wall loomed in front of us. A guard in the uniform of the People's Liberation Army stood at the gate, a rifle over his shoulder. The cars passed through the gate and pulled up in front of a dirty, dismal building. "Get out," the female interpreter ordered. She had obviously taken over responsibility for me from the Cantonese interpreter.

We walked into a receiving area, a large room that reminded me of a rundown hotel lobby complete with shabby couches and chairs. The decrepit furniture sat off at one side in an area apparently set up for visitors to meet with prisoners. I was led up to a counter in the front of the room where a sour-looking prison agent was seated, staring at me with cold, hostile eyes. "What's your name?" he asked in Chinese, and the woman translated. You've got to be kidding, I thought. I'm the only American these people have captured in fifteen years, and this dumb shit is asking me my name? I held my tongue and gave my name.

"What's your crime?"

"I have committed no crime," I responded. The agent was astounded. His face flushed as he slammed down his pencil and repeated, "What is your crime?" I said it again. I had committed no crime, and I was furious that they were continuing to badger me. I'd already been interrogated by top intelligence agents in Canton. Who the hell was this obnoxious creep?

The agent wasn't about to give up. "What's your nationality?" Oh, God, I thought, and the female interpreter stepped in. My expression must have given me away. "Answer the question," she said in a mean voice. "Don't be smart. We don't allow smart remarks."

I took a deep breath and then decided I better cool it. More calmly I said that I had explained everything in Canton. If the man wanted to write down a crime, write it down; I wasn't going to tell him anything.

Finally the registration ordeal was over. I knew I'd gotten off to a bad start. For a few moments I had let anger and frustration show, and had done so deliberately, but I knew in the future I'd better be cautious and control my emotions or I would bring about unnecessary trouble.

The female interpreter and the guards led the way out of the receiving area. From there began a walk that took me from the unknown horrors of a nightmare into the very nightmare itself. The route they took was circuitous, winding through mazes of hallways, doors, passageways, sometimes inside buildings, sometimes outside. As we walked I looked around, and what I saw gave me cold chills. For the first time I was seeing what a prison looked like from the inside, and it was horrible. The prison was an old, old place; mortar was decaying and falling out of the bricks. My sense of doom deepened. If the condition of the buildings was so bad, would my treatment be commensurate with my surroundings? I was afraid I knew the answer. I was walking through a hellhole into what I suspected would be a dungeon of despair. Grim, I thought, wondering how much worse it could get.

I could see that the prison was constructed with a series of rotundas, interconnected cell blocks extending out from them like fingers. Supervisors could be stationed in the center of each rotunda to insure prison security. As we wandered through this desolate prison it was clear that my captors were trying to keep me from being seen. A guard walked ahead of me at all times. If any other person came into sight, the procession was stopped until the way was clear, and then we proceeded.

At one point, as we walked through the maze, I noticed an area off in a corner where there were several hundred little old rusty stoves piled under a lean-to. I wondered about those stoves. They gave a look of total abandonment to this place of desolation. Was I the only prisoner being held here? Would my cell have heat?

Finally we arrived at the door of a cell and stopped. One of the guards opened the door and motioned me to go in. Hesitantly I stepped in. At 5'11" I had to duck to get through the thick wooden cell door, which was only five feet high and about thirty inches wide. The guard closed the door of the cell and then very dramatically slammed the bolt closed. The sound of that bolt sliding into place was the most dreadful sound I had ever heard. There was a *clang* and then a deadly silence. The sound would stay with me forever. I was a caged animal; sensations of doom and hopelessness made me feel faint.

I stood still, looking at the cell. It was ten feet by twenty feet, with an eight-foot-high ceiling. In it were a bed on a wooden frame—no springs, just boards with a small thin pad and some quilts—a small table, a chair, and, over in the corner, a little wood-burning stove with a stovepipe that went up into a hole cut through the wall. I realized then what the old stoves outside had been used for, and it made me feel even more alone in this desolate place. Most of the cells must be empty, I figured. The floor of the cell was concrete, the walls whitewashed. I reached out and touched the wall, and the whitewash flaked off. In the wall opposite the door were two windows, each fifteen by thirty inches, the glass painted to obstruct the view.

That was it. I was in prison, with bars on the inside of the windows and the door slammed shut and bolted. Clearly this was no temporary arrangement. I was going to be here for a long time. I knew they wouldn't have sent me all the way to Peking just to talk to me some more. The door had slammed shut, all right . . . on my life.

At that moment my emotions were no longer under control. I was too far down to care. How could I stand this kind of treatment? Why were they doing this to me? Why had this happened? Anger and anguish and self-pity flooded over me. A dam of despair had broken, and I couldn't stop it.

Through my torment, though, as I stood in that barren cell, I heard voices out in the hallway. Were those bastards staring at me through the peephole in the door? I couldn't tell, but I suspected they were. They were probably waiting to see what I would do. They had put a tiger in a cage; would he charge around, beating his head on the walls? They didn't know. And once again, it was my determination not to show weakness before the enemy that began to bring me around. I knew I must try to pull myself together. If I could help it at all, and I vowed I could, I must not let my tormentors know the depths to which I had sunk.

Since I had arrived in this hellhole I had been horrified by the condition of the prison. Even more horrifying, however, was the attitude of the people. Everyone I'd seen in this prison was cold and grim and harsh. The prison atmosphere was a deadly one, and it hadn't taken long for it to begin to seep into my consciousness.

Doom, despair, hopelessness . . . an animal in a cage. I realized that, and I realized something else. I was a proud American military officer. I had been willing to give my life for my country in battle, and this was battle. These beasts were not going to break my will or my spirit. I swore I would not give them that satisfaction.

A guard entered the cell, carrying water in a thermos jug. There was no water purification system, I later learned, so all water was boiled and kept in thermos jugs. I drank some of the water and wondered what would happen next.

Several hours later the female interpreter came into the cell. She was a very ugly Chinese woman whom I would always think of as The Hag. She was short and squat with strange bobbed hair and an attitude of utter contempt for me. In voice and manner she was harsh and arrogant and showed real hatred for her prisoner. In every way she was the exact opposite of Shu, the Cantonese lawyer who had met me at the airport in Canton and been with me for the first few weeks. Shu had been a civilized human being with intelligence and compassion. The Hag was a monster who wasted no time in establishing her tyrannical authority. She handed me a piece of paper and a pencil. "I will explain the rules to you," she said brusquely. "You must write them down. First, you must obey all prison rules."

The bitch, I thought as I interrupted. "How can I do that?" I asked. "I don't know the prison rules."

The Hag snapped back. "Shut up and listen and write them down like I told you to do. You must do as the warders [guards] say. Do not get in a fight. Get up when the whistle blows in the morning. Go to bed when the whistle blows at night." On and on she went. As I listened I began to wonder about her. Her English had an American accent to it. All the other Chinese I had talked to had had British accents.

I was trying hard to compose myself, but I couldn't imagine a lower point in my life than what I was going through right then. That terrible woman going on and on . . . the walk through the prison that had been so grim, all the sounds and noises and smells and the stern looks on everybody's faces . . . all of it was far worse than I had imagined when I was on the train. Then I had still hoped that I might not be put in an actual prison. This was not only a prison, I thought, it must surely be the most horrible and smelly one in this godforsaken country. The smell alone made me feel sick. It wasn't that of rotten food or dead things lying around; it was the smell of must and wetness and mud and despair.

I had entered the pits of the Chinese prison system, and none of it seemed real to me. I was confined in a squalid prison cell, in the pits of despair, dignity and self-esteem gone, perhaps forever. A soundless cry shook my body; this was a nightmare beyond anything I had ever imagined.

11

"Instructional Persuasion"

Flight Commander Harvey Quackenbush: "Losing Phil Smith was a hell of a loss to our squadron, and especially to those of us who had gone to Vietnam together. No matter where we were, it was something that was always with us, in our minds. We all agreed on one thing: Of the seven of us, if such a dastardly thing had to happen, Phil Smith was probably the best equipped of any of us to handle it, psychologically, physically, in every way. We all believed that.

"We felt so helpless. There wasn't a bloody goddamn thing we could do for Phil Smith. We rotated home on schedule at the end of October 1965. We came back to the States with the terrible sensation of leaving a comrade behind, and knowing we were helpless to do anything about it. That does something to you. It's a dreadful feeling. Our lives went on; his, in effect, stopped."

As the prison routine closed down around me in the winter of 1966 I wondered how I was going to survive. I was like a beast in a cage, stripped of everything known to civilized man. My living conditions were crude, cold, and monotonous; I was treated with anger, scorn, and contempt by Chinese captors who debased and demoralized me at every opportunity. Sometimes Communist propaganda was available for me to read; other times I had nothing at all in my cell to occupy my time.

Whether I had reading material or not, however, the facts of my existence didn't change and didn't improve. I was incarcerated in one of China's worst hellholes, hidden away in an isolated cell block all by myself. I existed, knowing I couldn't go out the door and look at the stars or smell the air or lean against a tree at will. I was caught in a nightmare that never ended, restricted in everything I said and did, and those restrictions preyed heavily on me.

There were times when I didn't know how I could go on. I can't take any more, I'd think in a frenzy, and then I forced myself to calm down. What were my choices? I would not permit myself to lose my composure and go berserk. To yell and scream and beat my head against the wall would show those Chinese bastards that they had gotten the best of me, and I wasn't going to do that. The other alternative was to give in and yield to their demands, and that was even more unacceptable to me. I was in a trap, and outwardly, at least, I knew I must demonstrate to my captors that I was firmly in control of myself at all times.

Inwardly, the awful sense of being imprisoned hung over me every moment of every day. It dulled my senses, making it difficult for me to think reasonably and clearly. The walls and bars of my imprisonment never changed, but my emotions and reactions fluctuated wildly. Sometimes, without warning, I'd be overcome by self-pity, doubt, and fear, and there wasn't anything I could do about it. I was never allowed to make a decision or to have a voice in the direction my life was taking. I was a puppet, being manipulated, cleverly and diabolically, by the Chinese communists.

I'd seen wild animals in the zoo, some of whom paced up and down, restlessly, nervously, wanting out. Others lay down in the sun and went to sleep, totally accepting their confinement. I knew I had to accept the cruelty of the prison system, but I wasn't willing to prostrate myself like an old lion in the sun, and it was never easy. I tried my best to tolerate whatever I encountered—the isolation, the weather, the confinement, the brainwashing, the discomfort, the lack of food, the horror of it all.

My first year in Peking was devastating to me. I tore myself apart asking the same questions: What was going to happen to me, and when might it happen? I analyzed my case and everything that had befallen me, reviewing everything again and again and again, my emotions in turmoil. The more I agonized over my predicament, the more I knew I had to stop. I was torturing myself by asking questions that I could not answer, and doing that only made my morale plummet. How long are you going to keep this up, I'd ask myself, and gradually, over many months, I was able to ease up on myself and to stop asking the unanswerable. During those times when I was able to accept the conditions of my life my morale improved.

I spent the vast majority of my time alone in my cell, and even then I tried to give the impression of being in good spirits. I did that because I knew my captors might walk in at any moment, and I knew I was being watched through a peephole in the door. The peephole was covered on the outside with a piece of black cloth that the guard could pull up by the corner to look in. It was difficult for me to know when I was being watched, especially at night, and it incensed me to know those bastards could peer in at me at all hours. It was further degradation that I viewed as an invasion of my life and my privacy. Sometimes, when I didn't know whether I was being watched or not, I went over to the door to see if the corner of the cloth was raised. If it was, and I saw a Chinese eyeball only inches away, it gave me the creeps to know that I was that close to such a barbarous creature.

And if it took great will to hide my feelings from my captors, it took equally great determination to hide them from my family. In those early days in Peking I was allowed to write one letter a month. Many times when I sat down to write that letter home I had to force myself to take pen in hand. I was so depressed and distraught, it was difficult to pretend that everything was fine, and I knew there was nothing of importance that I could write that would get by the censors. I would have liked to have described my treatment, my cell, what the Chinese were telling me, and how they were dealing with my case. I would have liked to have told my family that the Chinese had presented criminal charges against me, that they were making unreasonable demands for me to confess to alleged crimes and to denounce the U.S. government and the war in Vietnam.

None of that was permitted, and that made me feel even less like writing. If I couldn't write what I wanted, why write at all? I asked myself that question many times, and I always came up with the same answer. If I didn't write anything at all, my entire family would suffer. They would pay the penalty by worrying even more about me. If I was wallowing in the misery of captivity, even though I tried hard not to, I couldn't take it out on my family. It was my duty to write, to sound as optimistic as possible, to show my love, my concern, and to demonstrate that I still had my mind and my sanity. I tried in every letter to be very careful not to misspell words, to use proper English, and to make sure my handwriting didn't get sloppy. I wanted my letters to reflect calmness and control. If I didn't really feel that way, and I usually didn't, I would do my best to put up a false front.

My captors were watching me and reading my mail, and if I let them know how deeply depressed I was, they would never stop trying to make me feel even worse by creating a sense of hopelessness and doom. Their strategy, I knew, would be simple: Convince the American that he was lost and they were the only ones who could help him. They would try to grind me down so low psychologically that I would give up, unable to take it anymore, willing to do whatever they wanted me to do.

The very thought of doing that, of giving up, was repulsive to me. If I couldn't fight the war in Vietnam in my F-104, by damn, I'd fight it here in this Chinese hellhole. I wasn't going to let my Chinese captors drag me down to the point where I couldn't live up to the expectations of my family and friends. Fighter pilots had always tried to ease the fear of being killed by accepting a basic truism: "You have to accept losses in a big operation." At this moment I was one of those losses, unable to fly and fight and win with my fellow pilots, but I had no intention of groveling before the enemy. I would die first.

Soon after being sent to the north of China, a prisoner of the Chinese communists, I was called upon time and again to use everything I had ever learned about thinking clearly and expressing myself logically and persuasively.

During my early days in Peking feelings of doom and despair continued to overwhelm me. I knew I was being held in this crumbling, isolated prison area because officials didn't want anyone, including their own people, to know where I was or that I was there at all. They had made me as invisible as possible. I knew that since the communists had taken over in 1949 the country had been beset by internal division, controversy, and bickering, and I was sure that officials wanted to make sure that no one else got their hands on me. The government wanted no problems from me or from anybody in or out of the country. Conditions within the country were volatile and unstable; the whereabouts of the foreign captive would be kept as secret as possible, and the effects of that treatment on me were profound. I could not have felt more isolated or more cut off from humanity.

In Canton interrogators had repeatedly tried to obtain information from me about the war and U.S. involvement in it. Once they had me locked away in the prison in Peking they changed their tactics. They no longer seemed interested in what I knew about the war in Vietnam. Their focus had shifted; they now seemed intent on using a hard-line approach to gain political objectives. They had moved into the "instructional persuasion stage," which they called reeducation or remolding ideology and I called brainwashing— trying to convince me that the capitalist system was wicked and evil, the communist system good and pure. They began their "rehabilitation" by giving me communist propaganda to read and then quizzing me on it.

Initially the female interpreter I called The Hag came in every day, sometimes twice a day, to bring me reading material. One day she arrived carrying all four volumes of *The Selected Works of Mao Tse-tung,* chairman of the Communist Party of China. These were thick hardback books, and she warned me to be very careful with them, to keep them covered and to wash my hands before I read them. I wondered where they had come from. They were brand-new copies, never opened or read before. Everything in my cell was usually covered with dust from my coal stove, but I enjoyed reading anything I could get my hands on, so I did my best to keep the books clean.

The books were a history of China from Mao's point of view, and even though I knew little about the country since the communists had taken over, I had a reasonable knowledge of its history before 1949, and it seemed obvious that Mao had slanted his writings to further his own ideology.

As I read those books in the winter of 1966 conditions in China itself began to change. Even to a prisoner in the country it was apparent that the ideological split within the Communist Party of China was intensifying. All the material I received continuously stressed the importance of following Mao's teachings as opposed to what was called the "Russian Revisionist Road." As events unfolded Mao launched the nation into what he called "The Great Proletarian Cultural Revolution" that squelched the opposition. Ultimately that revolution resulted in chaos and violence, unlawful arrests and imprisonments, even executions. Radicals called the Red Guards ran wild in the streets and virtually seized power in all domestic and foreign affairs for a time. Every person in China, including me, was ultimately touched by the evil forces that were unleashed by Mao and his followers.

The prison authorities, out of fear or a sense of duty, seemed caught up in the furor that was sweeping the country. Peasants in the fields, workers in the factories, soldiers in training—all were depicted in every Chinese publication as ardently studying and worshiping Mao's thoughts. If ordinary citizens of China needed Mao's guidance in all they did, then even more so did a foreign prisoner charged with crimes against the state. Ruthlessly they increased their efforts to force-feed Mao and his teachings to me. Their brainwashing began in earnest.

The Chinese interpreters used various techniques in trying to convince me that their system was right and mine was wrong. They told me in detail their version of the race riots in Watts, claiming the U.S. was trampling over the people of the world, sucking the blood out of the working classes. They backed up their claims by giving me copies of *The Guardian,* a left-wing newspaper published in New York City that dealt extensively with labor problems in the U.S., sweatshops, and reports on how various workers were being persecuted and underpaid. They showed me lengthy articles about black people who had supposedly been railroaded into prison, innocent victims of the capitalist system. "You pretend to believe in freedom and democracy, and yet you persecute the blacks and the Spanish and all the other minorities," they charged in harsh, derisive voices. "Things aren't fair in the U.S. Look at these cases."

On and on they went, trying to beat down my beliefs as they derided my country and its government. Each day, after the interpreter had left, I reviewed everything that had been said and tried to think of things I should have brought up and points I hadn't made so I would be prepared the following day to rebuff their allegations and strengthen my own arguments.

I was surprised that I was permitted to express my own

feelings at great length in response to their harangues. Sometimes I admitted that conditions were not perfect in my country; then I would tell them that they really didn't know what they were talking about and launch into my own theories and explanations.

I was back in Thelma Wilkinson's speech club, where I had placed fifth in a statewide speech contest, with an opportunity to organize my thoughts and present them as simply and logically as possible, and that gave me a big boost. Gradually I began to believe I was doing a better job of educating the Chinese than they were doing with me, and that was one of the few bright spots in my grim prison routine. These "instructional persuasion" sessions were the only break I had in the loneliness and isolation of captivity, and I looked forward to them.

Each week I received an English copy of *The Peking Review,* and this was of special interest to me. The weekly newspaper was the official organ of the Communist Party, and I knew the news was slanted accordingly, but it gave me two vital pieces of information: It helped me keep track of the days, since its issues were dated, and it confirmed that the Vietnam War was still going on. This was of extreme importance to me. If the war had ended, and I'd been left to rot here in this hellhole, my chances of ever getting out were even grimmer than I had feared.

At first, when I read reports on the war in *The Peking Review,* I was suspicious. Were they trying to hoodwink me? Was this a phony newspaper? I finally decided that it wasn't phony, that they wouldn't print a special edition of *The Peking Review* just to make me think the war was still going on when actually it had ended. I understood that the news I was reading was heavily slanted, but any news from outside the prison walls gave me a boost.

I was also given newspapers written in English from New Zealand and other countries. These were radical publications that consistently criticized the U S. and praised Mao and his judgment and insightful leadership.

119

The Chinese augmented the written material they gathered up from around the world with a daily radio broadcast, which they required me to listen to and then discuss. Each morning at ten A.M. the guard out in the hall turned on the radio that sat on his desk, and the sound was piped into my room through a speaker above the cell door. This was Radio Peking, a one-hour broadcast in English extolling the virtues of Mao Tse-tung and the Chinese communists. I listened, as required, making mental notes of the issues I could rebut. Several times the guard, who could not understand English, turned to the wrong broadcast by mistake, and I got to listen to the BBC (British Broadcasting Corporation) rather than to Radio Peking, and what a blessed relief it was to hear even a few words of real news from the free world.

Through it all I never really believed that the Chinese expected to persuade me that their system was right. What they really expected, I was convinced, was for me to pretend to believe their propaganda, thereby taking the pressure off all of us and maybe even gaining me some favors—more food, perhaps, or even an earlier release. I could not go along with their game. My life and my honor were at stake, and I never stopped arguing against them or trying to come up with new points to make in our discussion sessions.

One day I was amazed when the interpreter asked if I would like to go into another cell and watch TV. Had I heard correctly? A guard led me down to a cell at the far end of the cell block, and there was a small black and white television set. I blinked in surprise. Were they trying to keep me from going bonkers? I'd give it a try. At first I enjoyed the diversion and was permitted to watch TV about once a week. Sometimes there were patriotic song-and-dance troupes waving flags and kicking up their feet. Most of the time, however, I was watching a group of people jabbering in Chinese, no doubt about Mao and his communist ideology. I began to fidget and noticed the guard looked equally bored.

More than anything else, it made me uncomfortable to sit

in the cell with the guard. The interpreters who spoke English were hateful enough to me. The guards spoke no English, and there was a feeling of bestiality and raw, nonverbal, primitive hatred about most of them. They were the lower life in the jungle, and they made my skin crawl. They blew their noses with their thumbs, first one nostril and then the other, and flipped any residue from their fingers onto the floor, all of this without the aid of a handkerchief. Equally repulsive was the sickening sound of phlegm being sucked from their clogged throats and mouths and the splat it made when it hit the concrete. It made me feel sick to be anywhere near such animals.

Finally I decided I'd rather stay in my cell alone than watch political discussions that I couldn't understand while sitting with such creatures. The next time a guard came to my cell and motioned me out I used hand and body gestures to ask him what was on TV, a song-and-dance troupe or people sitting around a table yapping? People yapping, the guard indicated, and I shook my head no. At that moment that one guard showed a brief touch of humanity. He laughed, and I stayed in my cell. I knew I should be happy to do anything to pass the time, even watch a discussion program in a foreign language, but I didn't want to do it, and it was one more way I could demonstrate my scorn for the Chinese and all their ideological gibberish.

One day as I paced in my prison cell The Hag shuffled in and announced in her hateful voice, "This evening you're going to the hospital for an examination." I was surprised. There was nothing wrong with me, at least nothing that I knew about. What was going on? Were the Chinese playing games? Or did they just want to make sure their American pawn didn't get sick and die on them?

At seven-thirty that night I was taken out of the prison and put in a car with The Hag and two guards, a second car of guards following behind. The drive took about thirty minutes, the roads clogged with people on foot and on bicycles. I looked around with great interest. I had been held in solitary confinement for so many months; what an unbelievable treat to see real people going about their lives. I felt like an alien awakening from a deep sleep in a strange environment.

I wished the ride could go on forever, but it ended as we pulled up before a large building that was obviously a hospital, even though it looked to be in great disrepair. I was led inside and down long halls, and I was puzzled by what I saw. Many of the halls were lined with old stacks of lumber and bricks that had been shoved to the side; holes had been knocked in some of the walls. It looked as though the Chinese had started a major renovation project or expansion of some kind and then just stopped. It was a mess, with dirt everywhere. I was surprised they would permit a foreigner to see a building in such a state, especially a hospital. If I'd been doing it, I thought, I'd have taken a prisoner into the building some other way, even if we had to climb in through a window.

With The Hag giving instructions I was led into an examination room that appeared to be relatively clean. There several doctors in white jackets proceeded to give me a routine physical examination, checking height, weight, blood pressure, pulse, ears, nose, mouth, and throat. While I lay on the examining table one of the doctors thumped my rib cage, moved all my limbs, tested my reflexes with a rubber hammer, pressed my abdominal area, and checked my rectum. Then I was given a chest X ray and an eye examination that I found fascinating.

During the eye exam I was told to sit in a chair before a somewhat typical eye chart with a series of lines, each line becoming smaller as it went down the chart. What made it so unusual was that all the letters were the letter E, some turned to the left, some to the right, some up, some down. When the doctor said, "Read the smallest line you can see," I replied, "I can read them all. They're all E's." The doctor laughed and said in quite good English, "I know they're all

E's. Indicate with your finger which direction the E's are pointing."

I had qualms about the accuracy of this weird eye exam, but as I followed instructions and proceeded down the chart I discovered it was probably as accurate an exam as those I'd had back home.

As it progressed the entire physical exam had seemed normal and comprehensive. Then it took a very strange turn. Three rather pretty nurses had been sitting in an outer examination room when I had first walked in, and they smiled at me, not quite being friendly, but almost. I wondered if they knew I was a prisoner. They didn't act as if they did, yet guards were all around, and The Hag was standing at the door in the background.

During one part of the exam one of the doctors had carefully examined my penis and testicles. Once the doctors were finished I was told to get dressed, and the doctors left. It was then that two of the nurses came into the examining room and spoke to The Hag in Chinese. She turned to me and said, "They want you to take your pants off." I did as I was told, again taking off my pants and putting them on the table. "Take everything off," The Hag instructed, so I pulled down my shorts and let them drop to the floor. What the hell was going on?

I stood there, bare from the waist down, and both nurses got down on their knees in front of me, and one began examining my penis with her hands. I couldn't believe what was happening. I had never had such an examination. I tried to turn so I wasn't facing The Hag and was humiliated and furious when I saw that she moved around so she could clearly see what was happening. The nurse continued to examine me in great detail, taking each testicle, moving it, tugging it, rolling it in her hands, then she started working on my penis again. My body took over as my penis became erect and the nurse immediately stopped what she had been doing.

I was dumbfounded. What were they doing? Was this part

of the exam to determine whether I could still become excited and get an erection? Or had they done it just to harass and torment and tease me? Or were they setting me up, hoping my animal instincts would take over and I'd attack one of the nurses? If I did that, all hell would break loose, I knew, and there would be even more charges against me.

What a rotten thing to do, I thought. Here I'd been in prison, in solitary confinement, and hadn't had a woman for such a long time, and then they did this, playing with me, trying to get me aroused, and then stopping. If they were going to do that, why didn't they shut the door and have those nurses take care of me? I would have liked that. But this . . . this was just a dirty rotten trick. And The Hag stood there watching it all. I had never felt greater anger or bitterness toward anyone than I did toward The Hag at that moment. Month after month the Chinese had derided and degraded me in every possible way, and now this. Pure blind animal hatred welled up in me. I did not look at The Hag, the dirty bitch. If they had done this despicable thing to humiliate me, never, never would I give them the satisfaction of letting them know they had succeeded.

12

Solitary Confinement

After many months in solitary confinement I began to worry about my sanity. I had no cell mates and no one to talk to except the Chinese interpreters, and even their visits began to dwindle. I was still permitted to write one letter a month, but that letter could never be a genuine outpouring of my thoughts and emotions. I could never let myself go, never talk to a friend or share a moment of companionship. I continued to hold myself in rigid control and not let the Chinese bastards grind me down, but I wondered what kind of price I was paying mentally and emotionally. It was difficult to judge. I knew isolation could play terrible tricks on the human psyche, and I knew it had to be having an effect on me.

I had looked forward to the "instructional persuasion" sessions as a way of occupying time and fighting back, but as the months passed those sessions, too, became less frequent. The interpreters no longer came into my cell once or twice a day. Now they came in once a week, if that often, and I was bitterly disappointed to lose the intellectual challenge of those debates with the Chinese.

As the sessions tapered off I continued rehearsing all the

points I wanted to make, and the frustration at being unable to make them had a considerable effect on my morale and, I feared, on my mind. The sessions had been my only mental stimulation, and even though the Chinese never stopped treating me like a subhuman, at least during those political discussions I had been able to fight back verbally. Now I had no outlet for expressing my hatred of the communist ideology and no opportunity or necessity to organize my thoughts and use them persuasively in heated debates. Now I was preparing for debates that never came, and I became concerned that my reasoning abilities would wither away.

I was convinced that the Chinese interpreters had stopped their indoctrination program because it was acting as a tonic for me, nourishing one of my greatest needs: to win with words what I hadn't won in battle. I also came to believe that they stopped it because they knew so little about my country. When they talked about conditions in the U.S. they could only discuss what they had been told by all the publications of the Communist Party, and that appeared to be very limited and warped. Perhaps they had not expected me to fight back with the facts during their reeducation efforts. They were fighting an ideological battle on a subject they knew very little about, and ultimately they made themselves look foolish.

Once they stopped our debates and arguments I had no one to talk to. Sometimes for days and weeks at a time I didn't speak at all. Not one word to anyone, and no one spoke to me. How was I to keep my mind focused under such conditions? I had no way of knowing whether I was behaving normally or acting strangely. What was normal in this kind of situation?

I refused to let myself talk out loud, believing only crazy people did that. Even though I was in isolation, cut off completely from the rest of the world, I knew I must never let myself forget that I was, in effect, in a fishbowl, being observed every moment of every day and night. I struggled to maintain my equilibrium and my standards as best I could. All of my thinking and worrying were carried out silently; to do otherwise, I feared, would be an obvious sign of approaching insanity.

But no matter how I behaved, I didn't believe there was any way in the world that a person could be held in solitary confinement in a hellhole in Peking, China, being treated the way I was, and still be normal. I looked for telltale signs of strange behavior that would indicate I was becoming unbalanced, but it was difficult to judge.

I scrutinized everything I did each day, reviewing the way I ate, bathed, dressed, acted. Was I maintaining reasonable standards or getting sloppy and careless? Once I caught myself slurping my food like a dog. Be careful, I warned myself, and then sometimes I'd wonder what difference it made. Why did it matter how I ate or whether I combed my hair? Whom was I trying to impress? I couldn't see myself; why should I care how I looked to the guards?

As time weighed more and more heavily on me I discovered two diametrically opposed parts of my mind that were debating the question of my stability. One part seemed to think I was generally normal and stable, considering the circumstances. The other part was convinced I was crazy.

These two parts of my mind carried on fierce debates with each other. You're okay, said one. No, you're not, you've gone over the deep end, said the second. And then my own common sense surfaced and put an end to the senseless controversy. I really did not believe I was crazy, but if I let this mental bickering continue, I would be. Enough of this nonsense, I told myself. Why worry about something negative and destructive? Prepare yourself instead for the next real battle, whatever it might be.

One battle that was constant and intensified my concern over my mental stability was accepting the extreme contrast between my captivity in Canton and the cold, harsh, brutal treatment I was receiving in Peking. In Canton I had been held in a house, slept in a double bed with mattress and sheets, and been served Western-style meals on a tray in my room. That treatment gave me a ray of hope that I might soon be released. At times some of the interpreters had even shown signs of sympathy and compassion for my situation.

Once I was moved north to Peking I was offered no hope. I was thrown into solitary confinement and locked away from the world to rot. On one side of my cell, at the very end of the ward that held no other prisoners, there was a latrine ten feet by ten feet. Originally, I'm sure, that latrine had been used by all the prisoners on the cell block. Now there were no others. I was alone in that deserted area of the crumbling old prison except for some of the guards who slept in nearby empty cells. I knew the state had to provide housing for everyone and assumed the guards who slept there were bachelors who had been assigned housing in this old prison. The Marxist doctrine, I decided, was much in evidence here: From each according to his abilities, to each according to his needs.

An opening had been cut in the wall between my cell and the latrine so that I wouldn't have to go out into the hall where I might be seen by others. The latrine contained a very old commode, a bathtub, and a urinal. Everything was old, dirty, and rusty, but the cold water worked, and once a week or so hot water was brought in so I could take a bath. I never saw who brought the water because the guard closed the connecting door, but I assumed it was prisoners from another cell block. I could hear the steps of the dog trot they used as they carried the buckets of water on shoulder poles.

I tried my best to keep going. I ate all the food I was served, but there was never very much, and my weight began to drop. Often there was only a thin rice gruel and perhaps a few vegetables slopped into my bowl from an iron bucket. A kitchen worker filled my bowl and then left it on a table outside my cell door. It was tasteless, watery food, meted out in much the same way we had fed chickens and hogs on the farm. My sleeping accommodations were consistent with the quality of the food. I slept on a bed of boards with a thin pad for a mattress.

Each morning I tried to do calisthenics in my cell in an effort to keep my stamina up, and most of the time I was in relatively good health. Early in my captivity I realized that being held in solitary confinement had one advantage: I was exposed to very few germs. I tried to avoid catching cold by not letting my body temperature fluctuate. I kept my few meager items of clothing in a box in my cell and added jackets or took off sweaters or did whatever I could to stay healthy and not catch a cold.

Peking itself was very cold that winter of 1966, but my cell was relatively warm. Every morning a guard came in with a bucket of coal chunks and put them in the rusty little stove, all the time watching me as if I were a wild dog. Even though I wasn't a big man, I was considerably larger than my Chinese guards.

I learned very quickly that walking in my cell was far more beneficial than sitting still. Walking increased blood circulation and helped keep me mentally balanced. No matter how limited the space, I felt better when I was moving. When I sat I stared at the wall and my mind went black, but when I walked my eyes moved and my mind roamed at will. I could only take a few steps in each direction before turning, but I quickly got into the rhythm of it and found it soothing. Sometimes I walked back and forth for an hour or more at a time. Every instinct told me I must not sit and stare at the wall; that was one way, I was sure, to go crazy.

As isolated as I was, I was not completely cut off from human sound. Often I could hear the guards talking as they changed shifts, and I wondered what they were saying. I knew for sure what they were doing much of the time they were on duty: They were watching me and keeping a log of everything I did. There was ceaseless surveillance. I could hear the scratching of a pen, and many times when I took a quick look out the peephole I saw the guards writing in a notebook. Whenever I moved around in my cell I knew they heard me and looked in. Then I'd hear the scratch, scratch, scratch of the pen as they recorded what they saw.

During my first year in Peking I was permitted to go outside for exercise almost every day. Each morning at eleven A.M., after the Radio Peking broadcasts, I was led down the hall, out a doorway, and into a triangular area about one hundred feet long on each side, surrounded by cell blocks. The ground was barren and often muddy, but several trees and bushes grew in the center near a circular brick structure filled with dirt that at one time must have held flowers or vegetables. I thought of it as a wishing well.

No matter how cold it got that winter, I enjoyed being outside in that exercise area. It was dreary and lifeless and muddy, but being outside breathing fresh air made me feel one hundred percent better than sitting in my damp, musty cell.

I looked around as I walked and noted that the cell blocks enclosing the exercise area were empty. Their windows were always closed, lifeless, and quiet. I spent hours wondering how many poor souls had languished in those cells, losing precious years of their lives. I knew I was only one in a long line of wretched creatures who had been confined here, and I shuddered to think how many years of my own life I might lose in this godforsaken spot.

At one time the windows of the cells had been painted beige so prisoners couldn't look out. Now most of the paint had chipped and peeled off. It was like a ghost town, heightening my sense of absolute isolation. The windows of my own cell showed occupancy, for they had recently been repainted.

From the exercise area I could see army soldiers standing guard in the watchtowers surrounding the prison. As the months passed I began to suspect that parts of the prison were being used as army barracks. Sometimes, from my cell, I could hear army troops doing drill in the distance.

During the time I was outside I walked briskly, feeling

exhilarated and refreshed. I tried to use that time to exercise my mind as well as my body. In one of her letters my mother had sent a bookmark with Psalm 121 from the Bible on it. In my cell I read that psalm's eight verses over and over, trying to memorize as many of them as possible. Then, when I got outside, I tested myself and was horrified by how little I remembered. Obviously I was losing part of my faculties, and that worried my greatly.

In flying school great emphasis had been placed on memorizing minute details and specifications pertaining to all aspects of flying. On a continuing basis all of us were required to recite verbatim intricate emergency procedures that could spell the difference between life and death. I had been able to do that easily and well. Now I was having trouble remembering a short Bible verse that I had just rehearsed in my cell, and that added to my constant concern about my sanity.

Sometimes when I was doing my laps around the exercise area the guard on duty also walked around, but there was never any communication between us. We walked nowhere near each other, giving me a rare opportunity to get a good look at these creatures who were the symbol of my captivity, and I could see differences in their attitudes and expressions.

Some of the guards had a bitter, tight-jawed look to them; others appeared less hostile. One of them, the oldest one, didn't have any teeth, and he didn't seem to show the hatred in his eyes and face that the others did. Nonetheless, I grew to hate them all with a vengeance. They were the personification of a system I loathed and an enemy that had stripped me of everything but life itself. I was alive, but barely. And even though I had come to look forward to the brainwashing sessions as a kind of intellectual challenge, I didn't kid myself. The enemy was deadly serious in what it was doing. In those sessions the Chinese had hoped to turn me into a traitor to my country and to everything I had ever cherished and believed in. They were diabolical, all right, and I knew I must never let my guard down. Be careful, I reminded myself; you are alone, and you are surrounded by evil.

Their psychological warfare never stopped. My life was totally regimented. Get up when the whistle sounded, go to bed when it sounded. In between, every activity was routine and monotonous, dictated by rigid prison rules that captors and captive alike were required to follow. Always, when I slept, the ceiling light was kept on so the guard on duty could see me.

For a time in my early days in Peking I was allowed to rest after lunch, and I enjoyed that. It helped pass the time and gave me an opportunity to lie down, close my eyes, and try to blot out the world. The Chinese permitted that for a short time, then they took the privilege away, and I was not allowed to lie down on my bed during the day. The rules kept changing, and there was little doubt that the Chinese would do anything to keep me unnerved and uneasy.

In Canton time had passed relatively quickly. Interrogation went on almost continuously, and the interpreters came in to talk to me several times a day. The rest of the time I spent worrying about my case, my family, and what was going to happen to me.

All of that changed when I reached Peking. Confined to a lonely cell, cut off from the world I knew, the hours crept by slowly, and the days seemed endless. The mental agony of having so many empty hours to fill had a profound and depressing effect on all that I thought and did.

Equally demoralizing and difficult during that first year was accepting the reality of indefinite imprisonment. For some time I refused to believe that I was going to be incarcerated much longer, even though all indicators showed otherwise.

Soon after my arrival in Peking I received several packages from the International Red Cross. In them were canned peaches and pears, raisins, preserves, crackers, canned meat, coffee, and cigarettes. Later the Red Cross notified my family that they would be allowed to send me one eleven-pound package a month. Receiving the items in those packages made the prison routine somewhat easier to bear, and I was glad to get them, but those packages also made me realize in a dramatic and convincing way that I was there to stay. Those boxes represented long-range planning on the part of both the Chinese and the international community. I didn't want to accept what they symbolized, but I couldn't ignore their significance.

I continued to analyze my case and to observe very carefully everything happening around me. One day, when I was led out for my hour of exercise, I was taken to a different courtyard, one I had never seen before, and I was curious about the switch. Why was I being taken to a different area? Was something going on in my old exercise area that they didn't want me to see or know about? Whatever the reason, it was refreshing and intriguing to see a different part of the prison, and I looked around carefully, noting all the details of the courtyard, the adjoining walls, roof, doorways, and possible hiding places. If the opportunity ever arose to escape, I wanted to be familiar with as many different parts of the prison as possible.

The new area was smaller than my regular exercise area, and there were larger trees scattered about. It would be possible, I saw, to climb one of those trees and get up to the roof. As I walked around the courtyard, trying to be as observant as possible, I made a startling discovery. A window into a storage room was wide open, giving me a clear view of the contents of the room. In there, to my amazement, were stacks of cardboard boxes, obviously an accumulation of many years. And on some of the boxes was stamped: STANLEY TOOL COMPANY, NEW BRITAIN, CONN., USA. I had begun to receive packages from home in American boxes. Was it possible that somewhere in this terrible, desolate, decrepit prison there were other Americans who were also being sent packages? I was jolted by the thought that other Americans might be here who had survived longer than I had. Maybe somewhere, sometime, I might be able to see them and talk to them. That would be a huge boost to my morale. But the idea that other Americans were here, and had obviously been here for a long time, also frightened me badly, for it was one more indication that I, too, might be a long-term prisoner.

I knew I must find out if there really were other Americans being detained here, but how was I to do that? The Hag would never knowingly tell me; I would have to trick her into it. My mind came to life as I began to scheme and plot.

The next time The Hag came into my cell she made her usual snide remarks. She could never resist belittling me. "Your coat is dirty. When are you going to wash it?" she asked derisively. She knew I was permitted to wash clothes in the bathtub in the latrine whenever I wanted and was simply trying to be obnoxious. I planned to wash it that day, I told her. I didn't want to do or say anything that would make her suspicious. After she had given me new reading material she was about to leave when I called her back in a serious, questioning tone of voice. She looked surprised. Was I about to express some profound declaration? Had I had a change of attitude? She waited in anticipation, then I looked her straight in the eyes and said, "There are other Americans in this prison, aren't there?" She looked stunned, not expecting that question. I'd caught her off guard, at a loss for words. Her face showed it all.

After some moments she regained her composure and said in an ugly voice, "None of your business." Yes, it is, I told her in a low-key, confident voice. There were other Americans in this prison, and I had suspected it for a long time because she spoke with such a pronounced American accent. Others in the country spoke English with very pronounced British accents. It was obvious she had been around Americans for a long time, I declared, feeling pleased with myself.

The bitch didn't respond. She had regained her composure; the mask was back in place. She glared at me with hatred and contempt, then turned around and stomped out.

Had the authorities deliberately let me see those boxes as a way of tormenting me? Or had the window been left open by mistake? I never knew, and I never told The Hag or anyone else what I had seen. It was enough that I had tricked The Hag into inadvertently confirming that there were other Americans in this ghastly place; that was a moment of triumph for me, much like having the young Chinese soldier tell me I was on Hainan Island on the day of my capture. But this was sweeter because I tricked her into it.

13

Sinking Deeper

By November of 1966 I had been a captive of the Chinese communists for fourteen long, devastating months, threatened, interrogated, brainwashed, deprived of every kind of freedom, faced with psychological warfare of every kind. My emotional health was precarious, my physical health declining because of shortage of food and confinement to a small cell. Soon after I was captured I thought I had reached the bottom of human existence. How wrong I had been. The downhill slide had continued during every moment of my first year in captivity. The Chinese continued to insist that I was a criminal, not a prisoner of war, and yet there had been no trial, no sentencing, no indication of what the future might hold for me.

During that first year in captivity I had been torn apart by feelings of fear, guilt, anxiety, anger, and sheer loneliness and despair. I knew what the year had done to me; I could only guess from their monthly letters what it had done to my family. My wife Judy had left our home in Victorville, California, and taken our three babies back to her hometown of McComb, Mississippi. Increasingly her letters were reflecting unhappiness with everything—the weather, her health, her weight, all the work to be done, life in general. She didn't come out and say it, but I was sure she was blaming me for everything that was wrong in her life. Even before my capture she had become a chronic complainer, and now she had many more things to bitch about. In the early days after I was shot down she had no doubt become a media celebrity of sorts, being interviewed by TV correspondents and news reporters of all kinds, and she would have loved all that attention. But that was bound to have ended by now, leaving her with the simple drudgery of coping with everyday life. Judy was not a strong, independent woman, and she didn't want to be. She thrived on being pampered and cared for. How long would she survive my captivity by herself? In my heart I knew. Not very long. She would take care of our babies; she would also find the first available replacement for me.

I had spent the long, painful months in captivity worrying about Judy and the children, my parents and siblings, the men in my squadron, the progress of the war in Vietnam. Over and over I had agonized about everything that had been said and done. Had I handled myself properly? Was I still sane and rational? I had no guidelines to help me determine what the Chinese might actually do or what my response should be. I had tried very hard to keep myself clean, in good condition, thinking clearly, behaving normally. But I knew what a terrible thing the Chinese were doing to me. By keeping me in solitary confinement they were removing every standard by which I might judge myself. To the rest of the world they were claiming humane treatment of their only American military captive. They and I knew their treatment was anything but humane. They were trying to destroy a human being by locking him away, totally alone in the dark, deserted, decrepit wing of a prison where slowly, day by day, he would lose his mind, his standards of judgment, his health, and finally his will to live.

Dammit, I thought, as I had so many times, they were not going to succeed. I was still alive, still able to think and reason and refute their heavy-handed propaganda techniques, still able to write letters home that I hoped were sane and sensible. If at times I was overcome with feelings of hopelessness and despair, I continued to try to hide them from my captors, my family, and even myself.

I looked at the crumbling conditions of my surroundings and knew I could punch a hole through the whitewashed walls of my cell with little difficulty. Yet I did nothing, for I also knew that I would never make it out of China alive. I dreamed and schemed and plotted escape, even though I had no place to go, no hope of release, no chance to end the rigid monotony of my prison life.

I never knew what to expect next. One thing I had learned from my Chinese captors was to fear change of any kind. I had been moved from Hainan Island to Canton to Peking, and each move had sent me further downhill. Now, no matter how dismal and dreary my living conditions were, I knew they could always get worse. In November of 1966 they did.

Little did I know, that day when I heard strange sounds in the hall outside my cell, that my descent into hell was picking up momentum. The muffled sounds were those of furniture being moved: a table leg dragging on the floor, the side of a chair as it touched the door frame, the shoulders of the guards as they rubbed against the wall.

I knew that many of my guards slept in cells around me. Why would they be moving their furniture? And why were they doing it surreptitiously? I listened carefully. Being in prison, especially in solitary confinement, had had a profound effect on my hearing. I could see almost nothing of what was going on outside my cell. My ears had taken over for my eyes, however, picking up nuances of sound that I would never have heard before. I listened to the sounds in the hall and felt the old, familiar clutch of fear. The guards were packing up and moving out. Why? What did that mean? Was I also going to be moved? For so long I had worried about being put on trial, but certainly any trial would be held right here in Peking. Did all this activity mean a trial was imminent? If so, would I be given a fair trial, or would it be a mockery of justice as I knew it? Would I be defended by an attorney? Possible verdicts flashed through my mind: death, a life sentence, hard labor in a remote part of the country, permanent leg irons and solitary confinement. Or perhaps a verdict that was so wretched it was beyond my wildest imaginings. At that moment there was no way I could answer the frightening questions racing through my mind. I could only collapse on the bed, worry, ponder, and try to sleep for a few hours, which wasn't easy. Fear of the unknown is a powerful stimulant. Something big was about to happen; I didn't know what, and every instinct told me it wasn't anything good.

The next morning workmen arrived with hammers and chisels and went to work in the latrine next door. I could hear them pounding and prying, apparently removing the old rusty American-style commode that was in there. What in the world? New fears arose: Maybe I wasn't going to be put on trial after all. Maybe I was simply going to be put to death, and they were removing all traces of me.

I sat, restless and fearful, through that long day. Then, late in the afternoon, The Hag came into the cell. "Pack up your things," she ordered. "We're leaving tonight."

"Where are we going? What's happening?" I asked, trying not to sound alarmed.

"None of your business," she snapped. "You don't need to know. Just shut up and do what I tell you." I looked at her, wishing I could tell the nasty bitch how much I hated her, but I kept my mouth shut.

In a matter of minutes I had folded my few pitiful pieces of clothing into a cardboard box and put my toothbrush and other small items in a plastic bag with a drawstring. Then I sat and waited. Activity out in the hall was no longer being kept quiet. I could hear loud footsteps coming and going and a steady barrage of Chinese gibbering. Suddenly the door of my cell opened, and two guards stomped in, looking grim and officious. Without a glance at me, or any indication that they even knew I was there, they began moving out my furniture. When they got to the chair I was sitting on I stood up, and away it went. The cell had been stripped.

I paced the empty, desolate cage, trying to remain calm, knowing I would find out soon enough what was in store for me. Finally The Hag returned. "Let's go," she said, leading the way out of the cell. There was great commotion in the hallway. Any time a prisoner is out of his cell the guards become watchful and wary. This time I could sense an added air of anticipation among the people around me. This was a move involving all of us; whether permanent or temporary, I had no way of knowing.

We left the prison along dark, unfamiliar corridors. Once again I knew the Chinese were trying to smuggle me out without being seen. At one point we rounded a corner and ran into a Chinese prisoner who was summarily ordered to bow down and not look up until we had passed.

The route we took out of the prison was much shorter than the one we'd taken going in ten months earlier when I had first arrived. We went out a side door, and I was told to get into the backseat of a dark sedan pulled up near the door. Four armed guards and a driver got in the car with me; other guards, I assumed, were to ride in the car behind us. It was obvious, I thought wryly, that the Chinese were making very sure that their American prisoner didn't escape and go running wildly through the streets of Peking.

Winter darkness had fallen by the time we pulled away from the prison, even though it was still only early evening. I looked out the window and saw masses of humanity weaving, darting, moving about on foot and on bicycles. The sights, sounds, smells all assaulted my senses, so dulled by months in solitary confinement. Avidly I looked out at people going about their normal, everyday activities and wondered if I would ever again live the life of a free man.

I couldn't tell which direction we were going as we made our way slowly through the city. I realized where we were some thirty minutes later, however, when we pulled up before a large gate. Months before the sight of a prison gate had thrown me into a tailspin. This time I was prepared for it, though I wondered what my being here meant. In the darkness behind the gate I could see a massive three-story complex of buildings. This prison was obviously much larger than the one I had just left. Grimly I watched as we drove around behind the buildings to a door in the back, where I was told to get out.

I looked quickly at the building I was entering. It appeared to be forty to fifty years old, newer than my former prison, and in better repair, though still old, dirty, and dismal. The door we entered led directly into one wing of the prison, and as I walked down the dim hallway, surrounded on all sides by guards, I saw something that shocked and startled me. The hall was lined with wooden doors, about seven feet high and three feet wide, obviously leading into cells. Directly above each door was a window with bars, and what I saw in the darkness that night made my heart beat faster. I saw lights on in some of the cells. Lights meant people. Oh, God, I thought, perhaps I wouldn't be totally alone in this desolate prison wing.

Briefly I felt a small spark of hope. Maybe my living conditions would improve. Maybe I wouldn't be held in solitary confinement. Then I walked into my new cell. My meager possessions had been moved with me, including my furniture, and I looked at them and the cell, and I knew with cold, icy clarity that I was sinking deeper and deeper into a real-life horror story.

The cell was ten feet by twelve feet, eight feet shorter than my previous cell, with no sink, toilet, drain, or water facilities of any kind, just a five-gallon bucket sitting in the corner. I looked around, realizing with a heavy heart that this move meant one thing: long-term incarceration. I could no longer pretend that release was imminent. This was a big, active prison, not a holding pen for a short duration. Clearly my situation had deteriorated badly. Even though my first prison in Peking had been dreadful, at least a latrine had adjoined my cell, and no matter how old, rusty, and disgusting the john and sink had been, they had worked. Now I was reduced to a bucket and a tiny cell.

Eventually that first night a guard brought in a thermos of hot water for me to drink and use in my small washbasin. No one else came near me. Drearily I put my same old heavy quilts on the pad that covered my board bed and tossed in torment until the whistle blew at six A.M. I'd been in prison long enough to know what was expected of me. It was time to get up. I washed my face in the basin on the table and began to ponder my fate. Was this the day a trial would begin? Many times during my captivity I had felt despair tearing at me, dimming hope and darkening everything I thought and did. On the first morning in this Peking prison the tug was stronger than ever. I faced an uncertain day, fearful and despondent.

As time passed, however, I realized once again how remarkably resilient we are when we have to be. There was nothing I could do about my immediate fate; I could only hope for the best and prepare for the worst. Wallowing in self-pity would accomplish nothing; paying attention to what was going on around me might. I'd been so absorbed in myself, I realized, that I hadn't been paying attention to the sounds of increased activity outside my cell.

I'd noticed the night before that there was a guards' desk in the hall near my door. Now I could hear voices yakking away out there, asking questions and barking orders, and people moving about with determined footsteps. Several times, much to my surprise, my door was opened; various people peered in, then left. One looked like the guards' supervisor, another a kitchen official of some kind. Each time a new face appeared I tried to look calm, not rattled and afraid, and wondered if I was the only new prisoner in this cell block or if we had all just arrived—and how many of us were being held here. I could tell from the chatter I'd heard that the guards were enjoying this move to a different prison. I couldn't guess where they were sleeping, but the change to a new environment had obviously exhilarated them. I was sorry I couldn't share their sense of pleasure in our new adventure.

I could see that it was getting light outside. Two windows were set in the outside wall of the cell, each about four feet high and two feet wide, with the lower parts painted beige. Light came in the top of each window, and even down low the paint had chipped away in spots, making it possible to peek out. By walking up close and looking out through the bars I had a fairly good view of several trees, another building in the prison complex, and a massive brick wall with high-voltage wires running across the top. A high-wire acrobat might get over that wall and escape, I figured, but nobody else would make it over alive.

At about seven A.M. a guard opened my door and motioned to me. A kitchen worker stood in the hall, dipping a foul-looking mixture from a bucket into a bowl. I stepped out, and he handed it to me. I looked down at the unappetizing mess of thin, watery rice gruel, then took the bowl back into my cell and ate it, knowing lunch probably wouldn't be any better.

Shortly after breakfast my door opened again, and there stood a guard, his supervisor, and a very small, thin interpreter I later learned was called Wu. My heart dropped. Was this an official delegation, ready to take me off to be put on trial? No, it quickly became clear, that wasn't their purpose. They were there to teach me the routine of this ghastly place. One thing I had already learned was that prison life is totally regimented, for inmates and guards alike. My instruction was beginning.

"Pick up your bucket," the interpreter said, "and go empty it down in the latrine." No one else was in sight as he led the way down the sixty-foot hall to the latrine at the opposite end of the cell block. I opened the door of the latrine, went in, and closed the door behind me, knowing one of my captors would be watching me through the peephole in the door. What I saw was worse than I had feared. The latrine did not look fit for human use, but why should that have surprised me? To these Chinese barbarians I wasn't a human being. I was an animal they had caged, to be used or abused in any way they chose. And I had to admit, even in my first rush of disgust, that any latrine was better than none at all, even one that was filthy dirty and smelled worse than it looked. My biggest surprise came when I saw the old American-style commode from the prison I had just left. My God, I thought, was this the only commode of its kind in this whole country? Maybe it was.

The room also contained four revolting-looking Chinese-style squat toilets, a urinal trough running along one wall, and in one corner a cement basin with a water faucet and a drain that emptied into the urinal trough. Even though the whole scene turned my stomach I emptied my bucket into the urinal trough, took a brush I found near the basin, and tried to clean the bucket. Years of use, however, had calcified the metal; I did the best I could, leaving an inch or so of clean water in the bottom of the bucket. Then I used my old familiar American commode.

It wasn't until several days later that I spotted a mop hanging near the basin in the latrine. In sign language I asked the guard if I could use the mop to clean my cell floor. He nodded yes. I didn't realize it immediately, but the importance of that mop far outweighed its cleaning value. Ultimately, in fact, that mop played a major role in the lives of those of us who were held in that cell block.

For many months after I was moved I was allowed contact with no one but my Chinese captors, though I could hear doors opening and closing, footsteps coming and going, other prisoners down in the latrine, running water and brushing out their buckets. And I could hear the swish, swish, swish of the mop as it was used in surrounding cells and along the length of the hall.

One day I heard something that brought unexpected tears to my eyes. I'd been listening to the morning activity of the cell block, which I did every morning, when suddenly someone mopping the hall right outside my cell began to whistle very softly. It was only a few bars, but he was whistling the theme song of the United States Air Force, and I couldn't believe my ears. Someone was telling me that he knew I was there—and that someone had to be a fellow American. For so long I had felt totally alone; this was the hand of friendship being offered in a soft whistle. I didn't dare respond; I could only thank God that the wall of silence around me had been broken, if only for a moment.

Gradually I, too, learned how to play the mop game. The trick was to put as much distance as possible between the guard and myself. Each time I mopped my cell I made several trips up and down the hall, mop in hand, eyes and ears alert, coughing or clearing my throat whenever possible to make my presence known to anyone behind those closed cell doors. What I learned on those trips was of tremendous value to me. The doors of the cells were staggered, none directly across from each other. Above each door was the window with bars that I'd seen the night I arrived. Those windows, the width of the door and two feet high, were hinged at the top and could be opened for ventilation. But even more important, each door had a peephole at eye level—Chinese eye level, to be sure, which put it several inches below my line of vision. Sometimes those peepholes were left uncovered—whether accidentally or on purpose, I never knew. But one day soon after I arrived in the cell block I caught the guard looking the other way just as we passed an open peephole. I paused momentarily and took a quick look into the cell, where I saw a Caucasian male sitting in a chair over by the windows. What a huge lift that gave me. For so long I had seen nothing but hostile Oriental faces.

I soon learned, however, that there would be few such moments. My living conditions had been stripped to the barest, most elemental necessities: thin, watery, sugarless food; no heat; no outside exercise; no communication with anyone around me but Wu, the interpreter, and even those encounters were brief and spasmodic. Maybe it wasn't prison life at its lowest, most primitive level, but it was very close.

One day I asked Wu about going outside to exercise, and he answered vaguely. "Oh, I don't know," he said. "Do you want to go outside?"

"Yes."

"Well, that hasn't been decided."

With that, I realized I had better try harder to exercise in my cell, but it was very difficult to stay motivated. I had always loved active sports; doing calisthenics and running in place in a ten-by-twelve-foot cage took tremendous willpower, which I didn't always have.

The food didn't help my strength or stamina. It was consistently bad and sparse: rice gruel in the morning; usually a soup at lunch, made from what looked like weed stems; boiled cabbage, roots, or other vegetables in the evening. And almost always there was steamed bread that was unbelievably tasteless and terrible. My family was still permitted to send me one package a month, and sometimes two, and I frequently asked them to include jelly or peanut butter that I could put on the bread to help me swallow it.

I asked Wu about the bread, and that was one subject he was willing to talk about—rather proudly, in fact. Wheat, he told me, was raised in northern China, rice in southern China. People living in the north considered their bread to be a much finer foodstuff than the southern rice. Okay, I thought, perhaps there was a quality distinction there, but I sure couldn't see it or taste it. I ate what I was served, only because I had to or I'd starve to death. At least the food was always served hot, and I was permitted to eat it with a spoon they gave me.

I tried not to think too much about the food. When I was a kid growing up on the farm in Roodhouse, Illinois, my dad wouldn't always let us buy ice cream cones in town, but he would let us eat as much of our own fruits and vegetables as we wanted, with only one admonition: "Don't make yourselves sick." Big, juicy tomatoes right off the vine, a smattering of salt sprinkled on them . . . peaches, apples, grapes, strawberries, cherries. Oh, to taste such delicacies once more. And the vegetable garden . . . lettuce, onions, carrots, radishes, green beans, pole beans, cabbage, sweet corn, popcorn. Sitting in my cell in China, I didn't want to dwell on things I'd taken for granted all my life. I was hungry enough as it was without torturing myself with thoughts of our midwestern farm and how well it had always fed our large family.

It was winter now, though, and the crops in Illinois would have been harvested. My mother had never liked the short days of winter, and I knew that worrying about me would make the days and nights seem even colder and darker to her, though she carefully hid any sense of worry or concern in the letters she wrote so regularly.

From the moment I walked into the second prison in Peking I was cold. I knew Peking was on the latitude of Chicago, but my first prison cell had been warmed by a wood-burning stove. My new cell had a radiator that didn't work and windows that leaked badly, letting in cold air in the winter, dust and heat in the summer. I suspected the problem was cost-related—either no money to buy coal or no money to fix a broken boiler. I'd heard and read enough communist propaganda to understand that conditions throughout China were still in turmoil as a result of Mao's Cultural Revolution. Factions continued to fight for control of the country in battles that were real as well as ideological. Those in power, I was sure, were more concerned about saving their own necks than worrying about the creature comforts of foreign prisoners.

In my letters I was permitted to say that Peking—and my cell—were cold. My family did what it could to combat my lack of heat and food, sending me heavy socks and gloves, warmer clothes, instant coffee to put in the hot water I was furnished each day. The Chinese allowed food and clothing to be sent, I was convinced, because it was that much less they had to provide. As the winter progressed there were many mornings when I went over to the washbasin on the table in my cell and found a coating of ice on it. The cell didn't warm up much during the day, so I wore several layers of pants and shirts under a coat, with gloves and a hat on, and I knew what a strange sight I must be as I sat reading or writing at my small desk. I had few clothes available and wanted only the essentials. I preferred receiving food from home to getting unnecessary clothing. Almost every aspect of prison life was rigidly controlled, but I was allowed to change clothes when they got dirty.

For a time during the winter of 1966–1967 the Chinese permitted my family to send me magazines—*Outdoor Life, Sports Afield,* and *Field and Stream*—and what an exciting diversion their hunting and fishing articles were to a lonely, bored captive. My family also sent me a small dictionary, a pocket calculator, even a calendar. I treasured these items and pored over all of them for hours at a time. I suspected— correctly—that eventually everything would be taken away from me, but until the diabolical Chinese stripped me of my "toys" I was like a child on Christmas morning.

During the day the only light in my cell came from the two dirty windows along the outside wall. In the evening, or on very dark days, the guards turned on a fluorescent ceiling light of about forty watts. It wasn't great, but if I sat or stood right beneath it I could see fairly well. Often I kept a table under the light, with a cardboard box on it that I used as a kind of podium so I could stand or move about while I was reading. During the night a small light on the wall adjacent to the hall was kept on at all times so the guards could look in.

Always, except when I was asleep, I had learned to keep my ears attuned to sounds from the outside, in or out of the prison. Much of what I heard, or even saw, I didn't understand, but I realized that out of necessity I had taken on the characteristics of an animal in the wild, listening warily. At any moment the slightest unfamiliar sound or sight might mean danger or death. I'd been caught and caged, but I was still alive and increasingly alert.

For days I heard bricks being unloaded outside my cell. Finally, through the paint chips in my window, I could see workmen beginning to enclose the corners of two existing walls some two hundred feet from my cell block. I thought a great deal about what I was seeing and what was happening. I was curious—and it gave me something new to ponder. I knew two other cells were occupied in my cell block, and from what little I had seen of the prison complex I had the impression it was quite large, capable perhaps of holding several thousand prisoners.

What were they building? New cells? A storage area? A place where they could execute us all? I didn't know and didn't discover its purpose for six months, but I watched and listened and filed it all away with other unanswerable questions.

At night I tried hard to calm my mind, to turn off all worries and fears, but sleep was always restless and sporadic. I knew I was being watched through the peephole, and I didn't want to have nightmares or cry out or show any other kind of weakness to the Peeping Tom guards. The cell block was very quiet at night; prisoners were expected to go to bed when the whistle blew at ten P.M. and stay there.

One night I had a particularly haunting, vivid dream. I heard a mournful cry echoing down long, dark corridors, sounding lost and hopeless. Then the cry was gone, replaced by the image of a young boy walking way back in a wooded area he loved called The Hollow. There was a stream in The Hollow, and all kinds of animals, and one day the boy took a rifle back there and shot a squirrel. Even though he didn't like killing animals, squirrel hunting was an accepted sport, and he was proud of himself for his good aim. He took the squirrel home, skinned and stuffed him, and put him out in a little house on the property where his parents had lived years before while his dad was building the big house.

He put the stuffed squirrel up on a shelf where he could see him the minute he walked in the door. He got a big kick out of that squirrel; sometimes he even greeted him when he walked in the house. Unfortunately, his dad didn't share his pleasure in the stuffed creature. Each time his dad walked in the little house he was startled, thinking the squirrel was alive, and that made him angry. He tried his best to get rid of the thing, putting it away in a box or knocking it down on the floor, but the squirrel kept coming back. It was an unspoken battle of wills—the first time, in fact, that the youngster had ever stood up to his father. He did it without conscious thought. He simply liked animals, and he wasn't going to have that squirrel hidden away in a box.

I came out of the dream slowly, feeling sweaty and agitated. I hadn't thought of that squirrel for years. Why had the dream upset me? I shook my head; it all seemed so far away. Strange, I thought, that my first show of independence so many years ago had been over a stuffed squirrel.

That childhood recollection had surfaced from deep in my subconscious, I knew, and I wondered why; but this was not the time to dwell on such things, I reminded myself. I needed to stay focused on the present. My living conditions had changed in this second prison, and so had the communists' brainwashing techniques. They were still trying to "remold my ideology," but a new twist had been added. The female interpreter I called The Hag was gone. Small, thin Wu had taken over, and he was very different from The Hag. She had always looked at me as if I were the scum of the earth, a dirty, rotten, capitalist killer. When I refused to grovel before her she became more furious and obvious in her hatred. Wu was more controlled, more businesslike, and I discovered, more deadly.

Wu brought communist propaganda into my cell for me

to read, and he made sure I listened to Radio Peking each morning at ten A.M. He wasn't about to carry on lengthy discussions with me, however, which I might have enjoyed. He demanded that I write reports, and he made it clear what he wanted in those reports. He didn't want me to analyze or to think freely; he wanted me to regurgitate the communist pap that was being fed to me.

I looked at him and knew we were on very dangerous ground. In most ways I had survived the past months by conforming to the demands of my captors. I had accepted their regimentation: when to get up, when to eat, go to the latrine, read, listen, go to bed. But write reports that could be used against me or my country? No way.

Wu repeatedly came into my cell. "Give me your report," he'd demand, and my response was always the same: "I don't write reports."

"You have to. It's prison rules."

"No, I don't." It was a battle of wills that I knew could lead to trouble, but the time had come for me to take a stand and to resist their every demand.

One day I discovered another way to fight back, and I surprised even myself. Each morning the Radio Peking broadcast opened with the news. As slanted and biased as it was, it was still news of sorts, and I listened with interest. Then they got down to business on the program, with someone reading long excerpts from Chairman Mao's works and then a panel discussing his wisdom, his brilliance, his ideology. China—mankind!—would be saved because of the genius of Mao Tse-tung. On and on they went, and I couldn't take it.

For months I had refused to let myself talk aloud, fearing it would indicate impending insanity. But one morning, in an effort to drown out what I was hearing right then and had heard for so many months, I opened my mouth and started to sing, loudly and clearly. For several days I listened to the news and then sang my way through the rest of the broadcast. Come and get me, you bastards, I thought, singing away as loudly as possible. I knew they'd stop me, and I wondered how, but until they did I enjoyed myself more than I had for many, many months.

Finally the Chinese did come up with a response to my insubordination. The results of what they did, however, weren't what any of us might have expected.

14

Radio Peking and Two CIA Agents

If I had known I was going to be thrown in prison in China and kept there indefinitely, I would have prepared better before I dropped in from out of the sky. I knew little about the country, its customs, culture, politics, or people, and I knew nothing at all about how the Oriental mind worked. Being a China scholar might have helped me anticipate and understand their actions; as it was, I never knew what to expect. Western logic was of little help, for their thinking and mine seemed worlds apart. Sometimes they appeared clumsy and heavy-handed, even indecisive, in their treatment of me, and I began to wonder if they were playing a game of mirrors, showing me one thing and doing another. No matter how deeply I pondered and puzzled, I sensed that I was usually seeing the inscrutable Oriental mind at work, not to be judged or understood by me, their captive, or by many other Westerners.

At times, driven to absolute frustration, I deliberately tried to elicit a reaction from my captors. I wanted to fight back by creating a furor, no matter what the consequences might be. If I sat, docile and cooperative, I was sure I would

wither away and die. They could send me off to the great
beyond, but I wasn't going to go quietly. Being shot down
and held captive had already stripped me of an enormous
amount of my pride and self-esteem; I clung to what was left
by refusing to go along with their demands.

I tried my best to agitate Wu, the English-speaking
interpreter who was the personification of a political system
that was tearing the country apart and keeping me caged like
a wild animal. Unlike The Hag, Wu revealed nothing of
what was going on behind the closed expression on his little
ferret face. I never saw him lose control, and that only added
to my fear and hatred of him. I wanted him to stomp around
my cell, ranting and raving, threatening me, showing anger,
demanding that I write reports, confess to my crimes, repent
my capitalistic ways. I wanted, in effect, to see behind that
inscrutable Oriental mask he wore, and I never succeeded.

I sang through Radio Peking broadcasts for several days,
and nobody did a thing, so I kept it up. Did I know what I
was doing? I thought I did, believing I had figured out one
thing about the damn Chinese. Early in my captivity I had
thought they didn't know what to do with me, and perhaps I
had been right. Now I saw it from a different angle. I was
convinced they hadn't begun to pester, threaten, or torture
me into doing anything because they knew they had one
major advantage on their side: time. They simply weren't in
any rush. They could afford to be patient. If I wouldn't toe
the communist line this year, there was always next year . . .
or the following year.

So let them play their games, and I'd play mine, I thought,
singing away in my cell and listening to what was going on
around me. I was convinced from sounds I heard on a
regular basis—doors opening and closing and a soft mur-
mur of voices—that some of the prisoners were being
permitted to listen to the Radio Peking broadcasts together.
I wondered why, wishing I could be included.

Inscrutable Orientals, indeed. One day Wu opened my

cell door and said, "Bring your chair and follow me." I was puzzled. It was almost ten A.M., time for another enthralling installment of good old Radio Peking. Maybe I'd be lucky enough to miss it for a change. I picked up my chair and followed Wu, who turned left toward the latrine and stopped at a cell two doors down from mine on the same side of the hall. My heart quickened as he opened the bolt and led the way into the cell. There sat three men, obviously prisoners. Two appeared to be Americans, one Chinese. I was dumbfounded. Had my singing led to this? I had been totally isolated for so long; this was a stunning turn of events.

The cell, I saw at a glance, was the same size as mine, but much more crowded, with two beds, two tables, and now five people. And as I looked around I glimpsed something that made me blink in surprise—and shock. Stacks and stacks of paperback books and American magazines were piled in one corner. In my eighteen months in China I had been allowed to receive a few American magazines and no books at all except a dictionary and a Bible. Who were these prisoners? And, my God, how long had they been here to accumulate such a vast array of reading materials? I was appalled at the very thought of how long they must have been incarcerated.

I looked at the two Americans, at a loss for words. Nothing had prepared me for this. My joy at seeing them was almost forgotten in a rush of sympathy for what they must have been through. I hesitated, unsure of what to say or do, but they immediately held out their hands and introduced themselves as John Downey and Richard Fecteau. The Chinese prisoner also extended his hand and, in English, identified himself as Maha. We shook hands, then Wu turned and left the cell, and the Chinese prisoner switched on a big, old-fashioned radio that was sitting on his table. This was evidently a routine they had followed many times. Wu didn't trust me, but he obviously knew the other three would follow the rules and listen to Radio Peking as instructed.

I sat down, my mind in a whirl. To be in the company of other Americans after so long was beyond my wildest dreams, and it had happened when I least expected it. I'd been misbehaving—and now this. It was too much to absorb.

The two Americans were older than I, and I wondered if they were the captives I'd read about who had been held since the Korean War. The Korean War. Could that be? That conflict had ended fourteen years before. If they were those men, what harrowing tales they could tell. Would we have an opportunity to talk at any length? And who was the Chinese prisoner? He had greeted me in English; what was his role in all this? I looked at the three of them, feeling elated to be there, and yet puzzled and apprehensive at what was going on. What were the Chinese bastards up to now? I'd been in prison long enough to know they had brought me in here for a purpose. Whatever it was, I'd worry about it later, I decided. At that moment I was filled with curiosity about the two Americans—who they were, what they'd done, how long they'd been here, how they'd survived.

My mind reeled with questions, yet I held back, not daring to say a word. Patience, I told myself; let Downey and Fecteau take the lead. And as the radio broadcast neared its end, the two of them did begin to talk and to ask questions, and I was touched that they seemed concerned about me and my welfare.

They had heard reports of my capture on Radio Peking, they said, and when they discovered there was another American in their cell block they had assumed it was that same Air Force pilot. They wanted to hear all about my capture, my treatment, my health, and I poured out the details, being careful to stick to facts that the authorities already knew. The presence of Fecteau's Chinese cell mate bothered me, and I knew Wu was probably watching and listening through the peephole. As excited as I was to be talking to other Americans, I had been in captivity long enough to know I should be very cautious, and I realized that Downey and Fecteau were being equally careful. They asked no sensitive questions about the U.S. war effort in Vietnam, even though they must have been very curious, for they would have heard about it only from the Chinese and known they were getting a heavily slanted version. Nonetheless, it was clear to all of us that the Vietnam conflict was one subject we'd have to approach with great care.

Downey and Fecteau told me they had been captured in the fall of 1952, and I vaguely recalled news accounts that had listed them as civilian employees of the U.S. Army whose plane disappeared while flying in the Korean war zone. Nothing was heard of them for two years, but then China finally announced that it had captured them and was charging them as spies who had been dropping nationalist agents into the mainland. In November of 1954 China reported to the world that the two Americans had been tried, convicted of espionage, and sentenced—Downey to life, Fecteau to twenty years.

Our first meeting lasted such a short time—an hour of Radio Peking and a few moments of conversation. Long before I was ready to go the guard opened the door and ordered Downey and me back into our own cells, and I went with a heavy heart. What a letdown it was to return to my own lonely isolation. Would that be my only meeting with Downey and Fecteau? What a pleasure it had been. I'd forgotten what it was like to see friendly faces and carry on a real conversation. I'd forgotten, in fact, what it was like to *talk*.

My delight was tempered, however, by the reality of what I'd seen. It appeared that Downey and Fecteau were going along with the rules set down by the Chinese, the very rules I had been flouting. It was chilling to wonder what that might mean to me and my case. Why had I been taken into

Fecteau's cell? The answer was staring me in the face, and I knew it. This was one time when the Orientals were not being inscrutable. They wanted to be very sure that I understood exactly what they were doing, and I did. They were trying to scare me and whip me into shape. They knew I'd be overjoyed at the chance to meet other prisoners—and horrified to learn that there were Americans who had been held in captivity for so long. Downey and Fecteau were meant to be living proof that the Chinese weren't playing games. "You don't want to behave?" they were saying to me, "then take a look at how we treat criminals. This could happen to you." To an extent, their plan worked. Seeing Downey and Fecteau did scare me. Their fate was a grim reminder that I could rot here forever if the Chinese chose.

I slept restlessly that night, eager for morning to come. Would I be taken back into Fecteau's cell? I tried not to get my hopes up, but there were so many things I wanted to ask and to say to them. Just before ten A.M. the next morning my door opened, and my heart pounded as I was led back into Fecteau's cell.

My radio sessions with Downey and Fecteau and the Chinese prisoner lasted on and off for several months after that. On the days when I was permitted to join the three of them, the routine was always the same: Downey and I would be taken from our separate cells into Fecteau's cell and listen to Radio Peking, and then, if we were lucky, we'd get to talk for a few minutes after the broadcast. I was sure Wu was well aware of what we were doing and wanted us to have time to talk, hoping that Downey and Fecteau would influence me by their behavior and thereby help turn me into the agreeable and cooperative prisoner the Chinese wanted me to be, writing reports and at least paying lip service to communist ideology.

Behavior was one thing, words another. At all times we were extremely careful in what we said to one another, revealing only facts already known to the Chinese. From the beginning of our sessions together I sensed that Downey and Fecteau were playing a game of sorts with Maha, Fecteau's Chinese cell mate. They treated him politely, though rather aloofly, obviously aware that he had been put in Fecteau's cell to report to the authorities on everything they said and did when they were together. Maha was there to rat on them; he knew it, they knew it, and they didn't want to give him anything of substance to report. He was a prisoner, all right, having been sentenced to ten years for crimes against the state. He was also Chinese, and that took precedence over any feelings of friendship he might have had for any fellow prisoners. He was expected to inform on the Americans, and he did, knowing it was the Chinese who would ultimately let him out, and it was in China that he would spend the rest of his life.

It was Downey who was so good at getting around Maha. Downey was a master at nonverbal communication. He could say more with his eyes and facial expressions than anyone I ever knew. His face alone could tell a story, and when Maha wasn't looking, it often did. He also taught me how to play the game with Maha. Sometimes I'd slip and start to ask a question or make a statement that was not appropriate in front of the Oriental, and Downey quickly shut me up just by looking at me.

Because of Maha we were never able to speak freely, but very gradually we began to learn a great deal about one another. Downey, a bachelor, told me he'd been recruited to work for the Central Intelligence Agency (CIA) while he was in college. Six months after his graduation from Yale he found himself in the hands of the Chinese communists, charged with espionage. Fecteau was a graduate of Boston University, the father of twin girls; his second wife had died in a fire while he was in captivity.

The stories they told were incredible, and so were they. My weight had been dropping steadily since I arrived in Peking; I would have expected them to be skin and bones, but they weren't. They seemed to be in fairly good health physically and remarkably good health mentally. In everything they said and did when I was with them they communicated optimism that some miraculous event would take place that would bring them early release. "This is what happened, we're here and we're going to make it," they said, and they seemed to believe it. I wondered, if I were in their position, if I would have equal fortitude. I could only hope I would.

Talk about tragedy, I thought. These men had been in their early twenties when they were captured and had already lost fifteen vital years of their lives. How could Downey, in particular, be optimistic when he'd been sentenced to life in prison? That was a devastating idea to me, but whenever I asked him about it he replied calmly and quietly that he would never give up hope of being released.

For the first three years of their captivity they had been shackled. Even at night they had been forced to sleep with arms cuffed and ankles chained, and I knew there was only one reason for such brutal treatment. It wasn't to prevent escape; they were already locked in prison cells. The Chinese simply wanted to increase their pain and discomfort and despair. I shook my head when I heard that story—not in disbelief, because I knew every word was true, but in awe at Downey's and Fecteau's endurance. They spoke about their years so matter-of-factly, but the agony of what they'd been through spoke for itself.

Sometimes the horror of their isolation cropped up in ways that might have been funny had they not been so sad. Both of them were avid sports fans who loved to read and discuss sports news from home. After their first few years in prison they were permitted to receive sports magazines from their families, and as I had recognized at first glance, those stacks of magazines and books in Fecteau's cell were indeed an accumulation of many years. Downey, I learned, had equal stacks in his cell. The two of them especially enjoyed

Sports Illustrated and *Sporting News,* they said, and for some time they'd been having a friendly debate over one question that could not be answered by reading from the printed page. When they asked me the question it brought a lump to my throat. Their question—argument—was how to pronounce the name of a football player constantly in the news. One of them insisted it was pronounced Johnny Ú-ni-tas; the other said it was Johnny U-ní-tas, with the emphasis on the second syllable. It was the latter, I said, happy I could be of help, but feeling rage at how completely these men—and I—had been cut off from the simple pleasures of the world we had known. How I wished we could all get the hell out of there and move on with our lives.

I had to be very careful not to overreact to many of the things they told me. Maha, our Oriental shadow, was always there and always listening. But when they told me the food and treatment they were currently receiving were the best they'd had in fifteen years, I wanted to tear the place apart. They had to be eating the same food I was, and it was absolute slop, so I shuddered to think what they'd been fed over the years.

Early in their captivity they had not been permitted to see each other or communicate in any way. Then, sometime after their trial in 1954, the Chinese had evidently decided it would be easier for the authorities to handle them if they were permitted to be together for certain activities during the day. They had worked together and been captured together and knew each other so well, there was little they could tell each other that they didn't both know already. Their personalities were very different—Downey was much more extroverted, talkative, and ready to laugh than the more serious and subdued Fecteau. And yet both accepted their fate, and their outlook was far more upbeat than my own. I suspected they would have been friends under any circumstances, for they were sensitive and intelligent and shared a love of adventure, sports, and the dangers of their profession. They were never cell mates, they told me, and never alone together, but they had finally been allowed to go out for exercise at the same time and be in the hall together to get their food or their water or make trips to the latrine.

I was a different matter. I was a relative newcomer who knew nothing about Chinese customs and habits, and anything at all that they could tell me was of great benefit. I never ceased to marvel at their courage and their optimism and their help to me. Carefully I tried to reveal my feelings to them about my own captivity. Our cases were very different. They were civilians who admitted they were CIA agents, caught red-handed in espionage activities against the Chinese communists. I, on the other hand, was a member of the U.S. Armed Forces, captured during a conflict that had not ended. My contemporaries were still fighting and dying in that war, and how I wished I could be fighting with them. All I could do was fight my own battles as honorably as possible. As a prisoner of war I was expected to live up to the Military Code of Conduct. To me, that meant my response to captivity had to be different from that of Downey and Fecteau. And yet there were many times when I wasn't sure I was doing the right thing. The general guidelines of the Code of Conduct couldn't possibly cover every situation, and I knew mine was unique. I appeared to be the only military captive in all of China, and only my training and instincts could tell me what to do on a day-to-day basis.

Seeing Downey and Fecteau was supposed to scare me into submission, into writing reports and behaving properly, but it didn't really work that way. I discovered after several sessions with them, in fact, that the meetings were actually having the opposite effect. My morale was greatly boosted and my spirits lifted by the example they set in dealing with their long captivity. And perhaps I was kidding myself, but it seemed to me that if two convicted spies were still alive and hoping for eventual release, then maybe my case wasn't as dire as I had feared. I had not been tried or convicted of anything. The Chinese could claim whatever they wanted, but to the rest of the world I was a prisoner of war, and when the war ended I should be released.

Downey and Fecteau had settled into a routine that worked for them. After so many years in captivity they had obviously decided to go along with whatever the authorities demanded. They were simply serving out their time, and they figured they couldn't harm anyone by studying and preparing reports on speeches and writings by top government leaders, especially the thoughts of Mao Tse-tung, or doing anything else their captors wanted. They had been in prison so long, there was nothing they could say or write that could be used against their country, the CIA, or the war effort in Vietnam, which hadn't even begun until long after they were captured. They were paying lip service to the system, waiting to get out of there, and I tried not to say or do anything that would get them in trouble.

I longed to discuss my case with them and ask their opinions of my behavior. Was I being foolish to be so rebellious? I didn't dare ask. If they responded, the authorities would hear about it, and I couldn't put them in that position. They were supposed to teach me by example to behave, not encourage me to rebel. I did, however, tell them that I had been unruly and uncooperative, and that I didn't intend to change. I told them that, knowing full well that Maha was right there and would report my every word.

I tried to read their expressions to catch any sign of approval or disapproval, and perhaps it was my imagination, or wishful thinking, but the overall impression I got from them seemed to be: "Do whatever you think is right. Don't let our case and what we're doing influence you."

What they were doing worked for them, but both they and I knew I had to find my own way. We also knew that the Chinese wouldn't let us continue our joint sessions if I didn't show improvement in my attitude and behavior. How much was I willing to compromise to continue meeting with Downey and Fecteau? I was the only one who could answer that question.

The sessions would end, and before they did there was something very important I had to do. Alone in my cell, I thought it through very carefully. I plotted and planned and worked it all out in my mind. The next step would be to tell Downey and Fecteau.

15

Secret Communications

My dad always taught us to keep things simple. Whenever any of us had a problem, he'd say: Strip it down, think it through, look at it from all angles, get to the bottom of it. Then solve it.

Now, more than any other time in my life, I needed to heed his advice and be very sure I knew what I was doing. The Military Code of Conduct said that, as a prisoner of war, I was expected to make every effort to escape and aid others to escape. I knew from what I'd seen so far in this prison that escape was not likely, at least for the moment, for me or for anybody else. And I knew Downey and Fecteau, as civilians serving lengthy sentences, hoping for release, would long ago have reached the same conclusion.

Time was running out for my meetings with them. I knew I wasn't going to knuckle under to my communist captors, and ultimately I'd pay for it. They had tried to stop me from singing through Radio Peking by moving me into Fecteau's cell during the hour-long broadcast. And even though I'd stopped singing, my attitude hadn't improved, and they knew it. Maybe I'd rot forever in the pits of the Chinese prison system, but I had to follow my own conscience and take the consequences, as I had from the very beginning. Not meeting with Downey and Fecteau would be one of the consequences, and how greatly I would miss having the opportunity to exchange ideas with those two brave men who had been caught, as I had, while serving their country, and who were paying such a high price for it.

I was sure Downey and Fecteau would still be allowed to listen to Radio Peking together. It was I who would be sent back into solitary confinement, unable to communicate with anyone but the communist barbarians who were holding us in this hellhole. It was the thought of going back into total isolation that first sent me into a deep depression and then galvanized me into some serious thinking. Every instinct told me to do something and do it fast, or the opportunity would be lost. I didn't want to take any action that would cause repercussions in the treatment of Downey and Fecteau, but I was convinced that the three of us must not lose contact with one another.

Some months back Downey had whistled the theme song of the U.S. Air Force while mopping the hall outside my cell. But what if a sudden emergency arose and it became imperative for us to communicate in more than a whistle? As determined as I was not to give in to the Chinese, I became equally determined to stay in touch with Downey and Fecteau. Somewhere down the line, being able to communicate with one another might pay dividends that we couldn't even begin to imagine. If the three of us couldn't communicate in person, then we had to find another way, a system that didn't depend on personal contact. And if such a system was going to be set up, I was the one to do it. But how? That was the question I'd been pondering, for at first I hadn't seen the answer. The more I puzzled over it, the more I thought about my dad and his knack of being able to cut through all the nonsense and get to the heart of any problem. That's what I had to do, and I knew I must be very careful. We were captives in a cell block in China, being watched day and night; we must make sure we did nothing that might look unusual or out of the ordinary.

For several days I paid special attention to everything around me, watching, waiting, listening. Prisoners elsewhere had developed tap codes to communicate through the walls, but that would never work in this prison wing. There were empty cells between us, and always at least one guard to monitor only four prisoners. He would know immediately who was tapping and make us stop.

I looked around my cell. One thing the Chinese let us have, at least most of the time, was writing paper. Would a note-drop system be too risky? If not, how would we do it? One morning I saw the solution, and I wondered why it had taken me so long to see it. It was so simple, I didn't believe it would be detected—not by Maha, Wu, or any of the guards.

I wasn't sure Downey and Fecteau would approve of a secret communications system or ever use it, but before I had a chance to find out, our Chinese captors came up with a new brainstorm for "reeducating" us, and I temporarily put the idea aside. The change in our routine came one evening when Wu took Downey and me into Fecteau's cell and stayed there with us. He looked officious and arrogant, and my skin crawled. Be careful, I warned myself, these slant-eyed maniacs have come up with some new twist to gain what they want and keep us off balance.

Wu held out a book and in his sarcastic, know-it-all voice told us what we were expected to do. We were going to take turns reading aloud from that book. "Oh, no, we're not," I thought, but I said nothing as Wu handed the book to Downey, who read from it for a time, then passed it to Fecteau and Maha. Then it was my turn, and I reached out to give the book back to Wu. "No," I said, trying to sound polite, "I don't believe I'll read any of this aloud."

Wu's expression flickered, then settled back into place. "Why not?" he asked, though I suspected he already knew.

We had been through this so many times, I tried not to

sound disgusted. "I've told you over and over that I will not write or say anything that could be used against me or my country," I repeated. "You could record my voice reading this communist propaganda. I don't agree with it, and I won't do it."

How long were the Chinese going to keep this up? They and I had locked into our positions, and we weren't going to change. Wu insisted I was a criminal; I maintained I was a prisoner of war, bound by the Code of Conduct to give name, rank, serial number, and date of birth, and that was all. I was not required to write reports or read propaganda aloud. Survival training had warned that a POW should be very careful of giving the enemy anything that could be used against him, and if Wu didn't like that, to hell with him. He could send me to a labor camp in the outback.

After several evening study sessions Wu gave up, and the meetings ended. It wasn't Downey, Fecteau, or Maha they were after. It was my voice they wanted to hear reading aloud, and I didn't intend to give in to what they wanted, even if it meant I was also hastening the end of our morning radio sessions. Wu would report that I was as uncooperative as ever, that my sessions with Downey and Fecteau hadn't brought me into line, that the authorities' plans for me hadn't worked.

I had often wondered about Wu. Who were his immediate supervisors? Did he have any voice in determining my treatment? I was supposedly a captive of the great Chinese people, or so I'd been told over and over, but Wu was the only Communist official who saw me on a regular basis and could judge my attitude and behavior. Who received his reports on me? Who made the decisions? What might they do next?

From then on my morning radio sessions with Downey and Fecteau took on increasing urgency, not only because of my recalcitrant behavior, but because of events taking place around us. As I had suspected, Downey, Fecteau, and Maha had been in my original prison in Peking and had been moved to this second prison when I was. And they had indeed had a long relationship with The Hag, the female interpreter I had accused of speaking English with an American accent. I was as curious about The Hag as I was about Wu. What had happened to her? One day I asked Downey and Fecteau and learned that somewhere, perhaps from Chinese guards that Maha had overheard talking, they had reached the conclusion that she had been caught on the wrong side of the ideological battle as the Cultural Revolution intensified between Mao's supporters and his opponents. They had even come up with a fitting reward for her treatment of us: Maybe at that very moment she was languishing in a cell nearby, being "reeducated" just like the rest of us were. What a great idea, I thought maliciously, hoping it was true. Let the bitch have a taste of what she'd put us through. And the idea made sense to me. Wu's thinking was obviously much more radical than The Hag's, and she might indeed be out of favor as Mao's forces became more militant in their battle for power.

I had hated The Hag, but I hated Wu more than any other Chinese with whom I had come in contact. The Chinese guards were the lowlife of humanity, dumb, despicable beasts carrying out whatever orders they were given, and I tried not to even look at them. Wu, on the contrary, was not stupid. He was an evil, ultra-left supporter of Mao's most radical philosophies, and if he was dangerous to me, I suspected he was equally dangerous to any Chinese who didn't follow Mao's party line. He and The Hag had probably disagreed on many issues, including their treatment of me.

Downey and Fecteau and I didn't dare talk about it very much, but it was clear even to us that the violence of the Cultural Revolution was intensifying. Radio Peking talked in glowing terms of how the masses were diligently studying, heeding Chairman Mao's thoughts and stepping forward to ensure that the destiny of the country was in the hands of the people. That might be, I thought skeptically, but all the masses I saw must not have responded to Chairman Mao's call. From my cell window I began to see dozens of buses filled with Chinese civilians pulling into the prison complex. I watched in fascination and horror, wondering what was actually going on during this dreadful time in China's history. I noted, too, that the food supply in the prison seemed to dwindle by the day. They were feeding masses of their own citizens now and appeared to be running out of food.

And if it was a frightening sight to see so many civilians being herded into prison, it was even more frightening to hear what was going on outside the prison walls. It started one day when I heard what sounded like thousands of protesters chanting and screaming. Was a riot about to break out? How I wished I could see what was going on out in the streets around the prison. If a riot did break out, what might that mean to Downey, Fecteau, and me? Would the mobs turn us loose? Kill us on the spot? How radical were these demonstrators? If they stormed the prison, could we escape? I assumed their objective was to free the civilian prisoners who had just arrived, and I suddenly had an unnerving thought: Maybe we were safer in our prison cells than many citizens were in their own homes.

For several days the violence of the demonstrations seemed to increase, and then—I never knew how—the authorities obviously quelled the uprising, and once again it was quiet outside the prison walls.

Meanwhile, conditions in our cell block had also changed, and one of my unanswered questions was finally settled when I learned what they had been building outside my window. It was an exercise area, evidently built just for those of us in this one wing of the prison. Wu took me out there one morning, and it was a special treat to be outdoors again after so many months of being restricted to indoor exercise. It was a big, open area paved with cement that measured about thirty feet by seventy feet, surrounded by a fifteen-foot wall. Interesting, I thought, trying to take in every detail as quickly as possible. All of it I filed away to consider later.

At the moment I had more important things to think about. Day by day I lived in fear that my sessions with Downey and Fecteau would end at any moment, and I finally took action. In a brief note I described the communications system I had dreamed up, and why I thought it was important for us to have such a system. And one morning after Radio Peking, while the four of us were milling about Fecteau's tiny cell, I saw Maha turn his head. Instantly I bumped Fecteau on the leg and held out the note I had cupped in my hand. Fecteau's instincts were good; in a flash he'd grabbed the note and buried it in his palm. Maha hadn't seen a thing.

I knew, though, that I was putting all of us at risk, both by passing the note and by suggesting the establishment of a secret communications system. I believed it was worth it, however, and I hoped Downey and Fecteau would agree. I knew, as they would, that any note-drop system could be dangerous to use, but at least notes could be torn up and flushed down the john or burned or swallowed. Timing, of course, was critical. Notes must be passed, retrieved, read, and destroyed as quickly as possible. The longer they sat in the hiding place or remained in our possession, the greater the risk that they and we would be discovered and all hell would break loose.

We needed two things for the system to work: a flag of some kind to alert the others that one of us wanted to pass a note, and a safe drop, or place to hide the note. I had found both in the latrine. On the wooden frame beneath one of the windows I spotted an old rusty nail bent at a ninety-degree angle that had obviously been there for years. It was stuck and wouldn't turn. For several days on my trips to the latrine I turned my back to the door, hiding what I was doing, and worked it loose so it could be rotated. That was our flag—a nail that could be turned to four positions corresponding to the face of a clock, each position asking or answering very specific predetermined questions. The nail was old and unobtrusive, but tight enough not to fall out, and the system itself was simple and workable.

Position 1 (twelve o'clock, nail straight up): Normal position, nothing happening, keep watching.

Position 2 (nail turned to three o'clock): I want to send a note. Is it safe? If not, nail stays where it is.

Position 3 (six o'clock, nail straight down): Yes, it's safe. Plant the note, I'll watch for it.

Position 4 (nail turned to nine o'clock): The note is in the drop. Get it out of there right away.

Position 1 (return to the normal position): The note has been retrieved. The system is back to ready position for when it's needed next.

And where was the note drop? That was the second basic element of this plan, and very crucial, for the moment a note left our hands it became evidence of our insurgency that could be found by the Chinese, and it had better not be found. Once again I had looked over the latrine carefully. Attached to one wall was a porcelain washbasin. When I felt around it I discovered a space beneath it between the basin and the wall. I'd tested that space several times; I could fold the note, wrap toilet paper around it to make it thicker, and then jam it in that space. If by chance it fell out, it would look like a piece of toilet paper on the floor and hopefully not be picked up. You could reach the space when you were sitting on the john or standing at the basin, so the note could be put in or taken out in a matter of seconds; then you'd turn the nail and be out of there.

All of this I detailed as briefly as possible in the note I gave to Fecteau, which he later passed on to Downey. The next time we were together both of them made it clear, without actually saying so, that they were willing to have the system put in place. We tested it once, but it wasn't until several months later that we fully appreciated the value of our communications system. Then it proved to be of enormous benefit to us and to a newcomer in our midst. My joint sessions with Downey and Fecteau had ended by then, and I was back in solitary confinement, but I no longer felt totally cut off from the people around me.

In August of that year, 1967, I heard shocking news on Radio Peking. The Chinese announced they had just captured another American flier: Navy Lieutenant Robert Flynn. My heart dropped. The very idea that another American was going to be exposed to the treatment of the barbaric Chinese communists made me feel sick. I listened intently. The Chinese claimed Flynn was the navigator of a Navy A-6, which they had shot down, and the pilot had paid dearly for his crimes against the Chinese by being killed in the crash. I felt sicker by the minute. The A-6 had taken off from the deck of an aircraft carrier, hit its target, and been attacked on its way back to the carrier.

Soon after hearing those news reports on the radio I saw a picture of "the air pirate Flynn" in one of the Chinese magazines I was given to read, and it was a typical propaganda photo, taken from an angle to make him look downtrodden and defeated.

A month or so later I saw unusual activity in our cell block. On one of my morning trips to the latrine I passed the open door of an empty cell and looked in quickly. Several people were in there, busily sweeping and mopping. I walked on, my emotions mixed. For weeks I'd been wondering what had happened to Flynn, half expecting him to arrive here at any moment. Now it looked as if they were getting ready for him, and even though having another American nearby would be a huge morale boost for me, I hated to think of anyone else having to live this way, and I wondered what the place might do to him.

I had been in captivity for almost two years. I would never get used to it, but I had learned an invaluable lesson: The first year was the hardest. During my first year I had torn myself apart with doubts, fears, and questions of all kinds, pondering my case, worrying about my fate, almost overwhelmed by the intensity of feelings I could not control. Somehow that high level of stress and intensity seemed to have leveled off. I had survived, and the longer I was there, the stronger I got.

I knew Downey and Fecteau would also see that cell being readied for a new prisoner, and I was tempted to write them a note, but I held back, waiting to see what the next few days would bring. I was glad I waited, for activity began to pick up, and I sensed an increasing air of expectation around me. One day I heard furniture being moved into that cell, and I knew for sure that we were getting a new arrival. My excitement grew.

Much to my surprise, one morning I went into the latrine and saw that the nail had been turned. I couldn't believe my eyes! Quickly I turned the nail to the third position, indicating that it was safe to send a note; then I waited impatiently for my next trip to the latrine. I knew Downey and Fecteau would not use the note drop unless something major had happened. Did it have something to do with Flynn?

It did. The note was from Downey, who had once told me that he could look out his cell window and see the door to the exercise court. His note reported that he had seen someone new going into that area, and the person was a dead ringer for pictures he'd seen of Robert Flynn.

That was momentous news. So Flynn had arrived, though I didn't know exactly when. He couldn't have been here long, or I would have known it. There were so few of us in this cell block—Downey and I in separate cells, Fecteau and Maha together—that it was easy to keep track of how many cells were in use. Flynn was put in a cell by himself, and his arrival was an exciting event in our routine. It broke the monotony and gave us something new to ponder. Where had he been? What condition was he in? Did he need our help?

He was a military man; from Chinese news accounts I knew I was the senior officer, and I felt a strong obligation to reach out and help a fellow American as he began a struggle I had already been through. In addition to my natural desire to help him, the Military Code of Conduct required that I do so. I wanted to let him know who the other prisoners were and encourage him not to be despondent or fear that this was the end of the world. Downey had seen him walking, but I wondered if he had been injured or harmed in any way by the Chinese.

I was going to have to get a note to him. I couldn't be positive that it was Flynn, but Downey's note encouraged me to take the risk. If it was a Chinese prisoner, I'd undoubtedly be turned in and end up in serious trouble, but I'd take my chances. I wrote a note to Flynn, rolled it up, put it inside the top of my ball-point pen, and carried it every time I was out in the hall. For almost a month I carried that note, my heart beating like crazy, looking for an opportunity to throw it in the transom above Flynn's door. Sometimes those windows were open, especially in warm weather, and there were no screens over them, just bars. I needed Flynn's window to be open and the guard looking the other way just as I reached his door. Then I would quickly stand on my tiptoes and throw the note in the window as I carried my bucket down to the latrine. I didn't want the note to drop just inside the cell, or the guard might see it when he opened the door. I wanted to throw it in and have it hit something— preferably Flynn's head.

I had put the note in the plastic top of the pen so it would make a noise when it hit the concrete floor of the cell. I had no way of knowing how Flynn was adapting to life in prison. Maybe he was languishing in the corner, his head between his legs, oblivious to his surroundings. I had to attract his attention so he would pick up the object before the guard looked in and saw something on the floor.

One day it happened. The most lax guard of all was on

duty. When it was time for my morning trip to the latrine he opened my door, and I picked up my full bucket, which I emptied every morning, as I had so many, many times. I'd been waiting for this particular guard. I knew his habits and had planned my timing accordingly. He always opened the door and started walking very slowly down the hall in front of me. Most of the guards walked behind me, watching my every step. On this day I delayed a few seconds to give the guard a head start. I'd practiced this maneuver many times before and had the timing down perfectly. He had to have passed Flynn's door before I got there, and I knew he was usually too lazy to even turn his head to see where I was. If he did turn around when my hand was up, I'd be caught. I needed him to just shuffle down the hall and not look back.

On this day I came out of my cell, looked around to make sure no one else was in sight, and then headed down the hall. Just as I neared the cell of the new prisoner the guard turned his head, and my heart stopped. He took a quick look, then turned back around. In a split second I knew this was it. I was going to do it. The window was open, and I threw the pen top through it into the cell and heard it strike the cement floor. This was something else I had practiced in my cell, timing how to throw the note and cough just as it hit the floor so the guard wouldn't hear anything unusual. He kept walking, and I followed him.

I had written the note on a piece of paper about three inches by two inches, saying I was U.S. Air Force Major Phil Smith and I assumed he was Navy Lieutenant Robert Flynn. The main point of my brief message was to establish a communications system with him, as I had with Downey and Fecteau. It would be a separate though similar system with a different flag—in this case, a piece of rusty wire I'd found sticking in a screen window. The separate system was necessary so that Downey and Fecteau didn't pick up a note intended for Flynn. The fewer people who handled a note, the safer we were.

Once back in my cell I breathed a sigh of relief that I had written and passed the note without being caught. There was nothing more I could do at the moment. I wouldn't know for many hours, or even days, whether the plan I had worked on so meticulously for so long would succeed. I couldn't even be sure that the prisoner in that cell was Robert Flynn.

16

A Death in the Family

My note had hit its target, sailing in through the transom and landing at the feet of Navy Lieutenant Robert Flynn. Once I learned of its success I felt a sudden burst of energy and enthusiasm. There was a job to be done, challenges to be met, and what a heady, almost forgotten sensation that was. I felt more alert and awake than I had in many months. For a brief time, at least, there was once again a purpose to my life. Robert Flynn was a relatively new captive; he needed to know what to expect in this prison, who the other prisoners were, how I had been treated, how I had responded. Then he could determine for himself how to handle all the demands made upon him by our communist captors.

In a large POW camp the senior ranking officer is expected to look after the welfare of the prisoners, issue orders, make policy, organize resistance, negotiate with the authorities on the prisoners' behalf. Here in China Flynn and I were the only military captives. We needed no elaborate organizational structure. We simply needed to be able to exchange information, answer questions, and give each other moral support and advice. It was up to me to establish the guidelines for our communications system, and I did so happily, for I was as eager as Flynn to be in contact with a fellow American.

I urged him to be extremely careful. Downey, Fecteau, and I knew the guards and their habits, the routine, the rhythm of life in this cell block. Most of all, we knew when it was safe to try to communicate with each other. Flynn had no way of knowing any of that. He would have to learn, slowly and cautiously, or we'd all be in big trouble.

At first Flynn and I exchanged notes several times a week. It was extremely risky, I knew, and yet I also understood that Flynn needed to pour out his questions, his fears, all the uncertainties and emotions that I, too, had experienced. Would he be put on trial? Tortured? Held in solitary confinement? What would be expected of him? I tried to calm and encourage him and help him understand, as best I could, what we were facing and how I had handled it. I told him I had refused to write reports or read communist propaganda aloud, and I urged him to do what he felt was right for himself.

His notes were long, written in very small script on both sides of a piece of paper about half the size of typing paper. My notes were much shorter. Here again I had learned from Downey. His few notes had been masterpieces of brevity, clearly thought through and written in the fewest possible words.

As the weeks passed I began to fear that Flynn and I were jeopardizing our system. Vital information had been exchanged; now Flynn was telling me about his wife, his dogs, his hunting, and while I was interested in reading all that, I became convinced that our notes were too frequent and too long. My concern wasn't the bulk of any particular note; even wordy ones would fit in the hiding place in the latrine. What worried me was the danger of being caught writing or reading a lengthy message or trying to get rid of it. Several times a guard came into my cell when I was reading one of Flynn's long notes. Fortunately, I always hid the notes in a magazine or in *The Peking Review,* and the guard didn't catch on to what I was doing; but each time it happened my heart took a big jump, and I realized we had to slow down. Flynn agreed, and we let the system revert to its original purpose: to be used in an emergency or in the exchange of important information.

Strangely enough, at about this same time I began to sense a hardening in the prison environment. There was nothing I could put my finger on, yet I felt that something was different, and I watched and listened warily. I did not believe that Wu and the guards had detected our communications system or discovered that Flynn and I were writing notes to each other. Flynn smoked, so he always had matches and was able to burn the notes I sent him; I tore mine into tiny pieces and flushed them down the toilet.

Why did I have this eerie feeling? Was Wu about to pounce with some diabolical new idea? It was only a hunch until one day I returned from my hour of solitary exercise in the concrete court outside and found that my cell had been ransacked and everything taken except my Bible and family photographs. Gone were the magazines, books, calendar, thermometer, even the little protractor I'd enjoyed so much. I looked around in horror. It was a terrible, dreary, tiny cell, but it was mine. My space, and now I felt violated and defiled. Once again I was a bug to be squashed at the whim of the Chinese, and it made me feel sick to my stomach.

I was not going to give Wu the pleasure of complaining, however. If their political system was so fragile that they had to strip me of my few meager possessions to get me to behave, then their ideology was even weaker than I had thought. To hell with them. If I had nothing to read, then I'd make up stories in my head, or maybe I'd mentally build a dock for my brother Bob's house on the Mississippi River. I wasn't going to beg the Chinese for anything. But several weeks later, without warning, my possessions were returned.

It was a strange and unsettling experience, and I wondered if my involvement in setting up communications systems with Flynn and with Downey and Fecteau had distracted me into forgetting the one thing I knew best about the Chinese: Their harassment would never stop. If one thing didn't work, they'd come at me from a different direction. That winter of 1968 they found the weapon they'd been seeking, and I was so furious at what they did, I began a downward slide that I couldn't reverse.

I'd had my possessions—my toys—back for several weeks when the little weasel Wu came in one day and announced officiously that if I wouldn't write reports, then I was no longer going to be permitted to write letters or go outside for exercise or receive packages. Okay, you bastard, I thought, take away all the privileges you want. I'm not giving in.

The next day he brought in a letter from my brother Bob, knowing I wouldn't be able to answer it. The letter had been mailed on the twentieth of February but not given to me until the thirty-first of March. I read the letter, swept by emotions so strong I could barely see. Most of all, I felt absolute fury. I had always considered my captors the lowest form of humanity, but not letting me have this letter when it arrived, or letting me respond to it now without giving in to their demands, was worse than anything I had ever imagined they would do.

> Clinton, Iowa
> February 19, 1968

Dear Phil,

I believe this will be the most difficult letter I have ever written. You may have been informed of this by now, as we had the Red Cross send a cable, but I will write this as though you don't know. As I wrote in my letter of Jan. 28th, Dad had been in the hospital in Jacksonville for two weeks at Christmastime. He came home and was doing fine, we thought. On Saturday, Feb. 10th, he went up to feed his cattle, and while carrying bales of hay over to the feed trough he apparently had a heart attack and died within minutes. The neighbors were driving past and saw him and immediately went over to him, but he was gone. They found him right after he passed away, since he had been gone from the house only a few minutes.

It was a very cold day, and I guess the cold air and exertion were too much for his heart. We had all wanted him to stop feeding the cattle, but he loved to feed and care for them. I guess we have consolation in that he died doing what he liked to do most. It was the way he wanted to go—swiftly, peacefully, and as we know, with his trust and faith in God.

His funeral was Tuesday, Feb. 13th, at 2:00 P.M. at Mackey Funeral Home in Roodhouse. There were so many, many flowers, and it seemed hundreds of friends and neighbors who came to extend their sympathy. . . .

I'm afraid this hasn't been a very cheerful letter, but I know you want to know conditions here at home. We are doing and will continue to do all we can to take care of Mother.

As I have told you before, I haven't forgotten my promise to you to see after the welfare of your family. Judy and young Philip came for the funeral.

Phil, I hope my next letter will be more cheerful and contain better news. You are in our thoughts and prayers daily.

> Love,
> Your brother, Robert

Phil's brother Jim had gone home for Christmas in 1967, and his dad was in the hospital, so he and his mother spent much of Christmas Day with him there. It was a day that Jim would not forget:

"We talked a lot about Phil. I think Dad knew he was in pretty bad shape and wouldn't last much longer. He hadn't given up hope that Phil would come back; none of us had. He was mainly concerned about what shape Phil would be in when he did get home. Would he be broken mentally or physically? When we left that day, the last thing he said to me was, 'Please take care of Philip.'

"He died shortly after that. My sister, Irene, called me in Washington, where I was living, and I went home immediately. It was a very difficult time. We all knew how hard it would be on Phil not to be able to come home for the funeral and share in the family grief. We hoped it wouldn't absolutely tear him apart. In almost all of his letters he apologized for the grief he had caused his family; here was another family tragedy, and we knew how helpless he would feel. We were afraid, if he wasn't already crazy, he would be after this. At the funeral itself there was as much talk about Phil as there was about my father.

"When it came time to go to the funeral, something very strange happened to me. I walked out the back door of the house onto the porch, and suddenly I couldn't move. I couldn't go any further. I started to shake and get very emotional. Papa had always been so tough; even though he was dead, I think I was still afraid of him, afraid to see him. I don't know if I thought he was going to spank me or beat me or tell me I'd done something wrong or what, but it was a terrible moment.

"When we read my father's will, we discovered just how deep his concern for Phil had been. There was quite a bit of land in his estate; he'd left half of it to Mother and half to the children, then when she died, the entire thing would be divided among the children. The will stipulated, however, that none of us could sell any part of the property until Phil came home. Papa believed that Phil might want to come back to his childhood home and be taken care of there, and he wanted to make sure that home was still intact."

* * *

March 31, 1968, Peking, China. I read Bob's letter about the death of my father, knowing I had only two choices: give in to the Chinese or not be able to respond to that letter. My greatest worry was that my mother would think something was wrong with me, that word of my father's death had thrown me into such a tailspin that I couldn't even write letters. But the price I would have to pay to write to her was too high. She needed words of condolence, sympathy, encouragement, but I couldn't sell my soul to give them to her, and if she knew, she wouldn't want me to.

My father had been stern and unbending in his beliefs, and at his death I realized how greatly his concepts of right and wrong had affected my own. What harm would it do to tell Wu that I'd write reports? Or even write the so-called confession that the Chinese wanted? I'd spout nonsense and then be able to write to my mother. The more I thought about that, the angrier I became, because I knew very well what it would do. It would destroy me.

I was flabbergasted that anyone, even dirty rotten communist bastards, would resort to using the death of a loved one in an effort to coerce me into bowing to their wishes and accepting their ideology. Why couldn't they use logic and reasoning? I knew why: because their whole system and thinking were weak and shallow, and I had no choice but to say, to hell with you, I'm not meeting your demands.

Over and over the dreadful thoughts ran through my head: Those dirty bastards were using my father's death and making my mother suffer to gain their own objectives. How lowly and despicable could they be? My anger was so intense I wanted to tear every one of them apart, limb from limb. I had been sent to fight a war, and I had been captured in the line of duty. Maybe the Chinese as a whole were good people, but the dirty bastards in this prison had been infected with the disease of tyranny for so long, they would stoop to anything. Why should my mother have to be dragged through all this? I prayed that she would be given the courage and strength necessary to help her survive this terrible time and somehow know that I was alive and that she would hear from me again. She had lost her husband of more than fifty years; for me to add to her despair was something I couldn't bear to think about.

I sat in my cell, listening to doors opening and closing as the others went out for exercise, and I wanted to go out, too, just as I wanted to write letters. But I would not give in. And for some time I was so bitter and uptight that I could mourn for my father, but I couldn't weep for him. I did, finally, not realizing that the whole traumatic affair was the start of a downhill slide in my life that was going to be hard to stop. I survived it by drawing in on myself to gain strength and courage; as I did so, without my knowing it, I was beginning to lose control. My anger and bitterness were growing and festering.

It would have made me feel better to yell and scream at Wu, but I knew what he would do. He would laugh and walk away, and I wasn't going to give him that satisfaction. Instead I began to glare at the guards. Normally I didn't even look at them, but this was one nonverbal way of showing my hatred. And one of them must have reported me, for Wu came in one day and gave me a warning: I was not allowed to glare at the guards or be disrespectful in any way. Try and stop me, you bastards, I thought, but I said nothing.

After four months I was informed that I could write letters again and go out for exercise. I wondered what had happened. Had my captors realized that I was stubborn enough to sit in my cell until I died before I would give in? Or had the Red Cross begun to ask questions? Packages and letters were exchanged through the American Red Cross and the Red Cross Society of China. Had someone noticed that I wasn't writing letters and asked why? I never found out the reason, but it really didn't matter.

Throughout my years in China, in the back of my mind had been the fear that I might never get out of China alive, and that if I did, I might never see my parents again. Now one of my worst fears had been realized. My dad was gone, and I was no closer to getting out of purgatory.

17

"Out of the Bowels of China"

Being in solitary confinement meant endless hours of dead time—no one to talk to and nothing to do. And as the Chinese began taking away my reading material and other possessions for longer periods of time I knew that somehow I was going to have to fill those hours, or I would go crazy. Surprisingly, it took me a long time to come up with the solution. My captors could strip my cell of everything in it, but there was one thing they couldn't take away from me: my mind. And as the years passed I found I could use that mind to take me out of the prison, out of China, and put me down wherever I wanted to be. What I was doing was developing mental exercises that I called mind games, and the more I played them, the better I got.

I played several categories of games. One was thinking about each of my family members: how they were, how they spent the day, what they were doing at that moment, and I'd visualize myself being with them. I'd join my mother sitting on the porch looking out over the farm, or my brothers at work. We'd have long, detailed conversations, and in my mind I'd be right there with them. And if I began to feel sad, I quickly switched to another topic. I was trying to take my mind out of the prison, not add to the emotional strain of captivity.

Another category was going over my case in great detail, trying to remember every little thing that had happened since I took off from Da Nang that September morning so long ago. Then I developed a mental game I called reliving my life, and I spent months on that one. I began with the first thing I could remember as a child: standing on the front porch in Roodhouse asking my mother when the others would get home from school. "Just keep watching down the road," she'd replied. "They're walking slowly today."

I remembered myself back on that porch, then I went through my entire life, trying to recall every detail—activities around the house and the farm, the animals, dogs, cats, cows, and my part in all that activity.

I took myself through every grade in school, trying to remember each teacher's name, what she looked like (since all my elementary teachers were women), the names of my classmates, how many boys there were, how many girls. I pictured the classroom and the door leading into it. Which side of the door were the hinges on? How many windows were in the room? What did you see when you looked out the window? Where was the teacher's desk located? The blackboard? I tried to remember every little detail and was amazed at how much I could recall. As I got better at playing my mind games I saw things more and more clearly, even remembering that when Jim was in the fifth grade the door to the room opened one way; when I got there, it had been changed for some reason and opened the other way.

Highlights stood out, such as the first basketball game I played in competition against another school when I was in the sixth grade . . . the high school years, when I was so active in sports, music, and speech contests . . . the barbershop quartets I sang in during high school and college . . . so many memories, and I relived as many as I could recall.

And when I'd relived my life once, I went back through it all again, trying to recall additional things, and each time I was able to dredge up new memories of people and events. Then I went back and relived everything the way it might have been. This was imagination time, inserting all the "what ifs." What if I'd stayed on the farm instead of joining the Air Force? What if I'd dated different people and married a Roodhouse girl? What if I hadn't been shot down? The "what ifs" went on and on.

And as I learned to play the games to keep my mind active I also learned that I had to keep my body equally active. It was much easier to play my mind games when I was walking, rather than sitting, so I moved around my tiny cell in circles, going around and around very slowly. If I just sat in a chair, I'd discovered, my mind wandered and drifted, and I couldn't keep it on track. I never played my mind games when I was outside in the exercise court. When I was out there I concentrated on exercising, looking around, breathing fresh air. It was important, I believed, to save my mind games for the long hours when I was locked in my cell.

It took some time for me to come up with my favorite mind games. Once I did, I spent months working on construction projects of all kinds. I started simply by building a doghouse, measuring it in my mind, sawing the boards, nailing them up, putting on the roof. Then I built several one-room cabins using logs and tools that would have been available in the 1800s. Each project became more ambitious: a modern cabin, using up-to-date tools; then a three-bedroom house with two baths and a double garage, figuring out every little detail, including the number of drawers and cabinets in the kitchen. And then, of course, I had to think big, and I built a thirty-room mansion, and that took many months. Never did I scrimp on time or effort. If I had been precise and careful in my real life, I was even more so in my mind. I watched my time, not because I was in a rush to finish, but because I wasn't. I didn't want to complete any project too quickly. Sometimes the Chinese let me have my watch, then they'd take it away from me. Whether I had it or not, though, I'd say to myself, "Okay,

I'm going to build my house for two hours today. Then I'll quit, put down my tools, and stop."

I also built bridges, barns, decks, docks, anything at all. My family would write about things they were doing, and I joined them in their projects. My brother Paul was building a house in Urbana, Illinois, and periodically he'd give me a blow-by-blow description of how it was coming along. I built it right alongside him and, in fact, got ahead of him sometimes, and then I'd have to go back and redo it to his specifications.

The single most important requirement of my mind games was to go into the greatest possible detail. My mind wasn't fully involved and distracted unless I did everything spade by spade, board by board, nail by nail. My games couldn't be played halfheartedly. My tool box had to be there, everything in its place, and if I made a mistake, I had to do it over again until it was right.

When I got tired of building projects I decided to be a wagon master. What was life like back in the days of the pioneers? I gathered together a band of people on the east coast and about twenty covered wagons, pulled by oxen. We had cows, chickens, pigs, and we were striking out for the west, destination unknown. In my group were married couples, children, single men and women, and I had names for everyone. When arguments arose, I mediated. I was the boss.

I dreamed up the most difficult problems I could think of and then tried to solve them. There were no hospitals, no doctors, but plenty of sickness, disease, wild animals attacking, Indians, battles with arrows, deep rivers to be crossed. It was a harrowing trip, but my little band kept moving westward.

In a sense, my mind games were like going to the movies in prison. I could see everything as clearly as if I were seeing it on a screen. Playing my mind games filled an enormous void in my life by helping me keep things in balance. I couldn't physically escape from my cage, but I could think about a better, happier life, and I could see it in my mind, and that gave me hope that someday I would live that life once again.

In my mind I could be at home, streaking through the sky in a jet fighter or lying on the beach in Spain. And then, suddenly, there would be a noise—a guard clanking open the metal bolt of my cell, sounds from the hall, the food arriving—and I'd come jolting back to reality, shocked because I had projected myself out of my environment so totally that for a moment I couldn't remember where I was. I always ended up back in the same place—my dreary prison cell; but for a few hours I hadn't been there, and that gave me an enormous sense of satisfaction, for it was one thing the Chinese couldn't control and couldn't stop me from doing.

All of my efforts to fill the dead time in my life reminded me of something very poignant that I had once read. At one point, when we were listening to Radio Peking together, Downey and Fecteau and I had been permitted to exchange magazines and books, and even when that ended we had slipped one another an occasional book in a hiding place in the exercise court. One time Fecteau had left me a book of famous quotations, one of which I read over and over again because its two lines said it all: "The years go by like grace notes in a song. Only the days and nights are ever long."

With a tired, aching heart I knew how true that was. In amazement I'd look back and realize I'd been in prison three years. Four years. Where had all that time gone? How true it was that the days would never end, but the years were ticking by like crazy.

And no matter how much I played my mind games, horrifying questions hung over every moment of my existence, the most frightening of which was when—or if—I would ever be released. I tried to keep myself calm and focused, but I couldn't help feeling restless and rebellious. It was like thunderclouds gathering before a big storm in the midwest; the air became heavy and silent, and you knew a storm was going to hit and hit hard.

And then another new prisoner arrived in our cell block, and with him came a feeling, not of excitement, diversion, or anticipation, but of doom, and I realized with a shudder than even a prisoner locked away in solitary confinement can sense when something is wrong. The light around us seemed to dim, and our prison wing, always quiet, now had a sinister feeling to it. My antenna went up as I listened very carefully for the sounds of anything out of the ordinary.

And when I finally heard those sounds I wished I could blot them out. The newcomer had been put in a cell across from Downey's and from there I began to hear loud, high-pitched, emotional arguing, all in Chinese. I didn't have to understand the words to feel cold chills. One voice did much of the talking, going up and down, filled with fire. Hour after hour, day after day they kept it up, the arguments getting louder and more emotional. It was horrible and frightening to hear. Someone was in desperate trouble; I didn't know who it was or how I might help him.

Then one day something peculiar happened that I realized later had been very deliberately staged by the diabolical Chinese. The guards changed our routine with the mop. There was a small storeroom directly across the hall from the latrine that I had never been in before. And on this particular day the guard on duty opened the door to that storeroom and pointed. There was the mop, so I went in and got it, thinking it strange that the mop had been moved. Then I saw why. Right beside the mop was a stack of old, dirty, crumpled boxes, and on each box was the name Hugh F. Redmond.

Downey and Fecteau had told me about Redmond, another American who had been in Chinese captivity for many years. They had heard about Redmond but had never seen him or been in the same prison with him. They knew he had been serving a life sentence in Shanghai; he was a businessman who had lived in China before the communists took over, and he had stayed, only to be arrested in Shanghai in April of 1951. For some time there had been no word of his fate; then, in 1954, China announced that he had been given a life sentence, calling him the chief American spy in communist China.

Now Redmond had been moved from Shanghai to Peking and put in our cell block, and I wondered why. And what was all the loud arguing about? One day when Downey was mopping the hall outside my cell he whispered a few words in to me, saying he believed the new arrival was the American captive they'd told me about, Hugh F. Redmond, and he cautioned me to be very careful. Redmond was obviously in trouble, and we must not add to it by trying to contact him in any way. I knew Downey was right. It was Redmond, and I would do nothing that might harm him.

Shortly after that I got a quick glimpse of Redmond in his cell, and then one day when I was in the latrine the door opened, and in he walked carrying the mop. I was amazed. Had the Chinese let this happen on purpose? Did they want me to see Redmond for some reason? "You must be Hugh F. Redmond," I blurted out.

"Yes, I am," he replied. "And I know who you are."

Had he been communicating with Downey? I suspected he had. "How are you?" I asked, wishing I could think of something more significant to say.

"Well, I'm still around. I've been better."

I looked at the human being standing there and couldn't imagine that I would ever see anyone who looked any worse. He was gaunt, threadbare, and haunted-looking, a living death's-head. His dirty gray beard couldn't hide his sunken face, jaws, and eyes. He was pitifully thin, with tattered, ragged clothes hanging on him. What he was wearing had once been a Western-style business suit made of wool tweed. Now it was so torn in places that he had sewn other cloth on it to hold it together.

We spoke only those few words, and I never saw Hugh

Redmond again, but the loud arguing continued, and now it was far worse to hear because I could picture the wasted man whose life seemed to be hanging so precariously in the balance. Finally I could stand it no longer. It was time to use our emergency communications system. I wrote a note to Downey and Fecteau. What was going on? What was happening to Redmond? What could we do to help him? Was he all right?

The response came back from Downey, saying, in effect, Yes, we'd like to help him, but anything we do now might cause him more harm than good. Let's not muddy the waters by trying to smuggle anything in to him or contact him in any way. He's got enough to deal with already. If we got caught trying to help him, they'd probably go in there and just beat the hell out of him.

And so I did nothing but sit in my cell and listen in horror. Several times, walking by Redmond's cell when he wasn't in it, I saw through the open door that it had been stripped of everything but the bed, a chair, and the bucket. God help him, I thought. And then I received a note that was the most devastating communication we had ever exchanged. It was a note from Redmond to Downey that Downey was passing along to me with a covering message: Read, memorize, and destroy.

Redmond's note indicated that Downey had communicated with him in some way, whether in writing or in whispered conversation I didn't know. Redmond thanked him for his offer of coffee but declined it and said he was okay and appreciated Downey's kindness. I knew that Downey would not have contacted Redmond had he not known that Redmond was in deep, deep trouble, and Redmond's note confirmed that, telling Downey that the Chinese were reviewing his case and that his sentence was being increased. He indicated that his health was not good, and he wasn't optimistic that he would survive or make it out of China alive.

I read Redmond's words and knew, as Downey had, that

Redmond must have decided that either the Chinese were going to put him to death or he was going to do it himself. And I assumed he was hoping that Downey would figure out a way to let the world know what had happened to him. They were increasing his sentence. What did that mean? If he already had a life sentence, did that mean execution? Or two life sentences?

Redmond, who had been stripped of everything, had written his note on a piece of toilet paper, scratching it with straw from a broom he'd found somewhere. Even so, his handwriting was beautiful, and that made the whole thing even worse. It was a message of total despair written in flowing, artistic penmanship, and I wanted to cry.

I knew with a sinking heart why Downey had passed the note to me. Downey was serving a life sentence, and no matter what he said to the contrary, he could not be sure he would ever be released. He was hoping I would be, and he was giving me this responsibility. I might be the only one who could get the word "out of the bowels of China" about what had happened to Hugh F. Redmond.

I sent a very short note back to Downey, assuring him that I had destroyed Redmond's note and his by burning them out in the exercise court. Had I not been able to burn them, I would have eaten them, for they were as sensitive as any we would ever exchange.

The loud, emotional arguing continued. Then it stopped. Totally stopped, and the silence was as frightening as the arguing had been. One night soon after that I came awake to the sounds of people talking excitedly and running back and forth, and all the commotion was coming from the direction of Redmond's cell.

The next morning I walked by the cell, and Redmond was gone. In my mind I tried different rationales for what had happened. He had been taken ill, the guard had found him and called the doctor, and he had been rushed off to the hospital. Or he'd been sent off to the hospital for other medical treatment of some kind and was right then recuperating in a real bed. Instinctively I knew it was imperative to think the best. For me, a prisoner trying to hang on to my own equilibrium, the worst was too terrible to contemplate, but in the darkest part of my mind I knew that one brave American might have lost all hope of surviving his terrible ordeal and reached the point where he would take no more.

18

More Beastlike Every Day

In the months following my father's death I could sense that grave trouble was brewing, and I did nothing to stop it. My belligerence, hostility, resentment, and blinding hatred of my captors had overflown the banks of reason or compromise. I was looking for confrontation. More than ever before I wanted to show the utter loathing and revulsion I felt toward the Chinese communists, their ideology, their very existence on this earth. My years in captivity had not calmed me down; they had, in fact, had the opposite effect. The longer I was held and the more I got away with, the more determined I became to push to the limit. I wanted to prove that I had nothing to be afraid of. I was an innocent victim of circumstances, and I did not intend to become a meek, docile prisoner. I had started singing again during Radio Peking, and the Chinese had done nothing to stop me. How far did I dare go in showing my rage and contempt? I had been in captivity for so long; I was restless and ready for a fight, and I finally got it.

My captors and I came to blows, and it wasn't over ideology, the status of my case, the law, philosophy, democracy, communism . . . it was over cigarette butts, soap, toilet paper, and toenail clippers. Of such minor matters are wars begun, and my war escalated in September of 1969. By then I was deep into singing during Radio Peking, being obnoxious, hateful, glaring at the guards, doing everything I could think of to show disdain and disrespect. The guards responded by staying away from me.

I hadn't shaved in over a year; I didn't know what I looked like, and I didn't care. Once a month or so a prison barber came through the cell block. He was a rather pleasant fellow who appeared to enjoy his work and seemed to want to do a good job, even though he cut everyone's hair the same: short. It wasn't stylish, but it was practical. I cringed when I looked at him, however. His hands were filthy, as were his apron and the towel he used. I couldn't blame him for being dirty. Everything about the prison, the prisoners, even the air outside was sooty and unclean. Sometimes, when I was especially belligerent, I even took my fury out on that poor barber just to be hateful, telling him to go away, I didn't want my hair cut. Piss on all of you, I thought, I don't need your services—not for my hair or anything else.

Dirt and dust were constant problems. Each of us had been given a towel that we kept in our cell, and small bars of soap. We were expected to wash ourselves, our towels, clothes, and bedding, either in the latrine or in the small washbasin in our cell. Once a week we were permitted to go into a small room off the latrine that contained a big old bathtub and a washbasin and take a bath. I never saw who brought the warm water for the tub. I assumed it was Chinese prisoners from other cell blocks, for I knew that occasionally Fecteau's Chinese cell mate, Maha, did odd jobs around the prison until he was released in December of 1967. Taking a bath felt good, even though the water was so hard I always got out of the tub feeling like I had a layer of scum on my body.

But as the months passed and my frustrations mounted I

knew a storm was about to break, and it did on a day that began innocently enough. I was told it was my turn to mop the hall. Looking disgusted, I grabbed the mop and started to work. Never would I give the Chinese the satisfaction of knowing that I liked to mop the hall, as we all did, for it gave us something to do, it got us out of our cells, and it gave us an opportunity to snoop around, and maybe even whisper a few words to one another.

On this particular day the guard on duty was one who wasn't in our cell block very often. He was a terrible individual in manner and appearance—short, fat, gross. Just looking at him made me feel sick; that loathsome creature was running around free while I rotted in captivity, and I wanted to kill him with my bare hands.

Most of the guards smoked and disposed of their butts and ashes in a can or an ashtray, not on the floor. And most of them appeared to be relatively clean, but this slovenly beast was an exception. He wore a disgusting-looking dirty black undershirt pulled down over his fat gut, and he spent the day sitting at the guards' desk in the hall, feet propped up, smoking one cigarette after another, flicking ashes and butts on the floor beneath him. As I mopped my way along the hall I saw those butts, very carefully mopped around them in a neat circle, and went on my way.

The guard watched, then went crazy, yelling at me in Chinese and pointing at the mess at his feet. I didn't have to understand his language to know what he was demanding. And right then, whether from stubbornness, pride, patriotism, whatever, I knew I was not going to obey his orders. I was not going to clean up those cigarette butts. They would have to kill me before I would be a slave to that dirty, odious excuse for a human being, and they might as well find it out right now. I finished mopping the hall, washed out the mop, put it up to dry, and went back to my cell while the guard continued to yell and point at the disgusting pile of butts and ashes. I walked into my cell and sat down, then heard him calling out to someone. Very shortly Wu came in, looking furious and agitated, and ordered me to clean up the mess out in the hall. "No," I said, "I'm not going to do that."

Before I knew what was happening Wu had summoned several guards who came in, grabbed me, put my arms behind my back, and slipped on what I thought were handcuffs. Then I realized they were cuffs of a different kind. Regular handcuffs are put on with the palms of the hands together. These were put on with my right hand twisted so that both palms were facing my right side. And unlike handcuffs, which are normally left loose for circulation, these shackles were clamped as tightly as possible against the wrists. They were on and tightened before I fully grasped what was happening. Then I could only feel shock. It was unprecedented behavior on the part of the prison officials. During all these years no one had grabbed me or thrown me around. And shackled though I was, I felt a perverse satisfaction in having caused such a ruckus.

I guessed it to be four or five hours later when Wu and the guards returned and took the torture cuffs off. I felt great relief, though there had been relatively little pain during that short period of time. And the episode, I discovered, did nothing to calm me down. It made me wilder, in fact. Once again I had rebelled against their system by not picking up the cigarettes, and even though in this case I had been rather severely punished for such a minor infraction, at least I had gotten away with not picking up the filth of that slob of a guard. And in the long run the experience fueled the flames of fury within me and encouraged me to keep up the fight.

The tougher the Chinese got with me, the more I lost control. I thought I should press to the breaking point, and now was the time. Nothing else had worked, and the more I got away with, the more irrational I became. Was I acting like a madman? Perhaps I was, and I didn't care. I was tired of rationalizing. It infuriated me to know that the Chinese should never have held me in the first place. Our two countries weren't at war; I was not a spy; I was there by accident. Why should I humor these filthy communist pigs? Downey and Fecteau had to behave; they were civilian prisoners serving sentences, hoping to be released early for good behavior. I hadn't been tried or convicted of anything. My only crime had been to take part in a war against an ally of the Chinese. I'd been in prison four years, and I was sick and tired of it.

Then I ran out of soap in my cell and asked for more, but they wouldn't give me any. I kept asking. No soap. Maybe there wasn't any soap in this whole damn, dirty country, I told myself, livid with rage to be at the mercy of such a monstrous system. Next they began to restrict toilet paper. Instead of having toilet paper down in the latrine, they gave each of us our supply of paper for the month and explained that we were to use it sparingly and keep the extra in our cell. Fuck you, you assholes, I thought, and I took my month's supply down to the latrine and left it there. The guard brought it back, and Wu came in and explained again that I was to keep it in my cell.

Day after day I kept it up. Raising hell and fighting back made me feel good. I could be a meek little prisoner and get along, but I was far beyond that. If I caved in, that would indicate I'd given up, and they could all rot in hell before I'd do that. I wasn't going to lick the boots of this odious offal or try to get along with them in any way.

In January of 1970 the toenail that had given me trouble in Canton began to get sore again. My family had sent me clippers to trim the nail to prevent it from becoming ingrown, and the guards kept those clippers in their desk in the hall. Once a week or so I'd use sign language to ask the guard for my clippers, and he'd always given them to me. Then, for no apparent reason, my requests for the clippers were being turned down. No matter which guard I asked, the answer was no.

So one day on my way back from the latrine I stood in the hall and asked for the toenail clippers. The guard shook his head no, indicating that I was to go back in my cell. I shook my head just as emphatically. Give me the clippers, then I'd go back in my cell. The guard knew better than to get in a confrontation of any kind. He called for help, and Wu came on the run.

"Go back in your cell," he ordered.

"Not until I get my clippers."

"We'll give you your clippers as soon as you get back in your cell."

All right, I thought, I'll go back in the cell and stand by the door. Wu followed me in. "Sit down," he demanded. I stayed where I was. "I'm telling you to sit down," he repeated, his voice getting harder and meaner. I had to respond: "If you think you can make me sit down, go ahead and try."

With that, Wu reached out and gave me a push, and I braced myself against the wall. I was surprised. Wu had never laid a hand on me before. I wasn't foolhardy enough to push him back or attack him in any way; neither was I going to let him force me into the chair. He glared at me, then turned and left me standing there as he walked out of the cell, closing the door behind him. Seconds later the door burst open, and I was surrounded by guards and other prison officials, all of them grabbing and pushing at me, and in all the furor I fought back, throwing two of the guards who were mauling me to the floor. Instantly other guards overpowered me, grabbing me by the neck, arms, feet, and wrestling me to the ground. Once I was down they forced my arms behind my back, and I felt the torture cuffs being put on and tightened. And this time, once I was shackled and the commotion had quieted, I realized there had been a change in the attitude and behavior of the Chinese. It was as if restraints had been lifted from them and they could finally vent the brutality and ugliness they had been feeling for such a long time. They didn't want to humble me; they wanted to brutalize me as savagely as possible.

After three days in the torture cuffs I began to understand the pain they could cause when left on long enough. Unlike typical Western-style handcuffs, these were meant not only to restrain a prisoner, but also to inflict pain. Regular handcuffs are curved to fit the wrist; the Chinese torture cuffs were constructed so that one half of the device was curved to fit the wrist, the other half bent the opposite way so that it dug deeply into the wrist.

Despite the increasing pain my mind continued to function, and I suddenly understood the significance of something that had happened several months before. One day a doctor had come into my cell, listened to my heart, taken my blood pressure, looked at my eyes and mouth, and asked me if I was hurting anywhere. Then he left. Shortly after that the torture cuffs had been put on for the first time, and now I understood the meaning of all that. The Chinese knew the torture sessions were coming and had probably set me up for them, and they wanted to determine how much torture they could inflict without killing me.

I also remembered something else. As a young college student working in a funeral home in Urbana, Illinois, I had discovered that some of us loved to play practical jokes on one another. And one day I sneaked down to the main floor of the home, crept up behind the owner's son, who was polishing the glass on the front door, and gave him a quick jab to the ribs. He was so surprised he almost jumped out of his shoes, and I was delighted to have scared him. Score one for me, I thought.

Immediately after that he stomped away without saying a word and went into the men's room. I was concerned that he was angry with me, so I waited outside, wanting to make sure he had taken my joke as intended. Then suddenly I heard terrifying noises, and I peeked in the door. There he lay on the floor, his face purple, making horrendous gagging noises, his body jerking violently. My heart in my throat, I raced over and started throwing water from the faucet on him in an effort to revive him. He took it for a minute or two, then sat up, looked at me, and laughed. I couldn't believe my eyes. Not only had he faked a seizure, he had even managed to constrict his breathing to make his face turn purple. I had been outdone by a master.

Now, shackled in China, I thought about that friend and his fake seizure. Might that work here? It was worth a try. I'd had enough of the torture cuffs; they'd been on long enough. So I lay down on the floor of my cell and started shaking and making strange gurgling sounds in my throat, feigning a seizure, and making sure I did it loudly enough for the guard to hear. Sure enough, a worried-looking face appeared at the peephole, and I redoubled my dramatics. I didn't know how to make my face turn purple, but I got the response I wanted. Wu came in and unshackled me, and I pretended to be pulling myself together. I knew I would only dare pull that trick once; this time it had worked.

That following September 1970, the torture cuffs went on for the third time. Wu appeared in my cell one day and said he was going to read a list of charges against me. As he began I groaned inwardly, for he was reciting the same old litany of so-called crimes against humanity and the people of the world for taking part in the Vietnam War. That was crime number one, he said, and it was the same old garbage we'd been through so many times since I was first shot down. As he continued, however, I realized he was sounding and looking rather deadly and determined, and I began to pay closer attention.

Crime number two, he informed me officiously, was my violation of Chinese airspace. Crime number three: new crimes I had committed in prison; that is, writing derogatory comments about China and the Chinese government.

The third charge was a new one and a true one. For a long time I had kept a diary, which I knew the Chinese officials were reading when I was out of the cell. That was one reason why I kept the diary. I wanted them to know what I thought of them and their system, and the diary was one of the few ways I had of expressing myself. I had started it on the train coming from Canton to Peking, describing what I saw out the window: the squalor, filth, poverty, people in rags living in hovels. It was all the truth, but not the truth communist officials wanted to hear from a foreign prisoner.

I also described my beliefs about the political situation in China and how a totalitarian government could not last forever without the people eventually rising up. I didn't criticize Chairman Mao by name, but the message was clear. I poured many of my feelings and frustrations into that book, which I kept in the drawer in my desk, knowing full well that Wu and others were reading it when I was out for exercise.

Writing in that book was a crime, Wu now declared. I was not permitted to write derogatory comments about China or the Chinese government. And then Wu got to the heart of what he was after. I was to write a confession, admitting my crimes and denouncing the war in Vietnam and the U.S. government. They would not take no for an answer. They would put on the torture cuffs, and the cuffs would stay on until I wrote the confession. Instinctively I knew the first two torture sessions had simply been a prelude to this moment. This was what they had been after for five years, ever since the first day of my captivity. Write the confession. "Go to hell," I said, and the torture cuffs went back on.

Once again my arms were shackled behind me, the palm of the right hand turned outward. Okay, you bastards, I thought, I'll take this as long as I have to. Each morning, after a restless night of little sleep, I told myself this would be the day the cuffs came off, but that didn't happen. The days passed, and the terrible pain began in earnest. It started in a muscle of the upper arm, just below the shoulder, and seemed to radiate through my body. After several days the pain was far worse than if somebody had been sticking a knife in my arm; it was sharp, agonizing, and occasionally so excruciating I screamed aloud.

The cuffs were not taken off at any time. My bowl of food was brought in and put on the table, and I lapped it up like a dog. Going to the bathroom presented even greater difficulties. I struggled to get my pants down, and the more I struggled, the greater the pain. There was no way I could wipe myself after a bowel movement or wash myself in any way. I was becoming more beastlike every day, and all of it I could experience only through the blur of agony and pain.

Periodically Wu came in and in a rude, sarcastic voice inquired, "Have you had enough? Have you reconsidered? Are you ready to confess your crimes?"

"I've committed no crimes."

"Your punishment will not end until you change your attitude."

As I began to descend into hell, mentally and physically, I knew it gave the monstrous Chinese great delight to demand that I continue to follow the prison routine. Shackled, filthy, hungry, crazed with pain, I was nonetheless required to get up when the whistle sounded, get my bucket in my hands behind my back, struggle with it down to the latrine, and empty it, trying not to slop too much of it on myself. I spent much of each day restlessly pacing in my cell or trying to find a comfortable position to sit on the chair or gingerly lying down on the bed—anything at all to relieve the pain. But the pain was never-ending and so severe that I could not even consider my mind games. I was only trying to survive.

The guards yelled at me when I tried to rest on the bed during the daytime, but I ignored them. I was already being punished; how much worse could it get?

I was sure the invisible danger flag had gone up to other prisoners in the cell block. Downey, Fecteau, and Flynn would know I was in great trouble; as always in such cases, they would do nothing that might add to my torture. On the day of the fracas over the toenail clippers I had seen Flynn's head peeking out the transom above his door. To do that he would have to have been standing on his chair, and I knew he was risking reprisal in an effort to show his concern.

After eleven days I realized I was not going to be able to take much more. The pain was beginning to cloud my thinking. I found myself losing track of time, and my mind seemed to fade in and out. I knew from all the training I'd received that if I was going to have to do something, I must do it while I was still rational. It was clear by now that the Chinese were serious; they were going to force some kind of confession out of me or break me trying. I must give them something and do it quickly, while I was still able to think relatively clearly. Lose one battle, I told myself, and you'll stay alive to fight others. The next time Wu came into my cell I felt sick at heart, but I knew it had to be done. Okay, I said, I'll write your confession. Wu brought in a pencil and paper, and I asked to have the shackles removed. No, he replied, they would cuff my hands in the front. And so I sat down at my small desk, torture cuffs still on, and began to write. It was an unbelievably terrible ordeal. Slowly, painstakingly, I wrote, trying to give the Chinese as little as possible.

Certain things I didn't deny. I had not been a good prisoner, I admitted. My attitude and actions had been belligerent, and perhaps I had caused disturbances, which I should not have done.

I would not admit that I had intruded into Chinese airspace. I simply wrote what I had maintained all along: I had had navigational problems; I was over a cloud cover and could not see the ground from high in the air; if I had strayed over Chinese territory, which I wasn't sure I had, then it was not intentional, and I was sincerely sorry I had caused an international incident.

I totally ignored the charge of committing crimes against humanity, nor did I respond to the demand to denounce the

Vietnam War and the U.S. government. I did reply to the charge that I had written derogatory comments about the Chinese government and people in my diary, saying, yes, I had in fact written an account of what I saw out the train window and my views of the Chinese government, and if anything I had written seemed disrespectful, I was sorry; I hadn't intended it to be. That part of my "confession" was total bullshit; I had very definitely intended to be disrespectful in my diary, if not worse. Then I added that I came from a country in which people have freedom of speech, and that's what I had been doing in my little book—expressing myself.

On and on I went, the whole thing covering about one full page of my small writing. Filling that page with endless words, and doing it with shackles on, took many hours. And when I was finished, Wu took the paper and left, then returned and made me change several words. I couldn't say terrible conditions, he informed me, I could only say conditions. I scratched out what they didn't want, and he took it away. After doing this several times he finally came back and said, "All right, rewrite the whole thing, and do it neatly and correctly."

I did as directed, and Wu took the paper away. This time, when he came back, he rather ceremoniously removed the torture cuffs, and I felt nauseated as he told me that in keeping with their lenient policy toward prisoners who have repented, it had been decided to end my punishment.

When it was over and I was alone in my cell I felt a huge sense of relief; I also felt drained, exhausted, and traumatized. The physical pain had been brutal; the pain of having to write anything at all for the Chinese and having to admit that I had made mistakes was equally brutal.

I sat, feeling dirty and diminished, hurting inside and out, and asked myself if I would have been smarter to have given in sooner. Should I have spared myself so many days of torture? And I knew the answer was no. My own needs, my own sense of self, had dictated that I push to the limits of my sanity. I had done so, and despite my own personal sense of defeat, I also felt proud of what I had gotten away with and amazed that the Chinese had accepted so little. My greatest fear now was of how the Chinese might use that piece of paper against me or my country.

As I struggled through the darkness of this time in my life I was aware that a new prisoner had been moved into the empty cell right beside me. And sometime between my torture sessions Downey had communicated to me that the new prisoner was a British engineer named George Watt who had been working on a construction project in the northwest part of China, jailed in 1967, and convicted of espionage.

Even though I knew Watt was there, I made no effort to communicate with him. He was the only person ever put in the cell right next to mine, and I feared he was a plant, put there to catch me doing something wrong. I was also too deeply involved in fighting my own problems to communicate much of anything to anybody else. A few times we did bang our buckets on the radiator pipe that ran under the windows on the floor. It wasn't code, it was simply bang, bang, bang . . . prisoners saying hello to each other.

By the time I was shackled the third and longest time, Watt was no longer in his cell. It was quiet, and I assumed he had been released. And as the pain of the torture sessions faded and I could think more calmly I realized that the most fundamental questions of all had not been answered, and it was beyond my powers to answer them. What had the Chinese really been after by torturing me? If they had wanted a confession, why hadn't they demanded that I address each one of their charges? I had totally ignored the most incriminating charges of all, and I had not denounced my country or the war effort in Vietnam. Why had they let me get by with that? I had become wild, almost out of control; was it possible that their true intent had been to rein me in and calm me down? Had they feared I was going off the deep end, and they wanted to bring me back to sanity? I couldn't make sense of what they had done in the past—nor could I foresee what they would do in the future.

19

Fear—and Uncertainty

July 11, 1970. Communist China announces American prisoner Hugh Francis Redmond of Yonkers, New York, committed suicide three months ago with a razor blade. The Chinese also announce the release of Roman Catholic Bishop James Edward Walsh after nearly twelve years in captivity in Shanghai.

August 2, 1970. British engineer George Watt is released from a Peking prison by the Chinese communists. Prominently figured in all news accounts of his release are his comments about a U.S. pilot named Philip E. Smith. He later writes a lengthy article for a London newspaper. In it, he talks about that pilot. "During my time in the 'Remoulding Centre,' I was never beaten up, but Major Smith was. His defiance was too much for the Chinese.

"One morning we were due for our monthly soap supply, but it had not arrived. 'Why,' came Major Smith's voice loud and clear, 'is there no goddam soap? Do you hear me, you buzzards? I want soap . . . get me some goddam soap.'

"Astonishingly, this produced results. The soap arrived

later that day, and I heard the bars being piled up on the corridor tables from which, one by one, we would be allowed out to collect. As I waited my turn, bedlam broke out. From the corridor I could hear running feet, Major Smith swearing at the top of his voice and the guards chattering and barking orders.

"Dragging my chair up to the cell door, I stood on it to peer through the small glass fanlight above the door. There was the major, standing at a soap-piled table, throwing the bars with all his might at the guards and yelling, 'You know what you can do with your goddam soap.'

"Finally the guards jumped him, and the major disappeared beneath punching, kicking, clawing guards. But he was still fighting mad. They had quite a job to pitch him into his cell. I was detailed to clear up the mess. The corridor was like a skating rink with that litter of soap chips. As I mopped away, I was thinking, 'Poor old Smithy. He must have gone off his rocker.'

"Edging near his cell, I heard him coughing and gasping as he recovered from the beating. He must have heard me moving, too, for suddenly, I heard his voice, 'Whatever you do, you can't let them get you down.'

"I changed my mind. The major had not gone mad. He was just fighting his own battle his own way."

December 1970, Peking, China. If the Chinese wanted to rein me in by torturing me, they succeeded. Once I was unshackled I felt indescribable relief at being free of the torture cuffs, able to sit down and eat, clean myself, and perform all the small, commonplace activities of everyday prison life.

I also knew that I was defeated and was going to have to change my attitude. The torture sessions had taught me to respect the brutality the Chinese could and would bring down on me, and the wrath they would unleash. My insurrection was over, and I had lost. I didn't want to be punished again; it would accomplish nothing, and I recognized that I must put things in balance. I was a prisoner, and that wasn't going to change, no matter what I did.

I was going through hell, and as bad as it was, I was acutely aware that one thing more than any other was helping me endure this terrible time: my religious training and my faith in God. I had learned much more than I had ever realized from the strict teachings of my parents and my church. Locked away in my prison cell in China I gained strength and comfort from knowing that God was watching over me and that He would be with me to the end. I had not been forsaken. With each passing year my faith grew stronger.

There were so many things I could do nothing about. One of them had been staring me in the face for a very long time, but I didn't want to think about it too much, and I didn't want to ask questions in my letters to my family because I feared the answer—and it wasn't one I wanted to share with the Chinese, who continued to read all my mail. My captors had stripped me of every dignity and every sense of privacy, but this was something so personal that it touched a very deep chord in my ego and my self-respect.

The letters from my wife Judy had dwindled to almost nothing, and even without asking I knew she had probably found someone else. And strangely enough, it wasn't that I cared so much about what she did; I just didn't want to give the Chinese the pleasure of knowing that I was worried about my marriage. I received an innocuous letter from her on December 12, 1970, and that was the last one. I asked no questions, and I stopped writing to her, but I hated her for what I suspected she had done. I had been fighting to preserve some sense of integrity and strength. She had pretended undying love, then diminished me by cutting me out of her life. Evidently I was so unimportant to her that she didn't even bother to write, and she wouldn't know or care that her behavior was playing right into the hands of the Chinese communists. From the very beginning they had treated me as though I was less than a human being, and

Judy's lack of interest would simply reinforce that belief. "I'll love you forever," she had promised, and that had probably been bullshit all along. As brutal as they were, the Chinese had permitted us to exchange letters. Now Judy, of her own free will, had stopped writing, and I knew my captors would take great delight in that. But they wouldn't know for sure what was happening—nor would I—if I didn't ask. And so I kept my suspicions to myself. I didn't mention Judy or ask any questions in my letters to my family. Eventually I would find out what my dear wife was up to, and I was sure it was no good.

20

An American President in China

As my years in captivity passed I tried to maintain perspective, and at times it was almost impossible. I was well aware that I was one of the lucky ones; my family knew where I was, and we had been able to communicate, at least sporadically. Through the ages thousands of other prisoners of war had not been that fortunate. And yet, after I had been in prison four years, then five years, a certain sense of detachment set in. I continued to feel a great sense of responsibility to my country, my family, and myself, but sometimes I wanted to say, "Hey, turn all this off. No more packages. No more letters. There's no sense in going on any further. I'll never get out of here, so why bother with this facade of trying to pump up my morale all the time? Why continue to write letters assuring one another that we are all just fine, I had a cold last week, but now I'm better, and we must continue to hope for conditions in the world to improve, then all will be well . . . and on and on?"

My family had never given up hope, but I was sure they must be having many of the same doubts. Month after month, year after year they had continued to send packages and write letters, and, my God, what a terrible strain that had to be on them. Why should they have to keep it up? They were paying an incredibly high price for my captivity, and it wasn't fair. They should be living happy, fulfilling lives, unencumbered by worries about someone locked away in China. In my low moments I wished I could say, with all the love in my heart, "Why don't we give up and forget about it and not try anymore?" If I couldn't be free, I wanted to set them free, even though I knew, of course, that I couldn't do that. And so I plodded along, continuing to play my role in this ghastly charade, writing my monthly letters, expressing hope and health when at times I felt a devastating lack of both.

During the times that were particularly bad for me, especially before and after the torture sessions, I wasn't sure how—or if—I could battle the enemy one minute and then sit down and calmly write a letter home the next. I learned I could do it, however, by flipping an imaginary switch in my head. I could be an animal, yelling and screaming; then, when the time came to write a letter, I pushed all that aside, sat down, and tried to sound sensible and reasonable. I did all that because I knew what was going to happen to that letter. It would go to my mother and then be circulated to my entire family, and I had no right to add to the worries they had all felt for so many years. And so I wrote each letter very carefully and very neatly, then went back to battling the damn Chinese some more.

Several times I hit rock bottom, then had to fight my way back up again, and in 1969 and 1970 I didn't always get back up. The torture sessions had beaten me back to some kind of sensibility; the sheer longevity of my confinement, however, intensified those occasional periods of doom, despair, and self-pity that made me want to give up. I had already lost so much; why go on? My career, my wife, my father, so many years of my life . . . they were gone forever, so what was to be gained by pretending that everything was just fine? The prison environment itself, so terribly insidious and demoralizing . . . Downey and Fecteau and their plight . . . the agony that had been inflicted upon Hugh Redmond . . . all of it added up to one thing: We were in the depths of hell, and there were no indications whatsoever that we were ever going to get out. I was ashamed and disgusted with myself, but there were times when I wanted to say, enough. I didn't want to end my life; I wanted to end the pretense of positive thinking and put to death the lie that all was well. Those of us who were caged in this hellhole were wallowing in the mud, and no matter how many letters I wrote or mind games I played, the conditions of our existence didn't change and didn't improve.

As 1970 ended I knew I had hit rock bottom. I also knew that if I was going to survive, I had better do something about it. I felt tremendous guilt at having let myself sink so low. What about all those who had been killed in battle? How dare I dwell on the negative and feel sorry for myself? *I was alive.* What more did I want? And gradually I began to pull myself together, and my willpower, desire, and energy to keep going came back.

One thing that helped considerably was a technique that I had used periodically during my captivity. I pretended there was a TV camera in my cell; I was being watched by the President of the United States, my mother, my squadron commander, my buddies—how would they judge my behavior? Would they say I should ease up? Relax? I suspected they might. And so I tried to get myself stabilized. I wrote my letters, played my games, tried to keep myself healthy. At night, when the whistle blew to go to bed, I lay down on my board bed and thin pad and gave thanks that I had survived another day, and I told myself that was victory enough.

Even during the worst of my bad times I tried to keep track of the days and months. I felt somehow that if I lost track of time, I'd lose track of everything, including myself. I used *The Peking Review* to make my calendars; if they took that away from me, I poked holes in a box or anything else that was left in my cell and moved a pin from hole to hole in an effort to keep track of the passing days. Life was moving on, and I fought desperately to keep my sanity and my hopes alive.

And then, in July of 1971, there was a historic breakthrough in international affairs that sent shock waves through our isolated cell block. I learned about it one day when Wu came into my cell and told me to follow him. He led me into a cell across the hall, where he sat down rather formally at a desk and indicated that I was to sit in a nearby chair. And then Wu told me something that took my breath away. U.S. Secretary of State Henry Kissinger, he said, had just completed a secret visit to Peking. I couldn't believe my ears. U.S. officials had made overtures to the Chinese? And the Chinese had responded? For so long China had closed its borders to the Western world. What did this mean? It was momentous news, though I couldn't begin to guess what was happening. Wu hastened to explain that Kissinger's visit would have nothing to do with my case, but for the first time in many, many years I felt a deep stirring of hope. The Americans and the Chinese were talking—and that was a step in the right direction.

And almost immediately I sensed a change in the guards' attitude and treatment. Whether they realized it or not, they, too, had been affected by the news that there had been dialogue between officials of our two countries. The changes were small, almost unnoticeable, but they were there. The guards were less arrogant and brutal in their treatment of us, and there seemed to be a softening in the harshness of the prison routine.

Five months later, in December of 1971, there was another memorable development, and this one took place right in our cell block and had a profound effect on all of us. As usual, it came without warning, and my ears were the first to pick it up. Each day when chow arrived the noises were exactly the same—so many doors opening and closing, so many bowls being filled, the same footsteps, the same rhythm. And one day the rhythm was off. The beat was wrong because one cell door was not opened. I listened, and my heart stopped. The door that was not opened was Richard Fecteau's. I felt cold chills. Had something happened to Fecteau? Had he been taken to the hospital?

I dared not ask. I sat, fearful and agitated. I had never found out what happened to Hugh Redmond. Would this be a similar, unexplained disappearance? The next morning, as I sat listening to the news on Radio Peking, my question was answered, and I felt sudden tears of joy. Richard Fecteau had been released. Released. I couldn't even really comprehend the significance of that word. It was something we had wanted for each other for so long; its actuality was almost more than I could absorb. I listened carefully to the Chinese announcement that the American "criminal and culprit," Richard Fecteau, had been ordered out of the country. And I thought, ordered out of the country. Hallelujah.

And then my thoughts turned to John Downey, who had been left behind. How would this news affect him? Downey and Fecteau had never been cell mates, but they had been together for so many years, and I had always hoped they would be released together, even though Fecteau had been serving a twenty-year sentence, Downey a life sentence. Fecteau's release had to be traumatic for Downey, and I wished I could console him, but I knew he would handle this stunning news with courage and equanimity. For all of us, the release of one was an event to be greeted with the greatest possible joy and thanks.

Two months later, in February of 1972, China received one of its most important visitors in recent history, and this visit, unlike Henry Kissinger's, was widely reported in advance. I heard about it on Radio Peking, and when U.S. President Richard M. Nixon arrived in Peking on his much-heralded, unprecedented trip, I knew that an incredible wall of silence between two worlds had been shattered. It was a major news story in China, as I assumed it was throughout the world. Once again Wu warned me not to get my hopes up; none of this had anything to do with me or my fate. He explained in great detail what it all meant, and I listened with some skepticism. "We love and respect the American people," he told me, hastening to add that this did not change the long-standing policies of the Chinese government. The Chinese were not giving up their ideology; they were still opposed to the aggressive, imperialistic policies of the U.S. government. This was simply a gesture of friendship to the American people.

Clearly, Wu would have ignored the whole historic event if he could have gotten by with it, but that wasn't possible. Nixon's visit to China was too big a story, so one day Wu asked if I would like to see highlights of the visit on TV, and I jumped at the opportunity. Later that day he led Downey and me into a cell with a TV set where the three of us watched President Nixon on Chinese television. It was an astounding experience for two Americans who had been locked away from their country for so many years. We saw President Nixon at a formal banquet, touring the Great Wall, and seeing other ancient sights. Downey had to be wondering the same thing I was: Had President Nixon discussed our fate with Chinese officials? We had to believe he had, and just seeing him in Peking—nearby—gave us a tremendous lift.

I lay on my bed that night, thinking about the staggering power and responsibilities of an American president. His presence in this country had enormous implications on the world stage. And yet what it meant most of all to me was the simple fact that maybe—just maybe—Nixon's visit, his vision of a better world, his conviction that China should no longer be excluded from world affairs might ultimately convince the Chinese communists that they should release Downey, Flynn, and me—three Americans who had been in captivity for so very long.

And if our guards' treatment had softened somewhat after Kissinger's visit, there was an even more dramatic change in our lives after President Nixon's trip. Both the quality and quantity of our food improved considerably. Suddenly we were being given more vegetables, and sometimes even meat and fruit. I ate everything, wondering if I was being fattened up for market. If so, I was willing to cooperate. I guessed my weight had dropped from 175 pounds to about 145, and any extra food was greatly appreciated. I couldn't recognize everything I was eating, but I figured that was irrelevant. I ate it anyway.

But if the year 1972 began with optimism and encouragement because of President Nixon's trip to China and improved conditions in our cell block, it quickly disintegrated into a tumultuous year for me. I hadn't heard anything at all from Judy for several years, and I knew it was time to find out what had happened to her. I could take anything, I thought, but I didn't expect a year of such death and devastation in my life, and my family's. For so long we had clung to one another through the power of the written word, and as fragile and long-distance as that was, it had helped to keep me going. The letters we exchanged during 1972 were filled with so much hope—and pain—that I could only sit in my prison cell, read them, respond to them, and ache for a family that had been torn apart by world affairs, and brought together by joy and tragedy in our own personal lives. My brother, Bob, had done everything possible for me and my family during my captivity, and it was he who broke the painful news to me: My precious sister, Irene, had died, and my wife had remarried.

21

Peace Talks in Paris...
Hope in Peking

My dad, my marriage and my only sister had not survived my years in captivity. Irene's death had been a devastating blow to my family. My mother repeatedly asked for courage and strength to carry her through, and so did I. And yet, in the midst of my family's personal grief during December of 1972, events were transpiring elsewhere in the world that would ultimately be of monumental significance to us and to millions of others. Even I, shut away in my ten-by-twelve-foot cell in Peking, China, was aware that change was in the air, in my own prison surroundings and in the world beyond.

I warned myself not to become overly optimistic. Prison conditions had improved, and there were encouraging signs that the war in Vietnam was winding down, but the fact remained that John Downey, Robert Flynn, and I were still captives of the Chinese communists, who continued to insist that they were not accountable to anyone or anything but themselves and their own Chinese law.

The preceding spring I had let myself slip and had vowed anew not to let that happen again. At that time, on several occasions I was taken on sightseeing tours of Peking, always accompanied by Wu and a contingent of guards, and I had fallen into the trap of believing that the Chinese were showing me sights they were proud of because they were going to let me go. I should have known better. The outings were most enjoyable, and although Wu was never friendly during them, he was at least cordial. One day we even had lunch—a ham sandwich and a beer—at an outdoor café. During these tours I visited the Great Wall, the Ming Tombs, the Palace Museum, and other historic sites. All of it was pleasant and diverting, but it was not followed by release. Many months had passed since then, and Downey, Flynn, and I were still locked away in our dark, dreary, lifeless cell block. We still communicated with one another at times, either by note or in whispers, but there wasn't very much left to say. The world outside our prison had moved on; we had not. We were still trapped in the relentless, stultifying rigidity and monotony of prison life and in the silence of solitary confinement, only now it was more quiet than ever along our bleak corridor. Three of us left, each sitting alone in his solitary cell, fighting his own battle in his own way. Never again, without official confirmation, would I let myself believe that I or any of us were about to be released.

I marveled, as I had from the beginning, at the courage of John Downey, who had been a captive of the Chinese for twenty years. His strength never ceased to amaze me, and I never forgot that it was he who had first held out the hand of friendship so many years before. Mopping the hall outside my cell, he had whistled the theme song of the United States Air Force, and what a lift that had given me. He had done the same thing when Flynn arrived, whistling a few soft bars of "Anchors Aweigh."

When I thought about Downey I also felt a deep stab of fear. What if Flynn and I were released when the war was over—and Downey, the admitted CIA agent, wasn't? Were the diabolical Chinese capable of such cruelty? Of course they were.

For so long I had wondered about the true progress of the conflict in Vietnam, and that wasn't something I could learn from either Radio Peking or *The Peking Review*. I often thought sadly about the fall of 1965, just before my capture, when we had all bitched and complained about the progress —or lack of it—in the war we were supposed to be fighting. Seven of us had come to Vietnam together from George Air Force Base in California as part of the 436th Squadron. When we got there we discovered that we, and military forces stationed throughout Southeast Asia, were not going to be permitted to pursue and defeat the enemy, and we were bitterly resentful of that. We had come to fly, fight, and win, to blow the enemy to bits and destroy their means and their will to fight. Instead, at every turn we had been held back by rules and regulations laid down by Washington policymakers. Those restrictions made no sense to us and denied us the opportunity to do the jobs we had been sent there to do. My flight commander, Harvey Quackenbush, maintained then—and we all agreed with him—that if we had been allowed to go in, do our jobs, and get out, we would have been home by Christmas of 1965. I still believed that was true. Had we acted with resolve early on, thousands of lives and billions of dollars would have been saved.

Now Christmas of 1972 was coming up, and the war continued to drag on. I personally approached the holiday as I had all others. It would be my eighth Christmas in captivity; it would be sad, dreary, and emotional, and I would end up giving myself the same tired old pep talk: I hadn't made it home for Christmas this year, but I would next year. It was a prayer and a dream, and I made myself believe it.

And then suddenly, when we least expected it, all hell broke loose, and the hopelessness and despair of our cell block was shattered. I first heard the news on Radio Peking. I knew it was slanted because it always was; nonetheless, what I heard gave me chills. Wave after wave of giant B-52s had swept in and bombed Hanoi, raining death and destruction on the very heart of North Vietnam. Why the hell hadn't we done that seven years earlier, I thought bitterly, but I knew that mourning the past was pointless. What mattered was that we had finally unleashed our mighty power, and for that I was deeply thankful. It was the best news I'd heard in a long time.

I rejoiced at what I knew had happened, even though the Chinese had come up with a rather imaginative interpretation of the bombing of Hanoi. The American aggressor, they reported, had reached the end of its tether. The imperialistic beast was in its death throes, forced into the heinous crime of bombing the capital of North Vietnam with no regard for civilian casualties. The Chinese wanted the world to know that the raids showed weakness, not strength, and that the Americans would not succeed in bringing the heroic Vietnamese people to their knees. What utter nonsense, I thought as I listened, but I had become accustomed to the Chinese habit of spouting excuses and slanting any news story to serve their own ideology. I felt great elation at what I heard, then I cautioned myself not to get too excited. The U.S. could bomb Hanoi back to the Stone Age, and I might still be left right here in my primitive Chinese prison.

Without a doubt, though, the Christmas bombings of Hanoi gave a tremendous lift to our dreary holiday. It was clear, as we headed into 1973, that major changes had also taken place in China itself. It had been several years since I had seen buses of civilians being unloaded in the courtyard outside my cell window or heard the noises of protestors out in the streets surrounding the prison. News reports indicated that Mao's forces had quelled the opposition. Stability, or Mao's equivalent of it, was returning to the country. What that might mean to the three of us, I didn't know.

Our prison routine remained the same, and one day I looked at Wu and realized with a shock how long he had been with us—more than five years—and how much he had aged. His little ferret face looked thinner, bonier, older, and it made me wonder how I looked. The only time I saw myself was on Sunday, when we were permitted to shave. On that day the guard would bring in my razor and a small shaving mirror, and I shaved, using shaving cream I kept in my cell. I couldn't really see what I looked like, and it was probably just as well.

Late in January of 1973 long-awaited news came out of Paris, and the Chinese made sure I knew about it. On February 1, 1973, I wrote a letter to my mother that included one very cautiously written paragraph. I wanted my family to know I was aware of what had happened, but I didn't dare comment in any way or my letter wouldn't get past the censors. I simply wrote: "It has been reported that an agreement on ending the war in Vietnam was formally signed in Paris on 27 January 1973. A copy of the full text of this agreement plus the various protocols to the agreement were made available, and I have read them all. And so I wanted to let you know that I have received this information."

Even though I dared not write what I really felt, I hoped my family would somehow read between the lines and sense my excitement. I believed that the Chinese had given me a copy of the Paris accords because they were going to release me, just as North Vietnam was going to release its POWs. The accords said nothing about the two American POWs being held by the Chinese, but letting us read them was an encouraging sign. If the Chinese did release us, it would prove that what I had been saying all along was true. Flynn and I were military prisoners who should be released when the war was over. I also realized something else: Bold steps taken by President Nixon in improving relations with Communist China might well play a decisive role in our fate.

In all that was happening it was impossible not to get my hopes up. I believed the terrible nightmare was coming to an end, and that made me both reflective and cautious. Over and over I reminded myself to be careful and not do anything stupid. I had struggled through all these years; it would be terrible if I did anything irrational at this point.

I knew I had to face several grim facts. The world I had known before my capture was gone. I would go home again—I was convinced of that—but I didn't know how much of it would be recognizable when I got there. Seven years was a long time in my life—and forever in the lives of my children, one of whom I had never even seen. Those children were now seven, eight, and nine years old, and I suspected they were a part of my life that was gone forever. I was glad I knew what Judy had done. I would have liked to have gone home to a wife who had been loyal, faithful, loving, and willing to wait. Since that wasn't in the cards for me, I was happy to know about it before I got home. One thing was certain: No matter how much my life and the world had changed, or how much heartache and sadness I had to face, the joy of being free would overcome everything. For seven and a half years I had been deprived of almost everything. Now, if I could only get out of China, I would happily make the best of what was left of my life. There were so many questions. Would the Air Force want me back? Would I be returned to flying status? If not, what would I do? Would my actions in captivity be applauded? Or condemned?

Stop! I told myself. Don't get too far ahead of yourself. *You have not been released.* And maybe you won't be. Downey, Flynn, and I were players in a deadly drama whose final act we hadn't seen and didn't know. For so long we had sat in lonely isolation, and we continued to do that. Hope and expectation were in the air, but sometimes I shuddered in fear and agitation. We were close, so very close. Now all we could do was watch, listen, wait, pray, and be silent. The denouement was fast approaching; I was excited and I was afraid.

A Brother's Helping Hand

Jim Smith: "By 1973 I had been made vice president in charge of Far East operations for an international transportation and shipping company. My bailiwick extended from Korea and Japan in the north down through Okinawa, Taiwan, the Philippines, Hong Kong, Singapore, Indonesia, and Thailand, plus several of the islands, such as Guam.

"In Taiwan I became friends with many Chinese people who had fled mainland China when the communists took over. Some of them still had relatives living in Peking, and from them I occasionally received invaluable information. Family ties were very strong among these people, and though I was never given details, word was leaked from one family member to another. Someone's third cousin was a guard in the prison in Peking. Phil Smith was there and seemingly all right. 'Can we get him out?' I asked. 'No,' I was told. 'He could never escape. He'd be shot before he got over the first wall.'

"We had a large shipping operation in Saigon, where I spent considerable time during the war. It wasn't always easy to get there. International flights had been cut off, so I usually took little shuttle flights from Bangkok to Saigon.

When I was there I'd hear bombs and mortars and artillery . . . and I'd think about Phil. And sometimes I flew from Bangkok to Vientiane, in Laos, which was even closer to North Vietnam and China. It was a lovely, sleepy little town with wonderful small French restaurants. In the evening I'd have my dinner sitting outside and feel so close to Phil and wish I could just reach out over the mountains and snatch him back. I had wished so often that I could trade places with him. He had a family that needed him; I was single.

"And then one day in January of 1973 I was at the Hilton Hotel in Manila when I got a call from a friend I had known for many years. We had worked for the CIA at the same time; he was then stationed at the American embassy in Manila, and what he said was staggering. 'Your brother is coming out. We don't know when, but soon. Do you want to be involved in planning for his return?'

"Was I hearing the question correctly? Of course I wanted to be involved. This was what I had been living and breathing for for seven and a half years. 'Okay,' my friend said. 'I'll put you in touch with some people at Clark Air Base, Air Force and CIA people, who will take it from there.'

"During January and February I met with various people, usually over lunch at the Manila Hilton Hotel, and these were some of the happiest moments of my life. To actually be making concrete plans for Phil's return was not something I would ever have imagined I would be doing, and what a pleasure it was. I was very impressed with the efforts being made by the Air Force to find out everything possible about Phil. What did he like to eat? Did he smoke? Did I think he had lost much weight? What were his interests? They wanted to be totally prepared to do everything possible to help ease Phil back into the real world.

"I was overjoyed to be of help, but as the weeks went by I began to wonder when the release would take place. No one knew. Dear God, I thought, let it be soon."

* * *

February 1973, Peking, China. I sat in my cell, knowing the war in Vietnam had officially ended, the POWs there told they would be released within sixty days. I wondered, as I had so often, how many Americans had been held in North Vietnam, how they had been treated, how many of them I might know. I had been captured so early in the war, I had no way of knowing what had happened to the rest of my squadron or to any other friends in the Air Force. I had been out of touch for so long, hearing only the Chinese communists' version of world affairs, that I could only guess at what was really happening.

How did the POWs in North Vietnam feel, knowing they were about to be released? Overjoyed, for sure, and I was equally happy for them. For myself, the dark days of February 1973 seemed longer, emptier, and more endless than ever before. Still no word . . . no word . . . no word. Had the three of us in China been forgotten? Of course not, I assured myself, hoping I knew what the hell I was talking about. *The Peking Review* continued to print news that was encouraging. Henry Kissinger had made another trip to Peking, resulting in the announcement that the U.S. and China were going to set up liaison offices in each country's capital. Hopeful signs on the diplomatic front . . . no signs at all for Downey, Flynn, and me that our interminable waiting was coming to an end.

On March 1 I wrote my customary monthly letter to my mother, and then the vigil continued. It was so quiet; Downey and Flynn had to be sharing my impatience and my apprehensions.

And then, on March 10, Wu came into my cell and told me to follow him. I did so, puzzled at where we were going. Wu said nothing as he led me to a rather distant part of the prison and into an attractively furnished office. Seated at the desk was a prison official I had never seen before and, off at the side, his interpreter and a man with a camera. Wu, I noticed, did not stay in the room with us. The prison official gestured to a chair, and I sat down, looking closely at the three men. None of them showed any expression whatsoever. I was asked to stand and have my photograph taken, which I did; then I sat back down. I tried to keep my face as blank as theirs, but the whole scene seemed peculiar to me. This wasn't at all what I had expected. The atmosphere of this room seemed so grim and forbidding. Something big was happening, but they were giving me no clues as to what it might be. Maybe I was going to be released. Or maybe I had been tried and convicted in absentia and was going to be sentenced or put to death. What if I'd come this far and didn't make it out of China? U.S.–China relations were beginning to thaw. Was it possible that the three of us had been pawns in the negotiations between the two countries—and we were *not* going to be released? No, I didn't believe that was possible. Our government would not be part of such an agreement.

The Chinese prison official picked up a piece of paper from his desk and looked over at me. I took a deep breath. "I want to inform you that the Chinese government has made an announcement," he said in somber tones. I dared not move as he read the announcement to me. I didn't catch all the words; there seemed to be a loud pounding in my heart and my head. But I heard the usual derogatory words—culprit and criminal—and I understood the message. The culprit air pirate was to be released and ordered to leave China. And this time he was talking about me. I opened my mouth to say something, but suddenly I was speechless. I simply didn't know what to say or do. I knew, though, that those were the greatest orders I had ever heard. Call me anything you want, just let me out, and that's what they were going to do.

I was then asked to sign the piece of paper that had been read to me. It was all in Chinese, and I had no idea what it actually said, but I couldn't have cared less. I was happy to sign it, and to have my picture taken as I did so. All I could think was, Here it is, what you've been waiting for for so many years. You've made it. I felt dazed, delighted, almost overwhelmed by the magnitude of what I had just been told. I was happy when Wu came back in the room. The rather official ceremony was over, and Wu led me back to my cell. I desperately needed time to absorb what was happening. Had my family been notified? I thought of my mother and all she had been through. One of her wishes had been to see me out of prison before she died. Now at least one of her prayers appeared to have been answered.

Robert Flynn was to be released with me, Wu said, sometime within the next few days. What about John Downey? Wu didn't know or wouldn't say. Flynn and I would be put on a train for the two-day ride back to Canton and be released at the border between China and Hong Kong. Later that day, for the first time ever, Robert Flynn was led into my cell. I had never met Flynn face-to-face, never had an opportunity to talk to him. As he stood there in my cell I saw that he was a few years younger than I, taller and thinner—and very, very excited. Unspoken emotions were sweeping over both of us, and we tried to say everything at once. Wu stayed right there with us as we babbled about how happy we were and asked each other a multitude of questions. So long in silence . . . so much to say now, but Wu cut the meeting short after only a few minutes. We would have to wait.

The next two days were a blur of activity. I was told to sort through all my belongings and set aside those items that I wanted to take home with me. Very carefully I set aside the boxes of letters I had received, all the family photographs, and some clothing, including a scarf my mother had made for me. Other things—magazine articles and pictures, old clothes and shoes—would be left in the cell and disposed of—or used—by the Chinese. I would carry only a small bag of clothing and toiletries with me on the train.

Our final meals in prison were the best we'd ever had— meat, vegetables, and now some sweets—and this after I had long ago decided there must not be any sugar in all of China. In the midst of my own preparations a man came in my cell and measured me for a new Mao jacket. I was evidently going to go out in style.

And then a truly amazing thing happened. On March 12 Wu came in my cell and asked if I would like to go shopping. *Shopping?* At first I wanted to laugh. Why would I want to go shopping? Then Wu held out his hand, and I saw he was holding American money, the money I had been carrying when I was shot down in 1965. I also saw that Wu was serious; he was offering to take me shopping. Why not, I thought, and away we went—Wu, several guards, and I. In a department store in Peking I bought several trinkets, including chopsticks and a couple of small Chinese vases. That was enough.

On that same day I realized there had been another change in our cell block. John Downey was gone. He had been released early, Wu finally told me, because his mother in Connecticut was very ill. He was on his way home. When I heard that, I suddenly realized with a jolt that our cell block was truly being disbanded. This wasn't a dream. For the past few days I had functioned in a state of disorientation and disbelief, my mind watching from afar as my body went through the motions of packing, sorting, getting ready to leave. I had found it hard to believe that any of this was really happening. Downey's departure made it seem real for the first time. And if March 12 was a momentous day for John Downey, it was an equally memorable one for Robert Flynn and me. Late in the day Wu told us we would be leaving the next morning.

That night I slept very little. I lay on my board bed with its thin pad and heavy quilt and wondered how any of us had survived and what captivity had actually done to us. I felt joyous and thankful; I also felt shaky and emotional and hoped I was ready for whatever the next few days would bring. How would the actual release be handled? Who would be there? Would I do the right thing? I didn't have very much money. Where would I go? How would I get home? Perhaps I could spend a few days in Hong Kong and get caught up on a few of the pleasures I'd missed during the past seven and a half years. I drifted off to sleep . . . my last night in prison, silent and strange. Tomorrow my life would begin again.

Flynn and I walked out of our cell block the next morning accompanied by Wu and four of our longtime guards, who would make the two-day trip with us. I noticed this was a special occasion for them, too, for they were wearing new uniforms. Two cars were waiting for us near the exercise court, and as we got in them—Flynn in one, I in the other—I vowed I would not think back or look back, and I didn't. I was going forward.

It was an incredible feeling to be driving away from that hellhole of a prison—and to be leaving behind seven and a half long, miserable years of my life. And it was strange: Wu and the guards—the people who had been persecuting, tormenting, badgering, harassing, even torturing me—were now the ones who were helping me go home and were actually going part of the way with me.

Flynn and I were put in separate sleeping compartments on the train, Wu and the others in nearby compartments. And even though we were headed toward freedom, I quickly discovered that we were still very much prisoners, guarded at every moment. I had expected the time on the train to drag, but the very opposite happened. The hours flew by, filled with so many sights, sounds, thoughts, expectations, anticipations. Wu gave me a book to read, written in English, and I glanced through it, but I couldn't concentrate. There was too much happening around me. It was a shock to come out of a cell, with nothing to look at but four walls, and suddenly be able to look out a window and see cities, farms, people working in the fields. And I could hear the noises of the train, people talking, life going on around me. It was a joyous, movable feast of sight and sound, and I reveled in every moment of it.

I realized, even more than I had in prison, how much my eyesight had changed. I could see, but my distance vision had weakened considerably. I had noticed it in Peking when Wu first took me out to the new exercise court that had been built for the foreign prisoners. For many months we had not been allowed outside; having nothing to look at but the walls of a ten-by-twelve-foot cell had evidently had a great effect on my vision. Even so, I could see well enough to greatly enjoy the world going by outside the windows of the train.

Periodically Flynn was brought into my compartment, and even though Wu or a guard was always with us, we were able to talk at length about release, going home, our families, plans for the future. He, too, wondered how the actual transfer would take place, and I knew that he shared some of my fears. Our lives had been totally regimented for so long; anything new and different was worrisome. Would we know how to behave properly? Say the right things? Had we become weird creatures who would be viewed with alarm—or pity? I could see that Flynn was highly excitable, and so was I. I was also nervous, anxious, and fidgety.

Meals were brought into the compartment on a tray, and several times Flynn and I were allowed to share them. We were even permitted to order what we wanted from a menu the train provided for its many Western travelers. It was a dramatic change from prison chow slopped in a bowl. This food was excellent, served on plates and a colorful tray.

As we continued to head south I began to feel like a marathon runner coming closer and closer to the finish line—exhausted and struggling, but finally able to see that the race was almost over. Hang on, hang on, I told myself. You have made it to the end with honor. Soon someone would meet me and say, "Well done, soldier," and I would feel relief. Until then I could only feel joy and fear and worry about what was coming next. Freedom was now only hours away.

We arrived in Canton on the second night, and our entourage of Flynn, me, Wu, and the four guards spent that night in simple lodgings near the train station. We were only several hours from the border, but the release would not take place until the following morning, Thursday, March 15, 1973.

Jim Smith: "I was in my office in Hong Kong on March 14 when I received a call from the American consulate. The message was the one I had been waiting for. 'We believe your brother is coming out tomorrow. We cannot be positive—anything can happen with the Chinese—but he is on the train from Peking to Canton and will spend tonight in Canton. It looks good. Do you want to meet him at the airport and fly with him from Hong Kong to Clark Air Base in the Philippines?' You bet I do, I replied, and I quickly called my brother Bob in Clinton, Iowa, to give him the long-awaited news, cautioning him that things could change, the release could be delayed, we wouldn't know until we actually saw Phil. News media in the U.S. had reported that China was about to release Phil and Robert Flynn, and we had worried about our mother being alone in Roodhouse during this traumatic time, so Bob had gone to get her. She was with Bob and his wife, Marie, and I knew they wouldn't get much sleep on this night of March 14."

23

The Journey Back

March 15, 1973, Canton, China. I'd spent a restless night, rolling and tossing, and came awake feeling nauseated. It was nerves, I knew, and maybe the extra food I'd eaten on the train. I shaved and freshened up with a washcloth, and the sick feeling began to pass. I put on my same outfit—dark pants and Mao jacket—and I was ready. This was it, I thought, and then I began to feel queasy again.

It was early morning when we left our lodgings in Canton. In only a few hours Flynn and I would be out of China, and I wondered if he felt as tired and shaky as I did. I looked at him as we boarded the train, and I knew that he had to be sharing many of my fears. We were coming out of the black hole of solitary confinement into the bright light of freedom, and the shocking contrast was too much to absorb all at once. I had asked Wu what would happen when we got to the border, but he said he didn't know the details. His job was to get us to the transfer point, and other officials would take us from there. And as our train moved steadily toward Hong Kong I felt my apprehensions increase. Over and over I reminded myself that I must behave properly. I was no longer an animal in a cage; I was a thinking, rational human being, or at least I hoped I was. I must act sensibly, say the right things, show that I was in full possession of my faculties.

After several hours our train pulled into a small station near the border. This was our final destination in China. Dear God, after so many years I was about to get out of this place, and I felt relief—and panic. And as Wu led us off the train a grim realization hit me. For so long we had not been permitted to make decisions of any kind. Freedom of choice had long ago been taken away from us. Our captors told us what to do and when to do it, what to eat, what to wear. Wu said, "Follow me," and we followed him. Now we were doing it for the last time.

As we walked toward the station I saw in the distance the covered pedestrian bridge spanning the Shum Chun River. The middle of the bridge, I knew, was the border between China and Hong Kong.

Wu led us into a room that appeared to be a small, private waiting room. The four guards, I noted, did not follow us into the room, and I guessed that this was to be the transfer point. Wu confirmed it, for he turned to me and said, "Give my regards to your family." For a moment I was taken aback, and then I realized that this was a Chinese courtesy he was expressing. He could not offer his best wishes to me; for too long he had considered me a criminal and had treated me accordingly. Sending his regards to my family was his way of saying good-bye. It was a formal moment of farewell; I thanked him, and we shook hands. Almost immediately a man wearing the uniform of the American Red Cross strode up to Flynn and me and said briskly, "I'm Eugene Guy. I've been authorized to enter China to secure your release. Are you ready? Are you well?" We were ready and we were well, we assured him.

He had already signed the papers necessary for our release. It was official: Flynn and I had been transferred from the possession of the Chinese communists to the American Red Cross. Eugene Guy wasted no time. He shook hands with Wu and then led us out of the building toward the bridge.

This was the moment we had been waiting for. We would walk across that bridge to freedom, and our lives would begin again. We walked onto the bridge, and I saw, clustered in the middle, a large group of reporters and photographers, TV cameras, microphones, mass confusion. This was not at all what I had expected. I tried to keep my feet moving and my face calm, but more than anything else I felt an eerie sense of disbelief. For so long we had been treated like subhumans, there to be spit at or defiled in any way the Chinese communists chose. Now, as Flynn and I stepped back into the free world, there were lights flashing, TV cameras recording our every move, a barrage of questions being called out to us. We crossed the center of the bridge and were free at last, and what an awesome jolt it was. Questions, commotion, people jostling to get closer . . . and all I could do was keep walking, Flynn and Eugene Guy slightly behind me.

When we left the bridge we made a slight turn, and for the first time I saw three Royal Air Force helicopters parked nearby, their engines running. Obviously they were waiting for us, and I wondered why. Eugene Guy explained as we walked rapidly toward them. We were going to Hong Kong's Kai-Tak Airport, he said, where we would board a U.S. Air Force hospital plane for a flight to Clark Air Base in the Philippines. By the time we reached the choppers their engines were warmed up and their rotors whirling. They were ready to get us on board and get the hell out of there.

I was the first one to reach the largest of the helicopters, and as I came up beside it one of the crew members inside reached down to take my hand and pull me up. I took that hand, feeling my composure begin to crumble, for that simple gesture marked the end of a nightmare beyond description. A picture was forever engraved in my mind: Seven and a half long years ago an old toothless Chinese fisherman had paddled up to me in the Tonkin Gulf, reached out his hand, and pulled me into his small boat, and my life had stopped.

Now the journey had come full circle. An RAF two-striper was pulling me back to freedom, and as I climbed into the helicopter the pilot and copilot turned, shook my hand, and said the most beautiful words I had ever heard: "Welcome. We're glad you're out." Flynn and Eugene Guy boarded, and with no further delay I could feel the vibration of the helicopter and the increased speed of the engine as the rotors sprang into action and lifted us off the ground.

Many times in my life I had ridden in helicopters and airplanes that shook, vibrated, and rattled. But there had never been a moment like this. Hearing and feeling that helicopter take off meant only one thing to me: We were being taken back to freedom. All this effort was being made for us. I thought about that, and suddenly my control was gone. The sound, the vibration, the motion of the aircraft as it took off simply overwhelmed me. I sat buckled in my seat, tears streaming down my face.

The ride from the bridge to the airport in Hong Kong was a short one, fifteen or twenty minutes, but it was long enough for me to pull myself together. We came in quickly and landed immediately, and I was able to smile as I thanked the RAF crew. They knew, of course, that they had been part of a special mission, and I felt deeply grateful to them and to the Royal Air Force.

As Flynn and I stepped out of the helicopter we were greeted by British officials who welcomed us to Hong Kong and then turned to lead us to an aircraft sitting nearby. It was a U.S. Air Force C-9, and as I looked at that airplane I saw a Red Cross symbol on its tail, indicating it was a hospital ship. I also saw the familiar sight of the U.S. military insignia and the words U.S. Air Force printed on its side, and what an exciting moment it was for me. Those symbols represented a big part of what I had lost during my years in captivity. To see them now made me proud to be an American and grateful to a nation that had not forgotten us.

We walked toward the aircraft, and I noticed groups of people standing near the steps of the plane, but I paid no attention to them. My eyesight was so poor I couldn't make them out, and I wouldn't know any of them, anyway. I was fifteen feet away from them when I looked more closely, and then I looked again. Dear God, it couldn't be, but it was. My brother Jim was standing there.

Jim Smith: "I went to the American consulate at seven o'clock on the morning of March 15 and found a number of people gathering there to go to the airport, including representatives from the Air Force, the CIA, and the American Red Cross. During the ride to Kai-Tak I was so nervous and edgy. I just couldn't believe this was really happening, and I wouldn't let myself believe it until I actually saw my brother. I suddenly realized, though, that I was a businessman in Hong Kong and planning to fly out of there on a military aircraft headed for the Philippines. That meant my passport wouldn't be stamped properly. There would be no record that I had left Hong Kong. Fortunately, sitting right beside me in the car was the British chief of police of Hong Kong, and I mentioned my concern to him. 'No problem, chappy,' he assured me. 'Bloody easy job to do. Give me your passport.'

"He jumped out of the car at the main terminal of the airport, took my passport inside, and had me stamped out of the country. Then he got back in the car, and we drove out to the Royal Air Force flight operations facilities. What a scene it was out there. British officials were all over because they were coordinating the release of the two men from China into Hong Kong. We went into one of the operations buildings where all the action was being monitored and directed, and I stood off at the side, watching all the people milling about. There was a great sense of excitement in the air. I could hear radio transmissions, though I couldn't make out everything they were saying. They were evidently transmissions between RAF operations and the helicopters that had gone to pick up Phil and Flynn. I drank coffee, and we seemed to wait forever. I felt like a tightly wound toy needing to spring into action. We had waited for so long; every minute now seemed like an eternity. And then I heard a radio transmission that I could understand. A voice came in loud and clear: 'They're walking across the bridge. I can see them now.' It was finally happening, and I felt weak with relief.

"We all rushed outside and stood staring up at the sky, even though we knew it would take the helicopters at least fifteen minutes to reach us. And as I stood there I marveled at all the effort that had been made for this return. All around me were British and American citizens, many of whom had played major roles in planning this moment. On their faces were looks of such anticipation, it took my breath away. Two fighting men were coming home after such a long time . . . and these people wanted to be there to see them and to give them the welcome they deserved.

"And then, coming in over the mountains, I saw a large helicopter with two smaller escort helicopters on each side of it. As they came closer I felt buffeted by the strongest emotions I had ever known. To be standing there, watching and hearing those helicopters come in for a landing, was a thrill beyond description for me. This was my kid brother coming home at long last, and here I was watching the momentous event unfold before my very eyes. The choppers landed about one hundred feet away, and I started to shake as I saw the door open and the people on board jump out.

"An Air Force colonel standing beside me said, 'Do you know which one is your brother?' Oh, God, yes, I said. There he is. Phil was leading the way. I was seeing him with

242

my own eyes, and what a wondrous sight it was to watch him walking toward us. As he came closer I saw that he looked worse than I had feared. I had hoped that he would not have changed too much, but the long years in captivity had obviously had a profound effect on his appearance, his mannerisms, even the way he walked. He was wearing old threadbare pants and a fairly new Mao jacket. None of it matched, and all of it made him look like an escapee from the darkest dungeons of Peking. More than his clothes, however, were his physical appearance and the confused look in his eyes. His skin was very pale, like that of someone who has been seriously ill for a long time. His face and eyes were sunken, and he was so thin and gaunt, almost haunted-looking. Dear God, I thought, is he all right?

"Then he got close enough to see me standing there, and everything else was forgotten. He looked at me for one amazed moment, and then we both started to run. I saw one tear trickle down his face as we grabbed each other in a big bear hug, and I dissolved in tears of incredible relief and joy. Every day for seven and a half years my entire family had prayed, 'Please bring Philip home safely,' and now here he was. If he needed help, it was waiting, and I would go with him on the next leg of his journey home. He stepped back and said, 'Jim! What are you doing here?' We laughed, and I knew there had never been a happier moment in my life."

March 15, 1973, Hong Kong. I tried very hard not to break down when I saw Jim, but the emotion of this day was beginning to catch up with me. Never in my wildest dreams had I expected to see Jim there. We hugged and cried and talked, and then Jim pointed out that others were waiting to greet me. For the first time I noticed senior Air Force officers nearby who were standing back, letting the emotional reunion of two brothers take precedence over Air Force protocol. Jim tried to lighten the moment. "Don't you think it's time for you to report back to duty?" he quipped, and I was able to smile as I turned to the Air Force officials. We exchanged salutes and shook hands as they welcomed me back, and they, too, seemed moved by the events of this day. There was to be no delay in our departure from Hong Kong, however. The C-9 was ready to go. Jim and I walked quickly up the steps of the aircraft, Flynn right behind us, and I couldn't believe my eyes when I saw what was waiting for us at the top of the stairs. There stood two of the prettiest air force nurses I have ever seen, and each of them gave me a big kiss on the lips, which I didn't expect and thoroughly appreciated. Right then I could have flown to the Philippines without the C-9.

As soon as we stepped aboard I could hear the engines being started, and the moment we sat down the airplane pulled away from the parking ramp. Before I knew it we were at the end of the runway and had been cleared for departure, and we took off quickly and steeply. "Feel that thrust!" I exclaimed as we were pushed back into our seats. It was a tremendous sensation, and I was so thrilled and excited that I simply couldn't handle it. So much was happening so quickly that I started to weep with tears of joy. All the emotion that had been pent up inside me just came gushing out, and there wasn't anything I could do about it. I couldn't hold it in any longer. For so long I had forced myself to hide my feelings from my captors. Now I no longer had to maintain that rigid control, and what a relief it was to let all those feelings come pouring out.

And when I was finally able to talk I had the same urge to let everything come out all at once. During all the years of my captivity I had wanted so desperately to talk about what was really happening at home and relate all my experiences from the moment of my shoot-down in 1965 and tell everyone what prison life was really like. Now I had the opportunity to start talking, and I couldn't stop. I just couldn't grasp the fact that I didn't have to say it all in the first few hours. As the words came flooding out I realized I was talking too fast, and the words weren't coming out the way I wanted them to. I knew what I wanted to say, but I wasn't able to express myself coherently. My tongue was going like crazy, but it wasn't saying anything. I just couldn't find the proper words to communicate everything that I was thinking and feeling.

I seemed to be floating on a cloud—hyper, overly talkative, restless, jumpy. I knew I should try to calm down, but I couldn't seem to keep my feet on the ground. Flynn, I noticed, seemed to be having some of the same problems. Sometime during our years in China his wife had sent him a horn, which the Chinese hadn't let him have. Now he was walking up and down the aircraft tooting the mouthpiece of that horn. What a great pair we were, I thought, and then I went back to my talking.

Jim and I had so much to catch up on, but finally the flight surgeon tapped Jim on the shoulder and asked if he might speak with me. I tried to sit still and answer his questions sensibly. Was I in any pain? Did I need any immediate medical attention? Did I have any broken bones? Kindly, calmly, he asked me basic questions about my health. The aircraft and the Air Evac unit, I knew, could handle almost every kind of emergency, including surgery. I told him I was fine. Later another member of the medical unit took my blood pressure, listened to my heart, looked in my mouth, eyes, and ears. I talked with them all, and they told me how well I was doing, how happy they were to see me, how much they admired me. If they thought I was goofy, they didn't say so, at least to me.

And then someone asked me if I would like to change clothes, and I realized how much it would mean to me to get out of my Chinese garb. Jim had said nothing about my appearance. I knew, though, that I looked better than I had in a long time. If anyone had seen me a few years earlier, they would have been very shocked.

An area of the C-9 had been turned into a dressing room

roped off with curtains, and my eyes widened at what I saw. There were new uniforms in several sizes, shirts, shoes, belts, the works. Two airmen helped me find a uniform that fit perfectly, and what a thrill it was to put it on. I had been out of uniform since the first morning of my captivity in Canton, when the lawyer Shu took my flying suit away to be washed. He had returned it to me, but I had been forbidden to put it on. Now I stood, once again wearing the uniform of the U.S. Air Force, and I felt both humble and proud. And then, for the first time, I was given major leaves to pin on, something I had never done before because I had been promoted from captain to major while I was in prison. In addition to the rank, the planners of our return had even assembled the appropriate military awards and decorations that I was authorized to wear. The only thing forgotten was my name tag, but this group wasn't about to be thwarted in its efforts to make this return as perfect as possible. One of the crew members was also named Smith. He took off his name tag and said, "I would be honored to have you wear this," and he pinned it on me.

When I walked back to my seat I could see by the expression on Jim's face that I looked considerably better than I had in my Mao jacket and old pants. But even though I looked better, I was still having trouble grasping what was going on and what my responses should be. Someone came and asked us if we wanted coffee, and I thought I did. But when they asked me if I wanted cream and sugar, I didn't know. I couldn't make that decision. I wasn't used to making decisions, even simple ones. So I turned to Jim and said, "I don't remember how I like it," and he made the decision for me. "I think you like it with cream and sugar."

I didn't have to ask Jim's advice a few minutes later, however, when the aircraft commander came back and asked if I would like to come up to the cockpit. I jumped at the chance. What an incredibly long time it had been since I had been at the controls of an airplane. So many memories

. . . and as I sat in the pilot's seat of the C-9 I listened with avid interest while the crew explained the instruments and controls, which represented the latest in aircraft equipment technology. So much progress had been made while I was in prison. It was awesome, and I wondered if I would ever catch up on all the new advances and be able to fly again. Sitting in the cockpit made me realize how eager I was to return to active flying duty. Would that ever happen? Was I still physically qualified? Would there still be a need for my background and experience somewhere in the Air Force?

During the flight to Clark an Air Force psychiatrist sat down beside me and asked me some very general questions about how I had been treated by the Chinese, how the food had been, where I'd been held, how I had spent my time, what I thought of the Chinese officials and their government. I appreciated his concern, and I understood that he was trying to determine what captivity had done to me. Was I going to step up to a microphone and proclaim, "Long live the thoughts of Mao Tse-tung"? The Air Force had no way of knowing what shape I was in, mentally or physically, and they were doing their best to determine my overall condition.

I felt a tremendous sense of anticipation and excitement and a great fear of the unknown as we approached the Philippines. Every step of this journey back raised new questions and new concerns. What would happen at Clark? I would certainly be able to call my mother. What was I going to do about my children? My career? My life? How well would I be able to handle the transition from prisoner to free human being? Jim had told me that the American POWs in Hanoi were being released, and many of them would be at Clark, and I was very eager to talk to them and to compare experiences. I wondered how many of them I would know and how they had been treated by the North Vietnamese.

So many questions, but they would have to wait. We were

about to land at Clark, and the public affairs officer reminded me that in accordance with military protocol, the senior officer should step off the airplane first. There would be microphones there, he said, and television cameras would carry the arrival live to stations in the U.S. and around the world. If I would care to make a few comments, I was welcome to do so.

I paled at the thought of having to say anything, but I knew it was the appropriate thing to do. I would try my best to say something sensible and coherent. Then we landed at Clark, and I looked out the window and couldn't believe my eyes. Hundreds of military and civilian personnel had gathered at the flight line; schoolchildren stood holding placards welcoming Flynn and me back to freedom.

Oh, my God, I thought, am I ready for this? I had just come out of solitary confinement. I looked at all those people, and I was flabbergasted. What could I possibly say to them? I wasn't used to formulating and expressing my thoughts. For months I hadn't said a word to anyone. And right at this moment my mind and my tongue didn't seem to be connected. I'd been talking like crazy for the past few hours, but my voice wasn't at all steady. It sounded quavery and shaky and unsure of itself. I had little time to worry, though. The C-9 taxied in and came to a stop. The door was opened, and I stepped out and walked down the stairs.

So many thoughts whirled through my mind. This day had been so traumatic; I felt both weary and overwhelmed by everything that had happened, and incredibly happy to be back on a U.S. Air Force base. There were so many things I wanted to say to the wonderful, waving people who were there to greet us. I felt moved beyond belief at their outpouring of care and concern and joy that we were back. I wanted to say thank you . . . to them, to President Nixon, to all the American people for their years of steadfast determination to get us out of China. I wanted to tell everyone what it was like to come out of a dark prison cell into the sunlight of this kind of reception and what the moment meant to me. I walked to the microphones, and I wasn't sure what I should say first—or if I would be able to say anything at all.

24

Operation Homecoming

Nothing could have prepared me for coming back to freedom after so many years in solitary confinement. The contrast was simply too great and too overwhelming. I was thrilled to be back on the soil of a U.S. Air Force base, looking out at smiling faces and American flags fluttering in the breeze, and yet waves of conflicting emotions swept over me. I had not anticipated any kind of welcoming ceremony, and I had certainly not expected to be greeted by two of the senior military representatives in the area: Admiral Noel Gayler, Commander in Chief of U.S. Forces in the Pacific, and Lt. General William G. Moore, Commander of the 13th Air Force. I could only shake my head in disbelief as we saluted and shook hands, and then I turned to the microphones, took a deep breath, and found that I could only get out eleven shaky words: "All I want to say is it's wonderful to be home." How I wished I could have been more eloquent, but at the moment that was the best I could do. And perhaps my few words were enough, for the crowd clapped and cheered, and I could sense their mood of jubilation and joy. It was amazing—these people didn't even know Flynn and me, and here they were, giving us a hero's welcome.

We waved to the crowd and then boarded a bus for the short ride to the base hospital. As we did so I realized once again how hyper, emotional, anxious, and apprehensive I continued to feel. This journey back was not going to be easy. Each step of the way seemed to present new and different fears and uncertainties. I had been locked away for too long to make the transition back to freedom without experiencing grave doubts and misgivings about myself, what was expected of me, what I was capable of doing. Only this morning Flynn and I had been captives of the Chinese communists. Now we were free men, caught up in the hoopla and excitement of a huge homecoming celebration, and it was too much for me to absorb without feeling shaky and unsure of myself.

As Flynn and I walked into the hospital I realized how traumatic the next few hours and days were going to be—and how filled with both joy and pain. Standing there to greet us was a man who looked so thin and gaunt, almost skeletal, that I wanted to cry. It was Bob Craner, one of my best friends from the 8th Fighter Squadron. A lifetime ago we had flown F-100s together in France and Germany, and I'd had no way of knowing that he had been a prisoner of the North Vietnamese for six long, terrible years. I hoped he hadn't seen my look of shock, but it was difficult to hide it. Looking at him made me feel heartsick at the treatment he must have received to look so horrible. His eyes were sunken, his face hollow, his skin deathly pale.

And standing with him was a man who looked equally wasted. He, too, was gaunt, and he was also hobbling on a crutch. It appeared he had sustained a severe injury and not received proper medical attention. I had never seen the man before, yet he welcomed me with open arms and a huge smile, and I wondered why a stranger was greeting me so warmly. Craner introduced him as Navy pilot John McCain, and together they told me a rather poignant story. They had been in cells next to each other in Hanoi, and for years they had communicated by talking through cups held to the wall, though they never saw each other until they were released. And one day in their prison cells, having run out of anything else to talk about, McCain had said, "I wonder how that guy in China is doing." Craner didn't know how I was faring as a prisoner, but he knew plenty of other things about me. "I know him well," he told McCain, and he launched into a lengthy discussion of our escapades as young pilots. I was a new and different topic of conversation for two lonely men locked away in North Vietnam; now they had come to share this wondrous moment of freedom with me, and I was delighted and touched by their thoughtfulness, and deeply saddened by the treatment they had obviously received.

The hospital at Clark, I quickly discovered, was overflowing with POWs who had been released by the North Vietnamese. That night at dinner in the hospital cafeteria I looked around at those men and saw that almost all of them showed the effects of severe malnutrition. And as they laughed and joked and ate everything in sight with gusto I also saw deep lines of pain and weariness on their faces and faraway, distracted looks in the eyes of many of them. We were back, all right, but I wasn't the only one who was feeling strange and out of place. We had no way of knowing what the future might hold for us, and even though I was still floating around up on my cloud, every instinct told me that we were going to have to be strong and resilient, and I hoped we would be up to it.

Most of the men were probably going home to loyal, waiting wives, and I envied them for that, but I was happy to have been warned beforehand that my wife had left me. My life would go on without her. What I was going home to was my own large, loving family that had never given up on me during all those long, tedious years. I sat at Clark Air Base on my first night of freedom and knew how fortunate I was to be going home to them and to be going home at all, for the shocking reality of war was beginning to sink in: Many men had gone to Vietnam and would never go home again, and their families would never know the joy of their return. I would see my own family in only a few days. We would be at Clark very briefly, then be sent to regional hospitals in the U.S., and I had chosen to go to Scott Air Force Base near my home in Illinois.

A vast telephone system had been set up in the hospital to facilitate all the calls that were coming and going, and I was thankful that my brother Jim was with me as we waited for the call to go through to Clinton, Iowa, where my mother was waiting at my brother Bob's. When she came on the phone there weren't really any words that could convey the deep emotion of the moment. My strong, seventy-eight-year-old mother broke down, and so did I. Through tears I could only tell her that I loved her, I was fine, and I would see her in a few days.

Incoming calls were screened, and one I did not accept came from my ex-wife. I wasn't ready to talk to her and had no intention of doing so. Later I would talk to my children, but not yet.

One call I did accept came from Thailand, and I was touched and surprised by it. It came from a master sergeant we called Doc Blanchard, who was the maintenance line chief at Da Nang the day I was shot down. For all the years of my captivity Doc Blanchard had worried about me and wondered if there was anything wrong with my aircraft that day that he should have detected. I assured him that my airplane had been operating properly when it left the flight line, and I hung up, greatly moved by a line chief who had worried for so long that he had not done his job properly. He had wanted to hear directly from me that he had not failed in his duties, and I told him that he had not.

The few days at Clark were filled with medical exams to determine whether we were well enough for the long flights back to the U.S., psychological evaluations, military debriefings . . . and eating, sleeping, showering, shopping in the base exchange. So many things to do—and now we were free to do them. And many of the POWs out of North Vietnam stopped me in the halls or came to my room, filled with curiosity about the treatment I had received. Where there had been hundreds of them, there had been only two of us in China, and that was difficult for them to comprehend. At times, they told me, some of them had been penned up like cattle, forty to fifty prisoners in one room, and the stress of such close confinement had caused all kinds of problems. Several of them said they would have welcomed my solitary confinement just to get away from fellow POWs who were driving them crazy. I listened to that and knew they wouldn't understand how desperately I had wished for someone, anyone at all, to talk to.

My roommate at Clark was an Air Force pilot, Major Ken Johnson, who had just been released after being a POW in Hanoi for about a year and a half, and he proved to be of enormous assistance to me. So much had changed in my absence, and he knew all the right things to do. Even the uniforms we were issued were new and different to me; Ken was meticulous about pinning the wings and ribbons on just right. And because he had been a captive for a relatively short time, he was more knowledgeable than many of the returning POWs about the latest technology within the Air Force and what had transpired during the war in Vietnam, and that was a great help to me.

After our few busy days at Clark it was time for those of us who were healthy enough to continue our journeys home. I said good-bye to my brother Jim and boarded a C-141 cargo plane for the long flight back to Scott Air Force Base. We would stop in Hawaii, we were told, and then continue on to Illinois, a journey of about twenty hours. Each of the POWs on the flight was accompanied by a military escort, someone similar to us in age, rank, and background. Our escort would be with us each step of the way as we headed back to the continental U.S., available to answer our questions, give us advice, calm our fears, and just talk if that's what we wanted to do. My escort was an Air Force fighter pilot stationed at Clark, Major Nevin Heiser, and I would be forever grateful to him for everything he did for me. He had been involved for several months with my brother Jim and others in planning my return and had been with the C-9 crew in Hong Kong when Flynn and I walked across the bridge to freedom. He had familiarized himself with me and my background and had prepared very carefully to answer my every question, and that gave me a great feeling of comfort. He knew about my marital status, my pay, what would happen every step of the way during Operation Homecoming. His knowledge and preparation helped ease my apprehensions and made me feel calmer and more confident. I had so many questions—and he was ready with the answers to them. He knew that Roodhouse was about eighty miles from Scott and that a large contingent of my family and townspeople were planning to meet us when we landed. He explained in detail exactly what would happen when we arrived. Each returning POW would step out of the airplane, one at a time, walk down the steps to a microphone, say a few words to the well-wishers gathered there, then move on and let the next man have his chance to address the crowd. He even knew that a freedom tree had been planted in Roodhouse in my honor a few days before my release, and he suggested I mention that in my remarks. During the long flight he helped me tremendously in sorting out my thoughts and putting a few words down on paper. Much of the rest of the time, as we headed eastward, I slept and tried not to worry about what was ahead for me.

I stepped back on U.S. soil when we landed in Hawaii. During that brief stop all of us on the C-141 were presented with the traditional Hawaiian lei. And then we headed on; our next stop would be my home state. On March 18, 1973, we landed at Scott Air Force Base in southern Illinois, and I knew that at long last I was about to be reunited with my family. We would depart the airplane in order of senority, and I would be one of the first off. I watched the others descend the steps, and I could see a red carpet laid out adjacent to the aircraft, an honor guard displaying the colors, and masses of cheering people standing at the edge of the flight line. When my turn came I walked off the plane, feeling dizzy with waves of doubt and joy and hoping that I would say the proper things and do so in a reasonably articulate way. I walked to the microphone and said the words that Nevin and I had prepared. Then I turned and, for the first time, saw my brothers Joe, Bob, and Paul and Irene's husband, Tom, standing nearby. What a great moment it was as we hugged and embraced, and then Bob said, "Mother's over in the car." I saw an Air Force staff car about fifty feet away, and I walked over and got in the backseat. There she sat, tears in her eyes, holding out her arms. So many words had been written, so many prayers offered . . . all of them hoping that this day would finally arrive. With smiles and tears we hugged, and I told her how wonderful she looked, and then I said what I knew both of us were thinking—two of our beloved family members had not survived my captivity and were not here to share this joyous homecoming. "Yes, it hurts," she said quietly. I sat with her for five minutes or so, then I knew it was time for me to go out and greet the crowd that had made such a special effort to be here for our arrival. I walked along the lines of people, and what a thrill it was. There were relatives, classmates, townspeople, and we all laughed and touched, and I was deeply honored that they were there.

Then I got back in the staff car with Mother, and we were driven to the officers' quarters on the base where she was staying, and I realized how thoughtful the Air Force had been. She had been given the VIP suite, which included a living room, bedroom, bathroom, and kitchen, and it was big enough and private enough for all of our family members to join us for a very special reunion. Joe and Clara were there, Bob and Marie, Paul and Ruth . . . my siblings and their families and so many other relatives, and it was a joy to see them all. We talked and reminisced, and there was a din of happy confusion. But under it all there was a sense of awkwardness and strangeness. Here was my family, but how did I fit in? What was my proper role in all of this? And they, too, seemed to be groping for what to say and do. So many years had passed—we were strangers, in a way, and we would have to reestablish our ties, and that was going to take time.

I checked into the base hospital later that day and found that I would share a room with Ken Johnson, who had been my roommate at Clark. I was happy and relieved; with him, I didn't need to talk or answer questions or pretend to be anything but myself. This had been a momentous day, and I was thoroughly exhausted.

My family stayed at Scott for several days, and then it was time for them to go back to their own lives. I had work to do, and so did they, and we would see each other as soon as I was released. For me, each day at Scott was filled with physical and mental exams and hours and hours of military debriefing. I talked and talked and talked to the intelligence officer, sometimes until I lost my voice. And I talked to the psychiatrists and to all the doctors . . . and I continued to feel uptight and unsure of myself, and I worried about everything. I also talked to my three children on the telephone and felt greatly saddened by how difficult it was for a father to communicate with offspring of seven, eight, and nine who didn't even know him.

Finally, after thirteen days, I was given a convalescent leave. On March 31 my brother Joe came to the hospital and picked me up in his car, which displayed a WELCOME HOME sign on top of it. I would have the pleasure of riding with him through the countryside of southern Illinois and seeing the familiar farming communities as we approached Roodhouse. I had always believed I would go home again, and that was about to happen. This journey would end at our family homestead.

On the day that Phil Smith left the hospital for his first trip home in many years, his doctors recorded the results of their preliminary examinations:

USAF Medical Center, Scott AFB, Illinois
Psychiatric Evaluation *March 1973*
Operation Homecoming

Major Smith had considerable psychic trauma during his years of isolation. I think his situation is different from the POWs held in North Vietnam in that he had no one else going through the experience with him. At present he appears to be suspicious, anxious and has a marked sense of obligation to others. I feel that his sense of obligation is a neurotic reaction aimed at insuring that he is seen by others as a "good person," and hence he will avoid traumatic problems in the future. I think he perceives the captivity as punishment for his tendency to be rebellious.

Impression: Traumatic neurosis.

Recommend: I think that psychotherapy is indicated, although the carnival atmosphere surrounding his return tends to mask his symptoms and make him less amenable to therapy at this time. I think his problems will manifest themselves as the euphoria of reentry diminishes, and at that time outpatient psychotherapy would be indicated.

He was given a convalescent leave which started on this date, 31 March 1973, and he is to return on 29 April 1973. At that time it is planned to accomplish his flying physical.

Harvey Quackenbush: "I had been Phil's flight commander when he was shot down in 1965. When he was released in 1973 I was stationed at Luke Air Force Base in Arizona. I called Scott as soon as I heard he was there and asked if I could come see him. His psychiatrist asked me to wait; he didn't think Phil was ready for visitors. The psychiatrist and I talked several times, and finally, after ten days, he said, "Okay, come." Another friend, Joe Nevers, and I flew to Illinois to see Phil, and it wasn't a real happy trip.

"Phil knew we were coming, and we first saw him standing down at the end of a long corridor, waiting for us, and he didn't look too bad physically. He took us into his room and introduced us to his roommate, and his roommate looked terrible. He was skin and bones. But then we started to talk, and there was a shocking contrast between the two of them. The kid who had been in Hanoi was sharp as a tack, whereas Phil looked pretty good, but he just wasn't all there. It wasn't the Phil we knew. He couldn't seem to concentrate on anything. I wasn't surprised that his long captivity had changed him so much, but I was very depressed to see him in that state. It was a sad reunion."

I was happy and excited to be heading home to Roodhouse and absolutely overwhelmed by the reception we received along the way. People had been alerted that we were coming, and in every town we passed through there were signs in the store windows and cheering throngs lining the streets. Farmers had come in from the fields, and I was moved beyond words at the warmth of the welcome in each small town. By the time we reached Roodhouse our caravan had grown, and the sheriff was leading us in, his siren blaring. And as I looked with great interest at all the changes that had taken place in and around my hometown I heard music playing, and suddenly I saw the band and police cars and fire engines and a huge banner across the main street and people everywhere and dogs barking, and I wondered how I would ever be able to let these wonderful people know what all this meant to me. A midwestern boy had come home to his roots, and these people were what those roots were all about. They were cheering me, and it should have been the other way around. From them, as well as from my family, I had learned the values and gained the strength that had helped me survive so many years in a prison cell in China.

Several nights later they held a banquet in my honor in the school gymnasium, and I could not believe the time, effort, work, thought, and money that went into that evening. Classmates and teachers and friends from all around came to join in the festivities. U.S. Congressman Paul Findley spoke, and I had already learned how very hard he had tried over the years to secure my release. Everyone I had ever known seemed to be there, and in addition to the dinner they had taken up a collection and presented me with a gift that I would treasure forever, a diamond ring inscribed A GIFT OF LOVE.

And through all the festivities my family stayed by my side, knowing my homecoming would be joyous . . . and sad. Joe and I drove out to the family farm that first day, and I had to hold back tears. My father had almost never traveled. He was always there because he didn't want to leave the farm. And now his youngest son had come home, and a strong, vital heartbeat wasn't there. He was gone, a devastating loss that my mother had learned to accept, and so must I. And in all of our family gatherings there was another missing face and lilting voice, and I couldn't believe that Irene wasn't there.

In the mind games I'd played in prison I had often visualized myself being at home with my mother. Now I was actually with her, and what a busy, happy time it was. Friends came, bringing food and wanting to talk. The telephone rang continuously. I tried to visit with as many people as possible, in Roodhouse and in the surrounding towns. I wanted to thank all of them for their part in a homecoming that had touched me deeply.

And on April 5 the Institute of Aviation at the University of Illinois sent a plane for me so that I could arrive in style at the university's Willard Airport, where a reception had been planned. How strange it was, I thought as we flew into Champaign-Urbana. This is where I had gone to school, learned to fly, and decided that I wanted to join the Air Force. So long ago—and so much had happened since then. When we landed at Willard the first people to meet me were my classmates from 1954. And all of us were especially glad to be reunited with our favorite instructor, who had not only taught us aviation but had also instilled in us a sense of pride and purpose in ourselves and in all we did. His name was Lester Applegate, and having him with us made the day even more special.

And once again I was awed by all the thought and effort that had gone into planning this reception for me. Alumni, students, staff, and dignitaries were gathered with townspeople in Hangar 2, and there was a red carpet and a brass band, and there was also a very special touch. I had loved to sing in barbershop quartets when I was a student—and there to join in welcoming me home was a barbershop quartet, and hearing them was a wonderful, unexpected treat. The mayors of Champaign and Urbana were there and presented me with keys to their cities, and there were speeches, and it was a great day in my life. My brother Paul, who lived in Urbana, had helped coordinate everything, and I spent several days with him and his wife Ruth before I returned to Roodhouse.

My convalescent leave ended April 29, and as wonderful, exciting, hectic, and enjoyable as it had been, I was weary and ready to go back to Scott. I wanted to stay in the Air Force, but only if I could fly; and on my return to Scott I would be put through the very comprehensive flying physical. I wasn't at all sure I would pass. Was I mentally and physically capable of flying? If the answer was no, what would I do with the rest of my life? Physically, I felt fine and had passed earlier Operation Homecoming exams. Mentally

261

and emotionally, I was less hyper than when I first returned, but I knew I still had a long way to go in readjusting to the demands and responsibilities of being free.

USAF Medical Center, Scott AFB, Illinois
Medical Evaluation

<u>2 May 1973:</u> Major Smith went on convalescent leave for thirty days and returned 29 April 1973. The psychiatric evaluation finds that he has some traumatic neurosis, but there has been considerable improvement in this while he was on convalescent leave. It is felt that probably some psychotherapy on an outpatient basis might be indicated at a later date when the euphoria of reentry has diminished. The plan at this time is to put him on another thirty-day convalescent leave and reevaluate him in regard to his psyche at that time.

<u>29 May 1973:</u> Lt. Col. Smith was seen on 29 May 1973 for psychiatric reevaluation. He seems to be adjusting well back into society. There are at present no manifest symptoms. I must add, however, that Lt. Col. Smith's captivity was especially difficult in view of his isolation and his symptoms upon release more marked than those of prisoners in North Vietnam. I would think therefore that continued psychiatric evaluation would be appropriate—i.e., at three-month intervals for the next year.

<u>30 May 1973</u> Addendum: Lt. Col. Smith has remained asymptomatic while on convalescent leave; his spirits are excellent. He seems to have made a good adjustment on his reentry. Medical and psychiatric evaluations reveal no reason why he cannot perform duty on a worldwide basis and be qualified for flying.

25

The Lost Years

On a rainy night in Washington, D.C., in the summer of 1973, my mother dressed very carefully in the first formal gown she had ever owned. We had come to Washington at the request of the president of the United States, who had invited all the former POWs from Vietnam to a huge gala celebration. It was my mother's first trip to the nation's capital, and she was awed and thrilled by the city, its majesty, its history, its role in our democratic way of life. As a young girl in Arkansas she had been forced to quit school after the sixth grade and go to work; nonetheless, she knew what this beautiful city stood for.

Tonight we were going to dinner at the White House. Buses would take us from our hotel to the front door of the White House, where we would be shown out to the south lawn and into a huge red and yellow striped tent that was said to be larger than the main portion of the White House itself. The evening had been billed as "the biggest sit-down dinner" ever held at the executive mansion, and I knew it was one none of us would ever forget.

Patriotism ran high throughout the evening's festivities. President Nixon said, "Never has the White House been more proud than tonight because of the guests we have," and we all stood and cheered. Bob Hope, John Wayne, Jimmy Stewart, Sammy Davis, Jr., and so many others who had entertained the troops in Vietnam were there to entertain us.

Most of us had not seen each other since we had first been released and processed through Clark Air Base in the Philippines. Several months had passed since then, and I could see a marked improvement in our overall appearance. I wondered how well and how quickly the others were adapting to freedom. Some things we seemed to talk about, and others we didn't mention. We told one another what we were doing, but not how we were feeling. Did many of them share my sense of isolation, disorientation, insecurity? And as I looked around at the people gathered in that huge tent I was appalled at how many years we represented of lost lives, talents, accomplishments, dreams, and hopes. We had gone to Vietnam to fight and win a war; instead we had been captured by the enemy and taken out of the battle, a tragedy that could not have been easy for any of us to face or accept.

And as we sat at that beautiful, festive dinner party I realized that my mother's thoughts were momentarily elsewhere. Several times during all the local homecoming celebrations she had mentioned her concern and sympathy for the mothers and families of the men who hadn't come home from Vietnam. During my captivity two mothers who lived near Roodhouse had called her and said that their sons had been killed in Vietnam, but they knew her son was still alive. Was there anything they could do for her or for me? She couldn't forget that in the midst of their own terrible pain they had expressed concern about her. And on this special night, this homecoming party at the White House, she was thinking of them and all the other mothers and wives and families who had no homecoming to celebrate.

The years had taken their toll on all of us, POWs and families alike. I suspected there were scars that would never heal. For me, seven and a half years was a big chunk out of my life, my career, my marriage, my development as a thinking, rational human being. Captivity had changed me, as I was sure it had changed many of the others.

So many years locked away from freedom and civilization . . . so many years lost that could never be recaptured by any of us. My mother and I sat that night, surrounded by candlelight and flowers and flowing champagne, knowing that all around us were the monuments and the trappings of a way of life that any of us would have defended with our lives. We were there at that dinner—and then they began to play the theme song of each of the military services, and suddenly I wasn't there in Washington, D.C., at all. I was hearing John Downey whistle the U.S. Air Force song as he mopped a dark, dismal hall in a dingy prison in Peking, China, trying to give courage and hope to a downed Air Force pilot. My mind was far away when my mother turned to me and said, "I can't believe we're here," and I knew what she meant. Thank you, God, I thought, for this moment and for all you have given us. And from my heart, I could only say to my mother, "Neither can I," and she smiled and reached for my hand.

EPILOGUE

Return to China

In the spring of 1989 Chinese officials I had met in Washington, D.C., asked me to return to their country as their guest, and I was torn. For many years thoughts of a return trip to China had haunted me. The Chinese had held me captive for seven and a half long, devastating years during which I had been treated with hatred and contempt by my communist captors. Why would I want to return to such a miserable place?

I had asked myself that question many times over the years, even though I knew the answer. The pull of history is very strong. Veterans revisit battlefields and relive the horrors of wars we want to forget but never will, and we do so, in part, because we know we have left something of ourselves and our lives on those battlegrounds. For many years China had been my battlefield as I struggled to survive with mind and body intact.

I was thirty-eight years old when I was released from China in 1973, and I had resumed an active military career. I graduated from the Air War College and then completed Jet Fighter Recurrency Training at Randolph Air Force Base in Texas. That was another step in Operation Homecoming for me, and a dream come true. For the next three years, while at Holloman Air Force Base in New Mexico, I flew tactical fighters, and returning to the controls of a fighter airplane did more than anything else to restore my confidence and self-esteem. My next assignment was in Europe, where I spent two years at Headquarters United States Air Forces Europe and three years as the commander of Hellenikon Air Base in Athens, Greece. After my tour of duty in Europe I served at Bergstrom Air Force Base, Texas, as deputy and base commander, and my final assignment in the Air Force was with the Inspection and Safety Center at Norton Air Force Base in California. I retired as a colonel in June 1987, ending thirty-two and a half years of military service. I would never know what might have happened to my military career had it not been interrupted, but in prison I had learned to accept what I could not change, and I didn't forget that once I was free.

I also would never know what might have happened to my personal life had I not been in captivity for so long. The time with my children—Philip, Deborah, and Tim—could never be made up, and yet, though we saw one another very seldom, we had developed a warm and caring relationship. A second marriage had ended, but it had brought me a very dear daughter, Cindy.

My mother died in 1978, and I knew that she had always hoped I would one day come home and take over the family farm. That was not to be, but she got her wish that she be able to live there until the end, thanks to assistance from her nearby family and from wonderful, loving friends, especially her dear neighbor, Mary Akers.

And so by the spring of 1989, when I was asked to return to China, my mother was gone and my military career was finished. The time had come, but I wondered how such a trip would be viewed by the Air Force, the U.S. government, my fellow officers. What would it do to me? Would it reopen wounds that had healed or help cleanse me of the horrors of those terrible years in China?

I knew I wanted to go, though I recognized that the trip would be emotional and traumatic. And yet by then I had also become deeply involved in the writing of this book, and I wanted to renew feelings and emotions, revisit people and places, and bring out thoughts and remembrances that might have dimmed and faded with time.

During the summer of 1989, as I prepared for my return to China, I read with horror and agony of the massacre of pro-democracy forces in cities throughout that country, and I was reminded of my treatment in the squalid, desolate prison in Peking, now Beijing, where I had been held for so many years. My Chinese captors had treated me like an animal in a cage, stripped of everything but life itself. My skin had crawled whenever any of the guards came near me, and even the interpreters, who spoke English, had tried to brainwash me and turn me into a traitor to my country, and I had hated them all with a vengeance.

To go back to that country, I hoped, would put my experiences there into some kind of perspective. I flew out of Los Angeles on Friday, the thirteenth of October, 1989, and as the plane headed west I realized I felt calm and tranquil, not extremely excited and agitated as I had when I last crossed that coast on my return to the U.S. in 1973.

At the airport in Beijing I was met by a representative of BIISS, the Beijing Institute for International Strategic Studies, my host for the trip. And throughout my ten-day stay in China I was treated with great hospitality, warmth, and friendship by the Chinese people. There were luncheons, dinners, tours, even a performance by the Acrobatic Troupe of China. My Chinese hosts had obviously spent considerable time and effort trying to fulfill my every request as to who and what I would like to see.

On Monday morning, October 16, we headed for the place I feared the most: the prison where I had been held for most of my years in captivity. We drove to the southwest part of Beijing along narrow, crowded streets, pulled up to the main gate of the large, dark prison complex, and were given a pass to enter the outer gates. We drove a short distance and then walked the rest of the way into the prison itself.

As we neared the cell where I had been held I felt cold and afraid. The cell, ten feet by twelve, so small and desolate . . . how had I ever survived? Seeing it brought back horrifying memories, and I didn't linger long. That portion of the prison, I noted, was no longer being used to house prisoners. It was used instead as a work area for prisoners to assemble bicycles, and I couldn't help thinking how happy I would have been to have had a similar project to occupy my time.

Two days later we flew to Shanghai, and I met the Chinese pilot who had shot me down, retired navy pilot Gao Xiang. How strange it was, and yet how fitting, to have a long, detailed discussion with him about the events that took place on the morning of September 20, 1965. Fighter pilots traditionally debrief at length after every combat mission; to be able to do so with the enemy was of tremendous interest to both of us. Gao Xiang became a hero in his country for shooting me down. He was honored and praised while I languished, fighting for survival, in a solitary prison cell. Enemy animosity was gone when we met in 1989, however. We both accepted the fact that we were fighter pilots who had been doing our jobs; I only wished our roles had been reversed and I had been the one to shoot him down.

Shortly after that visit I flew to Hainan Island, where I had first been brought ashore. In 1965 I had been taken by boat to a tiny fishing settlement at the edge of the water. Twenty-five years later we approached the village over roads that were unpaved and deeply rutted. Rain was threatening when we arrived, and we walked fairly quickly through the run-down, miserable-looking settlement with its few dreary shacks. I wanted to see the hut where I was first held on that day in 1965, and we found it, looking just the same.

Seeing that part of Hainan Island again gave me a very strange sensation. My life had moved on, while time appeared to have stood still in this remote village. They remembered me, though, for I met one of the fishermen who had brought me ashore, and he recalled details of that day that I had forgotten.

The sight of that village, in its primitive simplicity, took me back very dramatically to when my odyssey had begun so many years ago, and I knew right then that my return was indeed going to help me. For so long I had been locked away in that desolate country, unable to live my life or pursue my profession, and I would carry the scars of those years forever. I had never fully overcome the sense of isolation, disorientation, and insecurity that I had felt when I first came out of my many years in solitude. My return to China had helped me recapture the intensity and the horror of that experience, and it had also served an even greater purpose, for I understood that at long last I could turn the page. The chapter was closed, the story told, and my life could move on. I had revisited the battlefield, and its memories no longer held me captive.

Postscript

John Downey received his J. D. (Juris Doctor) from Harvard Law School in 1976. He held several positions in state government and is now a state Superior Court Judge, assigned to juvenile affairs. He and his wife and son live in New Haven, Connecticut.

Richard Fecteau returned to his alma mater, Boston University, and served for eleven years as the assistant athletic director. He is now retired and lives with his wife in Lynn, Massachusetts.

Robert Flynn continued his military career, retiring several years ago. He is now living with his wife in Pensacola, Florida.

PEGGY DILTS HERZ grew up in Ames, Iowa, and is a graduate of Syracuse (New York) University. For 19 years, she was the television editor of Scholastic, Inc., in New York City. She has written countless magazine articles for major publications and is the author of 20 books. She lived in Saddle River, New Jersey, for many years and currently resides in La Quinta, California, where she is working on a new book.

THE EXPLOSIVE AUTOBIOGRAPHY OF THE
CONTROVERSIAL, DEATH-DEFYING FOUNDER OF THE
U.S. NAVY'S TOP SECRET COUNTERTERRORIST UNIT
SEAL TEAM SIX

ROGUE WARRIOR

RICHARD MARCINKO
WITH JOHN WEISMAN

Coming In Hardcover from Pocket Books March 1992

POCKET
BOOKS